THE EU ECONOMIC AND SOCIAL
MODEL IN THE GLOBAL CRISIS

T0347485

Studies in Modern Law and Policy

Series Editor: Ralf Rogowski,
Professor of Law, University of Warwick

Also in the series

Judicial Application of European Union Law in post-Communist Countries
The Cases of Estonia and Latvia
Tatjana Evas
ISBN: 978-1-4094-4369-8

Constitutional Evolution in Central and Eastern Europe
Expansion and Integration in the EU
Edited by Kyriaki Topidi and Alexander H.E. Morawa
ISBN: 978-1-4094-0327-2

Central and Eastern Europe After Transition
Towards a New Socio-legal Semantics
Edited by Alberto Febbrajo and Wojciech Sadurski
ISBN: 978-1-4094-0390-6

Democracy, Law and Governance
Jacques Lenoble and Marc Maesschalck
ISBN: 978-1-4094-0395-1

Judicial Accountabilities in New Europe
From Rule of Law to Quality of Justice
Daniela Piana
ISBN: 978-0-7546-7758-1

The European Social Model and Transitional Labour Markets
Law and Policy
Edited by Ralf Rogowski
ISBN: 978-0-7546-4958-8

The Changing Law of the Employment Relationship
Comparative Analyses in the European Context
Nicola Countouris
ISBN: 978-0-7546-4800-0

The EU Economic and Social Model in the Global Crisis

Interdisciplinary Perspectives

Edited by

DAGMAR SCHIEK
University of Leeds, UK

LONDON AND NEW YORK

First published 2013 by Ashgate Publishing

Published 2016 by Routledge
2 Park Square, Milton Park, Abingdon, Oxfordshire OX14 4RN
711 Third Avenue, New York, NY 10017, USA

First issued in paperback 2016

Routledge is an imprint of the Taylor & Francis Group, an informa business

British Library Cataloguing in Publication Data
A catalogue record for this book is available from the British Library

The Library of Congress has cataloged the printed edition as follows:
Conference "The European Union's economic and social model—still viable in a global crisis?" (2011 : Leeds, England)
    The EU economic and social model in the global crisis : interdisciplinary perspectives / by Dagmar Schiek.
        pages cm.—(Studies in modern law and policy)
    Includes bibliographical references and index.
    ISBN 978-1-4094-5731-2 (hardback)
1. Law—Social aspects—European Union countries—Congresses.
2. Law—Economic aspects—European Union countries—Congresses.
3. European Union countries—Social policy—Congresses.
4. European Union countries—Economic policy—Congresses.
5. Financial crises—European Union countries—Congresses.
I. Schiek, Dagmar, editor of compilation. II. Title.

KJE935 2011
341.242'2—dc23
                                                                        2013023954

ISBN 13: 978-1-138-27191-3 (pbk)
ISBN 13: 978-1-4094-5731-2 (hbk)

Contents

List of Figures and Tables

Figures

Tables

List of Contributors

Professor Philip Arestis

Philip Arestis is University Director of Research, Cambridge Centre for Economics and Public Policy, Department of Land Economy, University of Cambridge, UK; Professor of Economics, Department of Applied Economics V, Universidad del País Vasco, Spain; Distinguished Adjunct Professor of Economics, Department of Economics, University of Utah, US; Research Associate, Levy Economics Institute, New York, US; Visiting Professor, Leeds Business School, University of Leeds, UK; Professorial Research Associate, Department of Finance and Management Studies, School of Oriental and African Studies (SOAS), University of London, UK. He is holder of the British Hispanic Foundation 'Queen Victoria Eugenia' British Hispanic Chair of Doctorial Studies (2009–2010), and of the 'homeage' prize for his contribution to Keynesianism in Brazil by the Brazilian Keynesian Association (AKB), 15 August 2013 and served (2005–2013) as Chief Academic Adviser to the UK Government Economic Service (GES) on Professional Developments in Economics. He has published widely in academic journals and other outlets. He is, and has been, on the editorial board of a number of economic journals.

Dr. Katalin Cseres

Katalin Cseres is Associate Professor of Law at the European Law Department of the University of Amsterdam and a research fellow, both at the Amsterdam Center for Law & Economics (ACLE) and at the Amsterdam Centre for European Law and Governance (ACELG). Her main fields of interest include competition law and regulation, consumer protection, comparative law and economics and institutional economics. Her publications deal with the interplay between consumer protection, private law and competition law and the institutional and economic angles of economic regulation and law enforcement. She investigates these research subjects in the dynamic framework of European law and national law, with a special interest in the legal and institutional developments of the Central and Eastern European countries.

Professor Giuseppe Fontana

Giuseppe Fontana is Professor of Monetary Economics and Head of Economics at the University of Leeds (UK), Associate Professor at the University of Sannio

(Italy) and Research Associate at the Levy Economics Institute (USA). In 2006 he was awarded the George Shackle Prize, St Edmunds' College, Cambridge (UK). His research interests include the new consensus macroeconomics, endogenous money theory, and monetary and fiscal policies. He has recently co-edited two books with Palgrave Macmillan and published the monograph *Money, Time, and Uncertainty* with Routledge.

Dr. Petra Guasti

Petra Guasti is a senior researcher at the Department of Political Science at the Johannes Gutenberg University of Mainz and a senior researcher at the Department of Political Sociology, Institute of Sociology of the Academy of Sciences of the Czech Republic. She obtained her PhD at the Charles University in Prague in 2007 for her comparative work on civil society in the CEE countries in which she developed a comparative methodology for the assessment of civil society organizations as well as an index of civic and political participation. Between 2005 and 2008 she was a junior researcher at the Jean Monnet Centre for European Studies at the University of Bremen working on the issues of European civil society and public acceptance of the EU constitutionalization process in the old and new Member States. Her research concentrates on the study of the functioning of modern democracies and their institutions, political and non-political forms of interest representation and the issue of citizenship. She is a co-convener of the Standing Group on Central and Eastern European Politics of the European Consortium for Political Research. Her recent publications include the edited volumes *The Nexus between Democracy, Collective Identity Formation and EU Enlargement* (with J. Hronesova and Z. Mansfeldova, Prague, IS AS CR 2011) as well as *Euroscepticism and the Perception of European Integration Process in the Czech Republic 2004–2010* (with Z. Mansfeldova, Prague, IS AS CR 2012).

Dr. Charlotte O'Brien

Charlotte O'Brien is a lecturer in law at the University of York. She is an ESRC 'future research leader' award holder and her publications focus on EU social law and its implementation in the UK; particularly social security coordination, EU citizenship, discrimination and human rights. She completed an AHRC-funded PhD at the University of Liverpool, on free movement, equal treatment and citizenship in the context of migrant volunteers. She does specialist casework on cross-border benefit claims with Ripon Citizens Advice Bureau.

Professor Malcolm Sawyer

Malcolm Sawyer is Emeritus Professor of Economics, University of Leeds and Principal Investigator of the EU-funded project Financialisation, Economy, Society and Sustainable Development (FESSUD, www.fessud.eu). Previous appointments include Professor of Economics, University of York. He established and is managing editor of *International Review of Applied Economics* (published by Taylor and Francis) and has served on a number of editorial boards. He is the editor of the book series *New Directions in Modern Economics* published by Edward Elgar and is the co-editor of an annual publication *International Papers in Political Economy* (Palgrave Macmillan).

Professor Dagmar Schiek

Dagmar Schiek is Chair for European Law, Director of the Centre of European Law and Legal Studies at the University of Leeds and holds an *ad personam* Jean Monnet Chair in Law. Previously she was Jean Monnet Professor of European Economic Law at the University of Oldenburg (Germany). Her research interests lie in the field of European Economic and Social constitutionalism, new forms of governance in the EU involving civil society and European and international equality law. She is on the editorial board of the Maastricht Journal for Comparative and European Law and of Kritische Justiz (Critical Legal Studies, Germany). She has been a visiting professor and guest lecturer at various universities, including London School of Economics and Maastricht University.

Professor Annette Schrauwen

Annette Schrauwen is Professor of European Integration at the European Law Department of the University of Amsterdam and a research fellow at the Amsterdam Centre for European Law and Governance (ACELG). She is director of the Department of Public International and European Law and editor of *Legal Issues of Economic Integration*. The focus of her research is EU free movement law and the concept of Union citizenship. Her recent work is on subjects such as European dimensions of educational policy, voting rights for foreign residents in European elections and the concept of consumer citizenship.

Dr. Bal Sokhi-Bulley

Bal Sokhi-Bulley is a Lecturer in Law at Queen's University Belfast. Her current research interests are in human rights and governance, specifically in applying the concept of governmentality to understand rights discourses as techniques of (self-)

regulation. She has recently published on the role of experts, statistics and new agencies for human rights protection in the EU as new forms of governmentality.

Professor Amy Verdun

Amy Verdun is Jean Monnet Chair *ad personam*, Professor of Political Science at the University of Victoria in Canada. From 2010–2013 she served as the Chair of the Department of Political Science. She holds a PhD in Political and Social Sciences from the European University Institute Florence Italy (1995). She is author or editor of 17 books and has published in many scholarly journals. She is the author of *European Responses to Globalization and Financial Market Integration. Perceptions of EMU in Britain, France and Germany*, (Palgrave Macmillan 2000) and *Ruling Europe: The Politics of the Stability and Growth Pact* with Martin Heipertz (Cambridge University Press 2010). She is the co-editor of the *Journal of Common Market Studies* (with Michelle Cini).

Julia Vinterskog

Julia Vinterskog is an associate at Öberg & Associés. She holds an LL.M from the Lund University, Sweden, where she also worked as research assistant at the Faculty of Law, principally within European, national and comparative labour law. She was part of the Lund University team in the regional final of the European Law Moot Court Competition 2010/2011 in Barcelona.

Dr. Rebecca Zahn

Rebecca Zahn currently holds a lectureship in law at the University of Stirling. Before becoming a lecturer, she was a Max Weber Postdoctoral Research Fellow at the European University Institute from 2010 until 2011. She received her PhD in Law from the University of Edinburgh in 2011. Rebecca Zahn's main research interests and specialization lie in the fields of European Law and Labour Law (particularly European, national and comparative labour law).

Preface

The idea for this publication emerged from a conference convened by the Centre for European Law and Legal Studies at the University of Leeds in December 2011. Given the rapid developments around the currency crisis and the socio-economic visions that used to be associated with the idea of European integration, it is no surprise that choosing and rewriting chapters for publication took some time. Thus, my sincerest thanks are due to all authors for being patient with this process.

Further thanks are due to institutions and individuals who made this possible. First, the School of Law was the main sponsor of the conference, as it was approved as an adequate activity under its second century celebrations, which coincided with the inauguration of a new building for the school. Further contributions came from a number of publishers agreeing to have publicity included in the conference folders and the EU Jean Monnet Programme, which enabled public access to one of the panels. Andrea Gideon provided invaluable research assistance for convening the conference and during the whole editing process, in the latter stages further supported by Michael Randall. Finally, Alison Kirk at Ashgate publishers provided excellent editorial work again. I am extremely grateful for their professionalism and their very hard work.

Dagmar Schiek
Leeds

Chapter 1

The EU's Socio-economic Model(s) and the Crisi(e)s – any Perspectives?

Dagmar Schiek*

Introduction

This book originates from a conference that took place in parallel to yet another Council meeting on the euro currency crisis.[1] Speakers discussed how far any EU social and economic model would still offer normative and policy orientation after this crisis has been overcome. Since then, hopes of resolving the EU currency crisis in any near future have been dashed. Accordingly, the question of how EU socio-economic models pursued in the past will fare in an on-going crisis remains current.

It seems not yet possible to present the philosopher's stone in answering this question. Nevertheless, key issues warranting further discussion can be identified. First, the currency crisis has brought to the forefront of public consciousness the initial asymmetry of the legal and policy framework of the euro, and the recalibration or reform of this framework is certainly one of the key issues. However, the doubts regarding the EU socio-economic model(s) originated long before the common currency and its current crisis. Tensions between, on the one hand, values underlying internal market law and the competitiveness agenda of the Lisbon strategy and, on the other hand, the normative frame of 'social Europe' and the agenda of social inclusion constitute unresolved enigmas, stemming from the original Treaties. Since the EU's competences (and Member States' political will) to resolve these tensions at EU level are limited, they are frequently felt at national level. For any realistic opportunity to overcome the resulting danger of renationalization of politics and law, the role of civil society (including the two sides of industry, often referred to as 'social partners' in the EU jargon) emerges as another key issue. And finally, the EU's global aspirations as well as the expectations raised by it around the globe should be another key factor in making its socio-economic model viable.

---

*   This chapter owes to all the contributors, and the privilege of editing this collection. The usual disclaimer applies.

1   The Council on 9 December 2011 first endorsed what later became the Treaty on Stability, Growth and Governance. For an overview of the Treaty see Craig, 2012.

The subsequent chapters assembled in this collection offer two perspectives on each of these four key issues, while this initial chapter offers a connecting narrative.

Its second section discusses the notion of the EU socio-economic model, since what has been debated as the EU social model was always inextricably linked to economic policy. The section argues that such a socio-economic model constitutes a programmatic vision common to the EU and its Member States in spite of the diversity of its concretizations at national levels. This vision has always been underpinned by values expressed in the EU Treaties, a normative base that has been strengthened through successive Treaty reforms, and particularly by the Treaty of Lisbon.

The third section considers how the EU can fulfil its normative commitment to a socio-economic model that does not, in fact, prioritize the economic side of integration. Uncovering a confusing mix of socio-economic governance, it concludes that hard law and resulting judicial governance and so-called 'new governance' through targets that are not legally binding do not necessarily differ in efficiency. However, hard law, legislative competences and 'new governance' instruments tend to be more efficient in contributing to the economic aspects of the EU socio-economic model than in relation to the social ones.

Unsurprisingly, the viability of the EU socio-economic model has always been questioned,[2] and recently representatives of EU institutions have denounced the European social model dead.[3] The fourth section discusses the question of whether it can survive, relating to the wider academic debate and specifying what the subsequent chapters contribute to answering it.

The EU's Socio-economic Model and its Normative Base

While much debate still stresses the 'European Social Model', it should be intuitively plausible that there can never ever be a merely social (or a merely economic) model for any polity. Accordingly, the EU institutions (Presidency Council, 2012:1) and voices in literature (Barysh, 2006) have taken to using the term 'EU economic model' as well. Since the economy is part of society as much as a society without any economic base is unthinkable, economic and social aspects

---

2   Giddens (2006:15) confidently summarized that 'it is agreed by more or less everyone (…) that the ESM [here standing for European Social Model rather than European Stability Mechanism, D.S.] is currently under great strain or even failing'. This was based on much earlier debates in literature (see below, text accompanying footnotes 19–20).

3   ECB president Draghi stated on 24 February 2012 in an interview with the Wall Street Journal: 'The European Social Model has already gone', answering the question: 'Do you think Europe will become less of the social model that has defined it?' This quote has been picked up widely in academic writing, e.g. by Barbier (2013); Pochet and Degryse (2013: 114).

are always inextricably linked. It thus seems more adequate to develop an EU socio-economic model instead of either a merely social or a merely economic one. This section sets out to do just that.

Unity in Diversity – a Common Core of National Models

First of all, diversity is one of the key characteristics of any EU socio-economic model: with 28 Member States the EU is now[4] too diverse to allow any single socio-economic model to be established.

As regards the 'European Social Model', many follow Esping Andersen (1990; 1999) in distinguishing clusters of national social models.[5] In very rough outline, the liberal model (comprising Ireland and the UK) is based on individualization of risks such as illness, old age, unemployment and parenthood through means-tested benefits, market-based solutions and a weak public sector as well as adversarial and decentralized industrial relations, while being neutral towards the role of the family. The Nordic model (comprising the Scandinavian countries) is based on securing the ability to react flexibly to those same risks by universal provision of social services, strong public services, and actively promoting inclusion of mothers into the employment market, which is governed by the cooperation of social partners unencumbered by states. The conservative model (comprising countries such as Germany, the Netherlands, Belgium and France) is based on absorbing social risks through contribution-financed social insurance for those in employment, low women's employment rates related to minimal (public) institutions for care of children and the elderly (familialism), cooperative industrial relations with sector-wide collective bargaining and concertation elements. The Mediterranean model (comprising Italy, Spain, Greece and Portugal, Ferrera, 2010) is based on residual welfare state payments and strong familialism, adversarial industrial relations characterized by competing trade unions according to political affiliations and concertation at the same time, and a relatively weak public sector. Further, the Eastern European welfare states are on the one hand similar to each other in that they followed a path of welfare retrenchment guided by International Financial Institutions, but on the other hand they developed in line with models stemming from before the 'iron curtain' (Cook, 2010; Dyson and Quaglia, 2012: 196).

As regards European economic models, the classification of different varieties of capitalism (Hall and Soskice, 2001) provides similar categories:[6] the liberal (or Anglo-Saxon) model too is based on minimalist conceptions of

---

4   The six founding Member States of the EEC arguably were close enough to develop a true European-level dimension corresponding to all the elements of the national welfare states (Scharpf, 2002: 646). However, that opportunity has been missed.

5   For an overview see Arts and Gelissen, 2010 and subsequent chapters in the same volume.

6   For different varieties of categorizations see Scharpf, 2010: 233; Featherstone *et al.*, 2012.

the state, supporting competitiveness and decentralized industrial relations. The coordinated model (assembling the welfare capitalisms of the Nordic and the conservative models) is characterized by state interventionism, sector-wide or even national-level collective bargaining and some degree of concertation as well as the coordination of activities within market sectors, rather than on competitive structures. Mixed market economies contain stronger interventionist elements, while emerging market economies just emerge from other economic constellations. A further model of egalitarian capitalism (Thelen, 2012) divides the Nordic from the conservative model.

Despite all these differences, European national social and economic models converge on a common core: social models share the idea that there is a (possibly minimal) responsibility of societies for the individuals' well-being, which in particular informs policies of transfer payments for periods of loss of (employment-based) income, and maintaining institutional social services as well as correcting labour markets through legislation and collective bargaining (Schiek, 2008: 38). Economic models converge in that economy is also concerned with organizing society: regulation of markets to avoid distortion of competition as well as social injustice are common elements alongside provision of some services in the general (economic) interest, including an accessible and efficient justice system. These main commonalities can be appreciated in an EU socio-economic model (Delors, 2013: 176), which emerges as a competitive market economy with social institutions to mediate between state and market, the promotion of social solidarity and complementarity of state and civil society and social partner activity in economic policy (Busch *et al.*, 2013). These commonalities are also conjured in recent attempts to find new traction for the EU integration project in the wake of an on-going economic crisis. Promoting welfare and justice are held up by McCormick (2010); and recent critique of the EU's crisis management draws on the hope that Europe could redistribute wealth rather than insist on divisive models of capitalism (Beck, 2013).

Programmatic Notions

From this common core it is possible to derive programmatic notions, as has been done by the EU institutions first for the European social model and more recently for the EU economic model.

The term 'European social model' first emerged as a programmatic notion in the 1980s: the EU Commission, then headed by Jacques Delors, coined the term as complementing the internal market to be revived by the Single European Act (Jepsen and Serrano Pasqual, 2005: 234; Giddens, 2006: 16). The 1994 Commission White Paper on Social Policy contained the first definition, stating that it is a 'unique blend of economic well-being, social cohesiveness and high overall quality of life' (European Commission, 1994: 1a). The Lisbon Strategy of 2000 revived the notion with its initial aim of 'modernising the European social model (by), investing in people and combating social exclusion' (Lisbon European Council, 2000). Soon the European Social Model mutated into a policy tool focused on good economic performance, a high level of social protection and education and social dialogue (Barcelona European Council, 2002, paragraph 22). The Lisbon strategy's second edition of 2005 still referred to the European Social Model, albeit mainly in recalling its importance without a clear definition.[7] Its follow-up, the Europe 2020 strategy, again proposes a definition, stating 'social models (…) mean empowering people through the acquisition of new skills to enable our current and future workforce to adapt to new conditions and potential career shifts, reduce unemployment and raise labour productivity' (European Commission, 2010: 18).

Similar to the national traditions, the diverse perceptions of the EU social model share as a common core a close relation to economic policy. Already Delors' 'European Social Model' was coined as complementing and arguably legitimizing the Single Market Programme, which after all aimed at accelerating EU economic integration.[8] Since the launch of the Lisbon Strategy and its successor, Europe 2020, the interrelation between the EU social model and economic competitiveness and growth has become even more pronounced, while synergetic effects of a more dynamic economic development for social progress have been stressed.

Programmatic notions of an EU economic model are of more recent origin. While Europe 2020 still refers to the social model, the EU institutions also refer to the EU economic model in their more recent rhetoric. For example, the Commission assured other EU institutions that 'since the onset of the crisis the EU and its Member States have worked to overhaul the EU economic model and restore its competitiveness' (European Commission, 2012a), stressing that growth is an important element of the EU economic model (Presidency Council, 2012: 2). Similarly, Commissioner Lázló Andor conjured the relevance of social enterprises for the development of the EU economic model (Andor, 2012). Besides being based on growth and innovation, the EU economic model in these documents is also seen as based on competitiveness, as well as the social market economy and social inclusion. Much as the EU social model is linked to economic performance, social aspects are characteristic for the EU economic model as invoked by the EU institutions.

Accordingly, the programmatic visions developed by the institutions again converge towards a socio-economic model, whose main elements can be summarized as enhancing growth, competitiveness, social inclusion and solidarity.

---

7   See for example COM (2007) 803 final, whose introduction states: 'Europe has a unique opportunity to transform itself into a creative, modern innovation-friendly, low-carbon economy, with a dynamic business environment, a highly-skilled work force and high-quality education, underpinned by a strong social model.'

8   'Economic integration' is used here beyond the confines of monetary and fiscal policy pursued under the TFEU title 'Economic and Monetary Union'. The notion comprises integration of product and factor markets as well as a common currency and general economic policy (Schiek, 2012: 13–15).

Normative Base

Some of these values have also found their way into the EU Treaties.

The economic model has by far the stronger Treaty base. Economic policy has always been central to the EU's mission. From its inception as the European Economic Community in the 1950s, it has pursued the integration of national economies into a common market that is now known as the internal market. This was pursued through opening product markets by guaranteeing free movement of goods and services as well as labour markets by guaranteeing free movement of workers.[9] In addition, freedom of establishment enabled self-employed entrepreneurs and companies to freely choose their base of operation within the internal market. At the same time, rules on competition, including a prohibition of state aid, provided a legal framework for the operation of markets unencumbered by anti-competitive agreements and the re-instatement of national markets by business. As is well known, all this is based on directly enforceable Treaty provisions,[10] whose interpretation by an activist Court of Justice has attracted ample criticism for prioritizing market integration over other aims of the EU (Ashiagbor, 2013; Busch *et al.*, 2013; Everson and Joerges, 2012; Scharpf, 2010; Syrpis, 2007). A detailed analysis demonstrates that the Court at times also allows social values to prevail, in particular in its case law on citizenship, but also in some rulings on gambling and taxation (Schiek, 2012: 148–64, 138–42, summary 210–14). It thus seems justified to consider values such as equality and solidarity as part of the EU economic model as conjured by its Court of Justice (Devroe and Cleynenbreugel, 2011: 107–10).

The Treaty of Maastricht added to the constitutionalized economic model for the internal 'Economic and Monetary Union (EMU)' (now Articles 119–44 TFEU), which consists of a common currency (monetary union) and a coordination of economic policies. This 'asymmetrical character' of the EMU is today seen as one of its major design faults (European Commission, 2012b: 4, Verdun in this volume). Despite the absence of legally binding norms, the EU economic policy is nevertheless based on 'the principle of an open marketing economy with free competition' (Article 120 TFEU) as well as on the model of a 'highly competitive social market economy' (Article 3 (2) TEU). Again, we can see that this economic model is connected to social values.

While the Treaty base for any EU social model is weaker, the Treaties have always contained a principled reference to the European social models' value

---

9   For the development of stages of economic integration see Tinsbergen, 1954.

10   Free movement of goods is guaranteed by Articles 28–37 TFEU, with Article 34 TFEU constituting one of the most frequently invoked provisions. Free movement of workers is guaranteed by Article 45 TFEU, freedom to provide services by Article 56 TFEU and freedom of establishment by Article 49 TFEU. EU competition law comprises the prohibition of cartels (Article 101 TFEU), the prohibition of abuse of a dominant market position (Article 102 TFEU) and of granting state aid (Article 107 TFEU).

base. From 1957, the Treaties stated that the Common Market should achieve progressive improvement of living and working conditions (then Article 2 EEC). Subsequent Treaty reforms added more elements: the Treaty of Maastricht included social policy, consumer policy, health policy and educational policy among the policies pursued by the EC (Article 3 EC). It also acknowledged that Treaty aims would not be achieved merely by creating a common market and an economic and monetary union, but also by 'implementing the common policies or activities' that were referred to in subsequent Treaty articles. This was the normative demise of 'embedded liberalism', according to which economic integration at EU level is accompanied, and indeed enabled by social policy and social constitutionalism at national levels.[11] With the change in Article 3 EC, the Treaty makers had admitted that EU-level policies for all Treaty aims are indeed essential. From this time, no area in which the EU pursued aims should have been left to national policies entirely. The Treaty of Amsterdam added some competences to legislate in the field of social policy (then Articles 138 EC, now Article 153 TFEU), as well as a high level of employment to the EU's aims (then Article 2 EU) alongside an employment title (now Articles 145–50 TFEU), which provided for coordination of national employment policies instead of EU-level regulation.

The Treaty of Lisbon further expanded the EU's values and objectives in the field of social policy. Article 2 TEU complements the traditional values liberty, democracy and respect for human rights by a second sentence according to which these values are common to the Member States in a society in which (among others) solidarity prevails, which has been characterized as giving the EU a stronger social orientation (Craig, 2010: 312). Further, Article 3 (3) TEU tasks the EU among others with promoting social justice as well as social cohesion and with combating social exclusion. Furthermore, Article 9 TFEU requires the EU to take promoting employment, social protection and combating social exclusion into account in any of its policies. This horizontal social clause has been the basis for high hopes of enhancing the EU's social profile (Dawson and Witte, 2012; Ferrera, 2012). Taken together with pre-existing provisions, and titles II and III of the Charter of Fundamental Rights of the EU, which contain some explicit social rights,[12] the EU's commitment to social justice and social cohesion has been enhanced, with a new emphasis on solidarity and social justice (Schiek, 2012: 219–24). This suggests that the EU is under a general obligation to pursue an EU social model, while respecting the Member States' national ones.

Even more importantly, the Treaty of Lisbon connects the economic and social models in a common value base. This is apparent from Article 3 (2) TEU, which combines the internal market with 'sustainable development of Europe based on balanced growth and price stability, a highly competitive social market economy,

---

11   For more detail on embedded liberalism see Giubboni, 2006: 56–93. Frequently authors defend the view that maintaining embedded liberalism is the only opportunity to maintain any EU social model; see for a recent summary Ashiagbor, 2013.

aiming at full employment and social progress, a high level of protection', among others. The social market economy has been criticized as an oxymoron, precisely because it marries the EU social and economic model (Scharpf, 2010). While this normative step only mirrors the EU's political commitments under the Lisbon strategy to enhance competitiveness of the EU economy among others in order to increase social cohesion and combat poverty and unemployment, the Treaty of Lisbon does nothing to remedy the potential contradictions between these aims. The EU remains a contradictory polity, based on conflicting values, which calls for reconciliation of economic and social aspects of any EU model.

EU Governance in Economic and Social Policy

If this is the new normative commitment of the EU, the question is whether and how far the EU is equipped to contribute to realizing it by EU-level law and policies. TFEU chapters headed 'economic policy' and 'employment' maintain that the EU merely coordinates the activities of its Member States, leaving the main responsibility for these fields with the Member States. However, the EU claims exclusive competence for competition law and monetary union and shares competences in establishing the internal market and some issues of social policy with its Member States. This leads to the well-known phenomenon of excessive complexity of EU governance[13] in the fields decisive for its socio-economic model.

Within the EU polity, hierarchical governance modes are prevalent in a variety of forms: directly binding norms in Treaties and secondary law, coupled with the supranationality of EU law as acknowledged by the Court of Justice, lead to the EU-specific phenomenon of judicial governance (Schiek, 2012: 235–7). Harmonization through directives (Andenas *et al.*, 2011) is the most complex form of governance: while hierarchical in principle, it maintains scope for Member States, sometimes even for social partners, to adapt the implementation to their national practices. 'New governance' EU style relies on a wide variety of coordination of politics without any regulatory competence for the EU. Best known under the term 'open method of coordination' (Armstrong, 2010; Dawson, 2011), these modes of policy coordination rely on targets defined by the EU Commission with other institutions as well as private actors, including norm-setting agencies.

For proactively realizing any social models, the EU can only rely on a limited range of legislative competences. After the Treaty of Lisbon, it can legislate in favour of (social) services of general interest (Dawson and Witte, 2012: 57–62), some aspects of health protection and (as before) some aspects of employment legislation, including equality and workers' and employers' representation, but excluding wages and industrial warfare (Craig, 2010: 178–81). This is very little to match the new normative commitments resulting from the new Treaty objectives

---

13   Obviously it is impossible to cover the full extent of the governance debate here (overviews are provided by Börzel, 2012 and Diederichs, 2011; see also Dawson, 2011).

(Dawson and Witte, 2012: 54). This lack of policy competences does not prevent that the different national social models are impacted upon by directly effective Treaty norms, and the judicial governance mentioned above. For example, with increasing marketization, national welfare states become vulnerable to EU competition law,[14] and labour market regimes have frequently been held as being in conflict with the economic freedoms of the Treaty.[15] In addition, the dynamics of economic policy coordination, especially in the context of negotiating a bail-out, have the potential of impacting on social security legislation (Pochet and Degryse, 2013) as well as labour legislation (Clauwaert and Schömann, 2012).

The often conjured asymmetry of EU integration (Scharpf, 2002; 2010) is thus still an adequate assessment of the European social model: while the EU is lacking some competences and the political determination to establish any EU-level elements of the socio-economic model to which the Treaties acclaim normatively, the impact of EU policy and Court of Justice case law on the national level at times threaten the pillars supporting the EU socio-economic model from below. Accordingly, negative integration has been said to outperform positive integration, leading to the danger of downward spirals or a general move of all Member States to liberal market economies. Received wisdom has it that it is the stronger legally binding character of negative integration through case law that achieves such movement, aided by the lack of legal bases and political will for positive integration through legally binding harmonization.

However, considering the EU economic model, this seems increasingly misconceived. As stated above, the EU internal market can rely on extremely efficient constitutionalization through direct effect and supranationality, which generates de facto judicial competences to disintegrate aspects of national law and policy making. In addition, the EU commands veritable legislative competences, in particular through Article 114 TFEU, as a base for any legislation harmonizing national laws with the object of ensuring that the internal market is established and functions well. This widely used provision is frequently exploited to cast into positive law principles developed by the Court. Thus, in relation to the internal market, the EU is in the comfortable situation of legislating in order to either outperform or confirm the results of judicial governance. In addition, the Commission is free to use other forms of governance in this field.

---

14 This has been demonstrated by the restrictions which the Court imposed on establishing third-pillar pension schemes through collective agreements (C-271/08 Commission v Germany [2010] ECR I-7087). Further, the maintenance of (social) services of general interest, which are important elements of many national welfare regimes, is seen as threatened by Commission policies (Neergaard *et al.*, 2013).

15 The 2008 case law around the restrictions of collective bargaining and collective action with trans-border dimensions by reference to freedom of establishment and freedom to provide services is illustrative of this (C-341/05 Laval [2007] ECR 11767; C-438/05 International Transport Workers' Federation (Viking) [2007] ECR I-10779 ECR; see also C-271/08, as referenced in footnote 14).

Only as regards economic policy in a narrow sense, the EU is thrown back on coordination of national politics exclusively. The relevant coordination mechanisms are seen as efficient in principle, although they do not differ fundamentally from the open method of coordination in social policy, whose practical implementation has been criticized as lacking in efficiency (e.g. Hatzoupoulos 2007). The mechanism consists of guidelines (broad economic policy guidelines – BEPG, Article 121 (2) TFEU), supervision and warnings on the basis of national programs (Article 121 (3, 4) TFEU). When it comes to combating 'excessive government deficits', warnings and recommendations are supplemented by the option to take a case to the Court of Justice (Article 126 TFEU).

The currency crisis has been taken as a starting point to tighten the enforcement mechanisms for these new governance styles. The so-called 'six pack'[16] introduced an automatic penalty for Member States whose currency is the euro in case of a macroeconomic excessive imbalance, and the Treaty on Stability, Growth and Governance establishes a similar mechanism. Similarly, the Member States in need of so-called 'bail-outs', i.e. the taking over of part of their debt by the European Union, have been made to comply with 'Memoranda of Understanding' (MoU),[17] which typically address matters such as wage-setting that are beyond the EU legislative competences. The desire to maintain 'conditionality' of any financial support of states mirrors the principles pursued by the International Financial Institutions such as the IMF. For the EU, it is enshrined in Article 125 (2) TFEU (Witte, 2011) as well as in the Treaty on European Stability Mechanism (ESM Treaty, Merino, 2012).

All these methods of 'new governance' in the field of economic policy presuppose that Member States in principle remain competent to formulate the specific measures which enable them to comply with targets such as a limit on budget deficits. Given the need of Member States to remain able to serve their

---

16   A set of five regulations and one directive reinforcing the stability and growth pact, consisting of Regulation (EU) No. 1173/2011 on the effective enforcement of budgetary surveillance in the euro area; Regulation (EU) No. 1174/2011 on enforcement measures to correct excessive macroeconomic imbalances in the euro area; Regulation (EU) No. 1175/2011 amending Regulation (EC) No. 1466/97 on the strengthening of the surveillance of budgetary positions and the surveillance and coordination of economic policies; Regulation (EU) No. 1176/2011 1 on the prevention and correction of macroeconomic imbalances; Regulation (EU) No. 1177/2011 amending Regulation (EC) No. 1467/97 on speeding up and clarifying the implementation of the excessive deficit procedure; and Directive 2011/85/EU on requirements for budgetary frameworks of the Member States (OJ L 306, 23.11.2011, pp. 1–47).

17   The publication of a list of demands established by the ECB and the IMF as a precondition of Italy's bail-out in August 2011 is still instructive (http://www.corriere. it/economia/11_settembre_29/trichet_draghi_inglese_304a5f1e-ea59-11e0-ae06-4da866778017.shtml). While not suggesting specific legislation, the letter details a number of measures which would, if taken at EU level, be well beyond the EU legislative competence.

sovereign debt, such institutionalized governance by cooperation generates a degree of coercion that may well outperform traditional hierarchical governance. It is thus not necessarily 'soft' in its effects, although it may be 'soft law' (Peters, 2011). That latter aspect has meant so far that it also escapes judicial review by the Court of Justice. However, in inducing national policy-makers from abandoning core elements of EU socio-economic models, it seems no less efficient than the Court's case law.

To draw an interim conclusion, the EU commands an incredibly complex array of instruments to realize its normative commitment to an EU socio-economic model. While 'hard law' and 'new governance' have often been perceived as representing two opposed end points on a spectrum of more or less efficient modes of action, the short overview of economic governance has shown that 'new governance', while not legally binding, is not necessarily less efficient. However, more efficiency of 'new governance' requires the existence of sanctions or other mechanisms to induce Member States to seriously pursue targets. As long as such mechanisms (or even targets) are not introduced in relation to social policy fields such as combating poverty or unemployment, the imbalance between economic and social aims is perpetuated (Cantillon and Mechelen, 2012).

Can the EU's Socio-economic Model Survive?

All this seems to question whether the EU socio-economic model can survive at all. Recently, such doubts have focused on the euro currency crisis, which coincides with a less positive appreciation of the EU generally.[18] This renewed EU scepticism is mirrored in academic writing, where an EU sceptic position seems on the rise generally (Tsoukalis, 2011; Usherwood and Startin, 2013).

The Currency Crisis and the Design of the European Economic and Monetary Union (EMU)

While there have always been pessimistic as well as optimistic views on the viability of any EU social or socio-economic model, the euro currency crisis has had a devastating impact on any remaining optimism (Jepsen, 2013). The pessimist views are most pronounced in relation to economic and monetary union,

---

18   Eurobarometer surveys confirmed that citizens in autumn 2010 still expected the EU to successfully govern the crisis (Standard Eurobarometer 74 Europeans, the European Union and the crisis – autumn 2010), while in December 2012 citizens' trust in the EU institutions and their positive appreciation of the common currency were suffering a steady decline (Standard Eurobarometer 78 Citizens and the EU, December 2012: 15 and 16). However, more detailed analysis suggests that the crisis is a mere trigger for increased public hostility towards the EU, whose causes lie in the rise of nationalism and populism (Serricchio *et al.*, 2013).

its intrinsic viability in spite of a focus on balanced budgets and the lack of federal style fiscal transfers (Arestis and Sawyer, 2011), as well as its negative impact on any EU social model (Barbier, 2013; Whyman *et al.*, 2012: 321).

These pessimist views chime with those that emerged upon the inception of EMU, predicting that the European social model would be 'sacrificed on the altar of the common currency' (Hay, 2000; Panić, 2005). After 2005, optimists seemed to be confirmed in their initial hope that EU national welfare regimes would prove resilient to the pressures that were predicted to result from the convergence criteria (Tolga Bolukbasi, 2009; Glennester, 2010). However, with the crisis, even those who were optimistic initially (Pochet and Vanhercke, 1999) have now come to the conclusion that fundamental policy changes resulting from changed compositions of the European institutions endangered any social policy (Pochet and Degryse, 2013). Such pessimism leads some authors to propose radical renationalization of all politics by leaving the EU (Whyman *et al.*, 2012: 266–80). Such a return to national protectionism with a 'Keynesian' profile does obviously not offer any perspectives for EU countries with weaker economies. Others impatiently demand to develop a true constitution of economic prosperity by stressing the obligations to maintain 'healthy budgets', if necessary by ignoring national electorates (Adamski, 2013).

In spite of the prolonged economic and currency crisis, proposals in favour of realizing the EU socio-economic model have been made. Above all, demands for more integration and credible steps towards a political union are made in order to decrease the democratic deficit inherent in the mechanisms based on Memoranda of Understanding described above (Habermas, 2012: 345–48). More substantively, it has been suggested to support the monetary union by complementing mere economic crisis governance with a new social pact (Begg, 2013). Specific proposals include the creation of a European pension fund to avoid losses of old age income as a consequence of future global crises (Zuleeg and Martens, 2009). However, it must be said that presently the design of a future economic and monetary union that allows developing the EU socio-economic model in line with its normative base is still nebulous. Much research and policy debate will be needed to achieve that aim.

The two chapters immediately following this introduction tackle the questions that still need to be answered from the perspective of heterodox economics and political economy respectively, while at the same time highlighting different points on the spectrum between pessimist and optimist assessment of the viability of the socio-economic model. The two chapters by Arestis, Fontana, Sawyers and Verdun agree that economic and monetary union is not perfect: it suffers from design faults (Arestis *et al.*) and an asymmetry between monetary union and mere economic policy coordination (Verdun). Arestis *et al.* provide a detailed critique of the recent policy responses to the euro currency crisis based on heterodox macro-economics. They show how the reinforcement of the euro-convergence criteria of 1993 (including a ceiling for government budget deficits of 3 per cent of GDP and for overall government debt of 60 per cent of the GDP) through the Stability and

Growth Pact and the Treaty for Stability, Coordination and Governance amount to strangulating any economically weak national economy, after having explained their view that the construction of economic and monetary union does not allow upholding the European Social Model. They conclude that so far, the policy responses to the crisis are ill conceived and a major policy change is warranted. Verdun starts her chapter by recounting the history of the EMU and the degree to which the social dimension had been addressed at its inception. She then recounts the various stages of development via the Stability and Growth Pact of 1999 and the responses to the 2008 crises. In concluding, she argues in favour of deeper integration in the euro area, and expresses concern about the lack of democratic accountability of the measures to contain the crisis. Her optimism that a solution will be found is based on the conviction that a leap to deeper integration will be made possible by the threats experienced presently.

The EU Socio-economic Model Beyond (and Before) EMU

While the debate at the time of writing is dominated by the currency crisis, the viability of the EU socio-economic model has been a matter of concern before and beyond the economic and monetary union. The recent assessments frequently rest on opinions formed long before the crisis, and not necessarily on the common currency only.

The optimists have stressed the positive potential of the Internal (Common) Market of overcoming national parochialism, and opening up a new world for the cosmopolitan citizens moving freely between Member States (Weiler, 2003). While this is a general statement, among those who analyze aspects of the EU impact on national welfare policies and national labour regimes more specifically, pessimism prevailed from the mid-1990s, conjuring the image of Member States' 'semi-sovereignty' (Leibfried and Pierson, 1995) in the field of welfare policy and the continued abstinence of the EU in this field (Streeck, 1999). Such scepticism has been a relatively dominant theme throughout a number of publications.[19] Today, some authors seem to have given up on the possibility of a true EU-level social policy and focus on defending the Member States' ability to retain scope for national policies in this regard (Everson and Joerges, 2012; Syrpis, 2007). Of course maintaining the national pillars of the EU socio-economic models is essential (Schiek, 2008). However, establishing the EU socio-economic model exclusively at national levels has been correctly labelled reverse ordoliberalism (Giubboni, 2006) – a strategy that is not tenable for Member States without a comfortable export surplus (Schiek, 2012: 230–32).

In spite of all this, optimist alternatives are possible and have been developed. For example, the decreasing capacity of Member States to guarantee the preconditions of national welfare has been identified as a viable driver towards

---

19   See for example most of the contributions in Dougan and Spaventa, 2005 and some of those in Shaw, 2000.

a new social contract at EU level (Poiares Maduro, 2000); a new constitutional principle of solidarity has been devised as a lever to overcome tensions between competiveness and national welfare state principles (Ross, 2010); and nesting of national welfare states in a European framework has been proposed as a strategy to overcome national closure (Ferrera, 2012). Positive visions of a new dynamic of EU social policy were also inspired by the initial Lisbon strategy, which endeavoured to coordinate national social policies (Daly, 2012; Dawson, 2011). It was seen as creating space for creative policy learning (de Schutter and Lenoble, 2010) and is still, together with enhanced social values, hailed as a starting point for new liberal welfarism (Ferrera, 2013). Such positive views could be developed further in the expectation that some of the suffocating aspects of socio-economic models in coordinated market economies with conservative welfare states could be overcome through such Europeanization: the normative commitment to equality and non-discrimination, for example, could be used to challenge gender stereotypes entrenched in welfare legislation. Above all, new orientations for EU-level social law and policy have been developed on the basis of the new normative framework established by the Treaty of Lisbon (Cantillon *et al.*, 2012; Dawson and Witte, 2012).

Current and future research must, however, neither forget to carefully analyze the impact of the CJEU case law on Member States' room for manoeuvre in maintaining social standards at national levels nor omit to analyze the mutual impact of preconceived (restrictive) conception of social solidarity and an EU social policy driven by competitiveness.

The next two chapters of this book work on these critical junctures of EU integration and national social policy. The commonality of these chapters is that they focus on the alleged intervention of the EU into national social policies, and at the same time show scope of manoeuvre for Member States – though this scope is more widely used in Sweden than in the UK. Vinterskog's chapter discusses the relation of the EU to international law regimes securing rights of workers, contrasting judicial governance and the content of harmonizing directives with Member States' (in this case Sweden's) wish to comply with ILO convention 94. This convention requires governments to ensure that their contracting partners and their subcontractors comply with local working conditions. The Convention could be seen as a new governance instrument as well, since the instrument for such compliance lies in contractual agreement rather than legislative imposition. Such government strategy can conflict with judicial governance by the Court, whose case law requires that Member States abstain from imposing social contract clauses, in particular if aiming to ensure that collectively agreed local conditions are applied. Vinterskog proposes to utilize the new social values of the Treaty of Lisbon as an additional argument to interpreting Treaty provisions and the public procurement directive in ways that allow for Member States to comply with ILO obligations. O'Brien's chapter focuses on the ambiguous character of EU social law and policy, which in her view betrays the de-commodification ethos of classical welfare state benefits. Discussing EU citizenship and related rules as well as the OMC's in social policy, she identifies a predisposition to embracing values such as individualism and competitiveness for granting benefits. The UK, she argues, as an emanation of liberal welfare states, is well disposed to being infiltrated by those values, and giving up its nominal autonomy in defining welfare provision in favour of 'neoliberalizing' it.

The EU Socio-economic Model and Citizens' Involvement

The apparent friction between expanding the normative demands on the EU to pursue its specific socio-economic model and refraining from adopting additional legislative and policy competences can be used as a starting point to develop the societal base of EU policy making. It can be argued that the lack of EU competences in fields such as wage-setting or combating poverty corresponds to another element characteristic of the European socio-economic model: that social and welfare policy is not only or even mainly pursued by the state, but partly or predominantly left to civil society in the guise of charity, consumer organizations and social partners. Such reading can be perceived as a necessary complementation of the EU's incomplete new constitution (Schiek, 2012: 238–40). Long before the Treaty of Lisbon, involvement of civil society and social actors has been one of the hallmarks of the 'new governance' EU style. The Open Method of Coordination, as developed on the basis of the employment chapter, offered ample room for including citizens and their organizations when Member States developed national policy goals and identified best practice examples. With the Treaty of Lisbon, citizens' involvement has also become an element of the EU's democratic legitimacy, in particular through the citizens' initiative (Article 24 TFEU) as an element of direct democracy. All this enhances the role of civil society, and poses the question of what role is adequate for civil and social organizations in contributing to the EU's socio-economic model.

Chapters 6 and 7 contribute to this debate. Cseres and Schrauwen discuss whether consumer empowerment as promoted by the Commission in its recent consumer policies satisfies the conditions of creating a new class of citizens who can enhance the legitimacy of EU consumer law and policy. The chapter's ambitions go beyond consumer law, though. The authors initially provide a critical analysis of the Commission's discourse around citizens' empowerment as emanating from policy documents issued on the Citizens' Initiative and the role of public consultations independently of such an initiative. Their interim conclusion is that both the Citizens' initiative and the public consultations empower the Commission rather than the citizens. Unsurprisingly, their analysis of the 'active consumer's' role in legislation on the electricity market and consumer redress concludes that these too do not exhaust the potential of truly empowering consumers to act as critical citizenry. Guasti analyzes the role of civil society in contributing to EU legitimacy. In defining civil society, she distinguishes between civil society organizations in a narrow sense and the organizations engaged in social dialogue, i.e. trade unions and employers and their organizations, and compares the respective influence of both these elements of European civil society on EU legitimacy. Her analysis is based on a dataset developed for media coverage of debates of the Constitutional Treaty. Relating to issues relevant to the socio-economic models, she finds that while civil society is an active player, social dialogue partners are more active and better networked throughout the EU. The confrontation of the research question with reality proves sobering: there is little proof of influence of both civil and social dialogue on the shaping of the EU socio-economic parts of the draft constitution, not least due to a lack of transparency. However, a glimpse of hope can be derived from the chapter in that civil and social dialogue offer an opportunity for networking to the participants and may thus contribute to the establishment of EU civil society.

The EU as a Global Model?

The currency crisis is not merely a European one,[20] as is among others evidenced by the IMF's involvement in its management. It impacts on the global economy – if only by relegating the European Union to a lower rank in that global economy than it had occupied before. This seems a regrettable development, since it was the European Union that had been seen as a protection against 'global winds of change' furthering a 'pure market form of capitalism' (Mistral, 2009: 2, 10). Arguably, it did fulfil this role in the very early stages of the crisis, when its politicians supported heterodox concepts such as Keynesian policies beyond mere quantitative easing, which were gaining traction globally. While this initially only lasted for two years, until 2010 (Wilson, 2012), at the time of writing, both the IMF and the EU Commission have demonstrated a renewed distance to overly draconian austerity measures. Thus, possibly the EU may once again have the opportunity to fulfil the role of holding up an alternative version of capitalism, perhaps by establishing a new social contract between its own citizens and, for example, banks having profited from the bail-outs, and propagating similar solutions globally (Wilson, 2012: 408).

Presently, these ideas appear as a very optimistic vision. However, it must not be forgotten that the EU Commission has from the 1990s portrayed the Union as contributing to a social face of globalization. The last two chapters discuss the EU's self-declared global role from two distinct perspectives that may well become decisive for any such export of the EU socio-economic model.

Zahn's chapter is concerned with the question of how exactly the EU develops its role as a global actor for the social side of globalization, and how this outward face in social policy matters relates to the inner-EU social policy. In the first part, she traces the development of EU internal social policy, taking a mainly critical position to the predominance of new governance which is not prone to creating legally binding instruments. In addressing EU external social policy, she finds that

---

20   However, the argument that an US and EU-based crisis has 'arrogantly been defined as a global one' (Tsoukalis, 2011: 25) deserves some thought.

while this is necessarily restricted to the indirect influence of non-EU states, the practice of conditionality of aid or cooperation has similar coercive potential as the MoU discussed above. Going further in discussing the (limited) changes of the legal framework for external social policy after the Treaty of Lisbon, and the practical use of conditionality within the EU in the financial crisis, the chapter demonstrates how the coercive force of conditionality is much better developed for economic aims internally. The external social policy could thus serve as a model on how to promote social policy aims through those same instruments. Sokhi-Bulley's chapter too tackles 'new governance' in relation to the EU's global role, taking the field of human rights as an example. Investigating the activities of the EU Fundamental Rights Agency in monitoring human rights compliance, the author exposes this practice as an emanation of governmentality in a Foucaultian sense. The EU utilizes and arguably demotes international human rights to instruments of control and monitoring, which may well run counter to their noble cause. Human rights become quantified by indicators, measurable and parts of a toolkit inducing Member States to constantly monitor themselves. The parallel to practices used to monitor performance in the field of economic governance is obvious, though not explicitly argued. In an eerie way, she manages to expose how governance without government can pervert the content of values central to democracy, such as human rights.

Outlook

If the EU is to maintain momentum beyond the current crisis, its official motto of unity in diversity must be taken seriously. The common currency arguably constitutes a halfway house on the road to deeper political and socio-economic integration. Deeper integration across this vast continent, however, should not only respect but also embrace the diversity of its regions, which presently comprise economies with stronger agricultural and touristic sectors as well as strongly export-based economies and egalitarian knowledge-based societies. Forcing any of Europe's regions to converge to another's socio-economic strengths would ultimately result in overall loss. In maintaining diversity, deeper socio-economic integration will need to establish sustainable interregional exchange and pan-European redistribution. The transnational solidarity necessary to achieve such sustainability would have to be tied into a common future of developing new directions for Europe's societies based on active citizen participation and democratization of its socio-economic model(s). In that way, the EU could once again contribute its visions to the world's future, instead of initiating ever further downward spirals in prosperity and societal integration. The chapters in this collection contribute to answering questions posed by these challenges, and while not providing complete answers, constitute starting points for future cross-disciplinary research on this.

Bibliography

Adamski, D. 2013. Europe's (Misguided) constitution of economic prosperity. *Common Market Law Review*, 50(1), 47–86.

Andenas, M., Baasch Andersen, C. and Ascroft, R. 2011. Towards a theory of harmonisation in *Theory and Practice of Harmonisation* edited by M. Andenas and C. Baasch Andersen. Cheltenham: Edward Elgar, 572–94.

Andor, L. 2012. *What can social enterprises contribute to the Europe 2020 Strategy?* [Online] Available at: http://europa.eu/rapid/press-release_SPEECH -12-677_en.htm [accessed 2 March 2013].

Arestis, P. and Sawyer, M. 2011. The design faults of the Economic and Monetary Union, *Journal of Contemporary European Studies*, 19(1), 21–32.

Armstrong, K.A. 2010. *Governing Social Inclusion. Europeanization through Policy Coordination*. Oxford: Oxford University Press.

Arts, W.A. and Gelissen, J. 2010. Models of the Welfare State in *The Oxford Handbook of the Welfare State* edited by F. Castles *et al*. Oxford: Oxford University Press, 569–83.

Ashiagbor, D. 2013. Unravelling the embedded liberal bargain: Labour and social welfare law in the context of EU market integration. *European Law Journal*, 19(3), 303–24.

Barbier, J.C. 2013. Europe Social: l'état d'alert. *Opinion paper: Observatoire social européen*, 13(4).

Barcelona European Council. 2002. *Presidency Report*. [Online]. Available at: http://www.consilium.europa.eu/ueDocs/cms_Data/docs/pressData/en/ec/ 71025.pdf [accessed 29 April 2013].

Barysh, K. 2006. East versus west? The European economic and social model after enlargement in *Global Europe, Social Europe* edited by A. Giddens, P. Diamond and R. Liddle. Cambridge: Polity Press, 52–69.

Beck, U. 2013. *German Europe*. Cambridge: Polity Press.

Begg, I. 2013. Are better defined rules enough? An assessment of the post-crisis governance reforms of the governance of EMU. *Transfer*, 19(1), 49–62.

Börzel, T. 2012. The European Union – a Unique Governance Mix? In *The Oxford Handbook on Governance* edited by D. Levi-Faur. Oxford: Oxford University Press, 639–52.

Busch, K., Hermann, C., Hinrichs, K. and Schulten, T. 2013. *Euro Crisis, Austerity Policy and the European Social Model*. Berlin: Friedrich Ebert Stiftung.

Cantillon, B. and Mechelen, N.V. 2012. Between dream and reality. On anti-poverty policy, minimum income protection and the European social model in *Social Inclusion and Social Protection in the EU: Interactions between Law and Policy* edited by B. Cantillon, P. Ploscar and H. Verschuren. Antwerp: Intersentia, 173–204.

Cantillon, B., Verschueren, H. and Ploscar, P. 2012. Social Protection and Social Inclusion in the EU: Any Interactions between Law and Policy? In *Social Inclusion and Social Protection in the EU: Interactions between Law and*

Policy edited by B. Cantillon, H. Verschueren and P. Ploscar. Cambridge, Antwerp: Intersentia, 1–16.

Clauwaert, S. and Schömann, I. 2012. *The crisis and national labour law reforms: a mapping exercise*. Brussels: ETUI aisbl.

Cook, L.J. 2010. Eastern Europe and Russia in *The Oxford Handbook of the Welfare State* edited by F. Castles *et al*. Oxford: Oxford University Press, 671–86.

Craig, P. 2010. *The Lisbon Treaty. Law, Politics and Treaty Reform*. Oxford: Oxford University Press.

Craig, P. 2012. The Stability, Coordination and Governance Treaty: principles, politics and pragmatics. *European Law Review*, 37(3), 231–48.

Daly, M. 2012. Social inclusion and the Lisbon strategy in *The EU's Lisbon Strategy. Evaluting Success, Understanding Failure* edited by P. Copeland and D. Papadimitriou. Houndsmills: Palgrave Macmillan, 68–87.

Dawson, M. 2011. *New Governance and the Transformation of European Law: Coordinating EU Social Law and Policy*. Cambridge: Cambridge University Press.

Dawson, M. and Witte, B.D. 2012. The EU legal framework of social inclusion and social protection: Between the Lisbon Strategy and the Lisbon Treaty in *Social Inclusion and Social Protection in the EU: Interactions between Law and Policy* edited by B. Cantillon, H. Verschueren and P. Ploscar. Cambridge and Antwerp: Intersentia, 41–69.

Delors, J. 2013. Economic governance in the European Union: Past, present and future, *Journal of Common Market Studies*, 51(2), 169–78.

Devroe, W. and Cleynenbreugel, P.V. 2011. Observations on economic governance and the search for a European economic constitution in *European Economic and Social Constitutionalism after the Treaty of Lisbon* edited by D. Schiek, U. Liebert and H. Schneider. Cambridge: Cambridge University Press, 95–120.

Diederichs, U. 2011. The dynamics of change in EU governance in *The Dynamics of Change in EU Governance* edited by U. Diederichs, W. Reiners and W. Wessels. Cheltenham: Edward Elgar, 1–20.

Dougan, M. and Spaventa, E. (eds). 2005. *Social Welfare and EU Law*. Oxford: Hart.

Dyson, K. and Quaglia, L. 2012. Economic and Monetary Union and the Lisbon Strategy in *The EU's Lisbon Strategy. Evaluting Success, Understanding Failure* edited by P. Copeland and D. Papadimitriou. Houndsmills: Palgrave Macmillan,189–206.

Esping-Andersen, G. 1990. *The Three Worlds of Welfare Capitalism*. Cambridge: Polity Press.

Esping-Andersen, G. 1999. *Social Foundations of Post-Industrial Economies*. Oxford: Oxford University Press.

European Commission. 1994. *European Social Policy – a way forward for the European Union. A White Paper*. Brussels: European Union.

European Commission. 2010. *Europe 2020. A Strategy for smart, sustainable and inclusive growth COM (2010) 2020*. Brussels: European Union.

European Commission. 2012a. *Action for stability, growth and jobs (COM (2010) 299)*. Brussels: European Union.

European Commission. 2012b. *A blueprint for a deep and genuine economic and monetary union: launching a European debate (COM (2012) 777)*. Brussels: European Union.

Everson, M. and Joerges, C. 2012. Reconfiguring the Politics-Law Relationship in the Integration Project through Conflicts-Law Constitutionalism, *European Law Journal*, 18(5), 644–66.

Featherstone, K., Kornelakis, A. and Zartoloudis, S. 2012. Conceptualising the Lisbon Strategy: Europeanisation and varieties of capitalism in *The EU's Lisbon Strategy. Evaluting Success, Understanding Failure* edited by P. Copeland and D. Papadimitriou. Houndsmills: Palgrave Macmillan, 50–67.

Ferrera, M. 2010. The south European countries in *The Oxford Handbook of the Welfare State* edited by F. Castles *et al*. Oxford: Oxford University Press, 616–29.

Ferrera, M. 2012. Modest beginnings, Timid progresses: What next for social Europe? In *Social Inclusion and Social Protection in the EU: Interactions between Law and Policy* edited by B. Cantillon, H. Verschueren and P. Ploscar. Cambridge, Antwerp: Intersentia, 17–39.

Ferrera, M. 2013. Liberal Neo-Welfarism: new perspectives for the European Social Model. *Opinion paper: Observatoire social européen*, 14.

Giddens, A. 2006. Social model for Europe? *Global Europe, Social Europe* edited by A. Giddens, P. Diamond and R. Liddle. Cambridge: Polity, 14–35.

Giubboni, S. 2006. *Social Rights and Market Freedom in the European Constitution. A Labour Law Perspective*. Cambridge: Cambridge University Press.

Glennester, H. 2010. The sustainability of western welfare states in *The Oxford Handbook of the Welfare State* edited by F. Castles *et al*. Oxford: Oxford University Press, 689–702.

Habermas, J. 2012. The crisis of the European Union in the light of a constitutionalization of international law, *The European Journal of International Law*, 23(2), 335–48.

Hall, P. and Soskice, D. 2001. *Varieties of Capitalism. Institutional Foundations of Comparative Advantage*. Oxford : Oxford University Press.

Hatzoupoulos, V. 2007. Why the Open Method of Coordination is bad for you: a letter to the EU, *European Law Journal*, 12(1) 309–42.

Hay, C. 2000. Contemporary capitalism, globalisation, regionalisation and the persistence of national variation, *Review of International Studies*, 26(4), 509–31.

Jepsen, M. 2013. Conclusions, *Transfer*, 19(1), 117–20.

Jepsen, M. and Serrano Pasqual, A. 2005. The European social model: an exercise in deconstruction, *Journal of European Social Policy*, 15(3), 231–45.

Leibfried, S. and Pierson, P. (eds). 1995. *European Social Policy Between Fragmentation and Integration*. Washington: Brookings Institution.

Lisbon European Council. 2000. *Presidency Conclusions*. [Online]. Available at: http://www.europarl.europa.eu/summits/lis1_en.htm [accessed 29 April 2013].

McCormick, J. 2010. *Europeanism*. Oxford: Oxford University Press.

Merino, G. 2012. Legal developments in the European Economic and Monetary Union during the debt crisis: the mechanisms of financial assistance. *Common Market Law Review*, 49(5), 1613–45.

Mistral, J. 2009. Shaping a new world economic governance: A challenge for America and Europe in *Liberalism in Crisis? European Economic Governance for an Age of Turbulence* edited by C. Secchi and A. Villafranca. Cheltenham: Edward Elgar, 1–23.

Neergaard, U., Gronden, J., Krajewski, M. and Szyscak, E. (eds). 2013. *Social Services of General Interest in Europe*. Vienna: Springer.

Panić, M. 2005. The Euro and the welfare state in *Social Welfare and EU law* edited by M. Dougan and E. Spaventa. Oxford: Hart, 25–44.

Peters, A. 2011. Soft law as a new mode of governance in *The Dynamics of Change in EU Governance* edited by U. Diederichs, W. Reiners and W. Wessels. Cheltenham: Edward Elgar, 21–51.

Pochet, P. and Degryse, C. 2013. Monetary Union and the stakes for democracy and social policy, *Transfer*, 19(1), 103–16.

Pochet, P. and Vanhercke, B. 1999. The challenge of economic and monetary union to social protection. In *Financing Social Protection in Europe* edited by J. Saari. Helsinki: Ministry of Social Affairs and Health Publications, 56–98.

Poiares Maduro, M. 2000. Europe's social self: The sickness unto death in *Social Law and Policy in an Evolving European Union* edited by J. Shaw. Oxford: Hart, 325–49.

Presidency Council. 2012. *Presidency Non-Paper Competitiveness Council and the Annual Growth Survey 2012*. Brussels: Council of the European Union.

Ross, M. 2010. Solidarity – A new constitutional paradigm for the EU? In *Promoting Solidarity in the European Union* edited by M.Ross and Y.Borgaman-Prebil. Oxford: Oxford University Press, 23–45.

Scharpf, F. 2002. The European social model: coping with challenges of diversity, *Journal of Common Market Studies*, 40(4), 645–70.

Scharpf, F.W. 2010. The asymmetry of European integration, or why the EU cannot be a 'social market economy', *Socio-Economic Review*, 8, 211–50.

Schiek, D. 2008. The European social model and the Services Directive in *The Services Directive – Consequences for the Welfare State and the European Social Model* edited by U. Neergaard, R. Nielsen and L. Roseberry. Copenhagen: DJØF Publishing, 25–63.

Schiek, D. 2012. *Economic and Social Integration. The Challenge for EU Constitutional Law*. Cheltenham: Edward Elgar.

Schutter, O. de and Lenoble, J. (eds). 2010. *Reflexive Governance : Redefining the Public Interest in a Pluralistic World*. Oxford: Hart.

Serricchio, F., Tsakatika, M. and Quaglia, L. 2013. Euroscepticism and the global financial crisis, *Journal of Contemporary European Studies*, 51(1), 51–4.

Shaw, J. (ed). 2000. *Social Law and Policy in an Evolving European Union*. Oxford: Hart.

Streeck, W. 1999. *Competitive Solidarity: Rethinking the European Social Model.* Cologne: Max Planck Institut für Gesellschaftsforschung.

Syrpis, P. 2007. *EU Intervention in Domestic Labour Law.* Oxford: Oxford University Press.

Thelen, K. 2012. Varieties of capitalism: Trajectories of liberalization and the new politics of social solidarity, *Annual Review of Political Science*, 15, 137–59.

Tinsbergen, J. 1954. *International Economic Integration.* Amsterdam: Elsevier.

Tolga Bolukbasi, H. 2009. On consensus, constraint and choice: economic and monetary integration and Europe's welfare states. *Journal of European Public Policy*, 16(4), 527–44.

Tsoukalis, L. 2011. The shattering of illusions – And what next? *Journal of Common Market Studies*, 49(1), 19–44.

Usherwood, S. and Startin, N. 2013. Euroscepticism as a persistent phenomenon. *Journal of Common Market Studies*, 51(1), 1–16.

Weiler, J.H. 2003. In defence of the status quo: Europe's constitutional Sonderweg in *European Constitutionalism Beyond the State* edited by J.H. Weiler and M. Wind. Cambridge: Cambridge University Press, 7–23.

Whyman, P. Baimbridge, M. and Mullen, A. (eds). 2012. *The Political Economy of the European Social Model.* New York: Routledge.

Wilson, G. 2012. Governance after the crisis in *The Oxford Handbook on Governance* edited by D. Levi-Faur. Oxford: Oxford University Press, 398–412.

Witte, B. de. 2011. The European Treaty Amendment for the Creation of a Financial Stability Mechanism, *Sieps: European Policy Analysis*, (6), 1–6.

Zuleeg, F. and Martens, H. 2009. Beyond the current crisis: How should Europe deal with government deficits and public debt in future in *Liberalism in Crisis? European Economic Governance in a Time of Crisis* edited by C. Secchi and A. Villafranca. Cheltenham: Edward Elgar, 148–77.

Chapter 2

The Dysfunctional Nature of the Economic and Monetary Union

Philip Arestis, Giuseppe Fontana and Malcolm Sawyer

Introduction

The Economic and Monetary Union (EMU) is confronted with a multi-headed set of crises – an unemployment crisis, a balance of payments crisis, a banking and financial crisis, a fiscal sovereign debt crisis and an existential crisis. The underlying argument of this chapter is that these sets of crises have arisen from or been exacerbated by the ways in which the EMU was constructed, rather than 'bad behaviour' by some Member States. Indeed, the 'euro crisis' can only be resolved through major policy changes, which permit the combination of the continued existence of the Euro with acceptable economic performance.

We deal with the design faults of the EMU in section two after this very short introduction. Section three discusses the economic performance of the EMU, while section four looks into the neoliberalism aspects of the European social model. Section five deals with the 'one size fits all problems' of the euro area (a term used interchangeably with EMU). Section six provides a critique of the 'fiscal compact' and the Treaty on Stability, Coordination and Governance (TSCG) in the Economic and Monetary Union. Section seven concludes.

Design Faults of the Economic and Monetary Union

The design faults of the construction of the EMU can be seen by reference to the convergence criteria for membership of the euro area. The Maastricht Treaty laid down criteria that should be met by those seeking to join the euro and indeed all the countries that met the criteria were obliged to join, though Denmark and the UK secured opt-outs from that obligation.[1] The Maastricht criteria included

---

1 The convergence criteria can be summarized as follows: (1) average exchange rate not to deviate by more than 2.25 per cent from its central rate for the two years prior to membership; (2) inflation rate should not exceed the average rate of inflation of the three community nations with the lowest inflation rate by 1.5 per cent; (3) long-term interest rates not to exceed the average interest rate by 2 per cent of the three countries with the lowest inflation rate; (4) government budget deficit not to exceed 3 per cent of its GDP; and (5) the

the convergence of the inflation rate and the interest rate in a country with the average experiences of other potential members. This has a clear rationale in that under a currency union there is a single level of interest rate (as set by the Central Bank) and the clear expectation of similar rates of inflation across countries. However, there was no attempt to assess whether the inflationary conditions in potential Member States were similar and that was significant in two respects. First, the inflation targeting regime of the European Central Bank (ECB) rested on the following linkage: changes in the interest rate → changes in the level of demand → changes in the inflation rate. However, differences in the price and wage determination processes between countries would lead to different outcomes in terms of inflation resulting from a common interest rate. Second, countries differed substantially in their past experiences, future expectations of and in their general attitudes to inflation (including the legendary German fear of inflation) which portended differential rates of inflation.

The convergence criteria also included some stability of the exchange rate prior to joining, which again had a clear rationale, but no attention was given to the trade and current account positions of each country. This was highly significant as clearly the formation of a single currency, which is the ultimate in fixing the nominal exchange rate between countries, permits no devaluation option to adjust a current account deficit (or revaluation for current account surplus) and, as is now readily apparent, a change in the real exchange rate of a country within a currency union can only be secured by internal deflation (or inflation in other Member States) or possibly exit from the euro area.[2] The general proposition is that a (national) trade deficit cannot be sustained indefinitely. It requires borrowing capital from abroad and hence willingness of foreigners to continue to lend capital, though experience suggests that a trade deficit can continue for many years. The borrowing to cover the trade deficit means rising debt and rising interest (and similar) payments on the debt and then a tendency for the current account (that is, trade account plus net income including interest payments) deficit to rise.[3] The creation of the single market, the removal of barriers to capital movement, and the removal of exchange rate risk for borrowing between members of the EMU all

---

overall government debt not to exceed 60 per cent of its GDP. The convergence criteria are decisive for each country's membership in the Euro area and were initially introduced in a protocol annexed to the Treaty of Maastricht, which has since then only undergone editorial changes. Protocol No. 13 on Article 140 TFEU has been consolidated recently (2012) OJ C 326/281, accessible under http://eur-lex.Europa.eu.

2   It should be noted that the exit of a country from the Euro area is not discussed in the criteria for countries joining the EMU.

3   Denote trade deficit (as proportion of GDP) by $(m - x)$, the foreign debt (D) to GDP (Y) ratio as $d = D/Y$, then $dd/dt = (m - x) + d(i - g)$ where i is rate of interest on foreign debt and g is growth rate of GDP (both in real terms, or both in nominal terms). The debt to GDP ratio will then tend to rise, though it can be seen that there are circumstances in which it would not; for example, g much greater than i, or d itself positive (see, for example, Arestis and Sawyer, 2011).

meant that it was rather easy for current account deficit countries to borrow capital to fund their deficits; indeed, many countries have been able to have continual and rising deficits through the 2000s. But the financial crisis presented major difficulties for the continuation of borrowing by deficit countries (and the counterpart lending by surplus countries). The consequences of the continued borrowing and the build-up of debts are now plain to see. The point to be made here is that this arose from a failure to consider current account imbalances at the time of the formation of the euro; and also a failure to have any adjustment processes whereby those current account imbalances could be adjusted (or arrangements for the long-term funding of those imbalances being made). It has long been known that in a fixed exchange rate regime (and a single currency is the extreme version of a fixed exchange rate regime between the Member States) there are severe difficulties in resolving current account imbalances without resorting to deflation in the deficit countries, and the EMU is no exception as regards Member States losing their freedom to change the exchange rate of the currency in use.

The Stability and Growth Pact (SGP) brought in an attempt to impose a common fiscal policy on all Member States, whatever their economic position. The fiscal policy would have been rather deflationary, if it had been implemented with a maximum of 3 per cent of GDP as a limit on budget deficits and a balanced or small surplus on the budget over the cycle, and this represented a tightening as compared with the 'convergence criteria'. There are a range of criticisms that can be made of the SGP. We would highlight the imposition of an arbitrary figure for the size of the budget deficit without thought for consequences and the attempt made to impose a common fiscal position on all countries.

The small scale of the EU budget at around 1 per cent of GDP and the requirement that it is balanced year by year clearly preclude any euro area (or EU)-level fiscal policy. This lack of euro area-level fiscal policy precludes fiscal transfers whether as a means of stabilizing the euro area economy or to effect transfers from rich regions to poor regions.

The 'independent' European Central Bank has also created a range of problems. We have elsewhere criticized the specific policies pursued by the ECB and more generally the inflation targeting regime (for example, Arestis and Sawyer, 2008). The main point to be made here does not relate to the specific actions of the ECB but rather the institutional arrangements. We highlight the main argument as follows: first, an 'independent' Central Bank has led to a non-democratic organization and the only one with EMU level macroeconomic decisions to pursue its own, generally neoliberal agenda; and in terms of its policy objective, the pursuit of price stability and nothing else. Second, coordination and cooperation over macroeconomic policies become more difficult with these institutional arrangements. Third, the relationships between the ECB and the national fiscal authorities do not parallel the relationships between a national central bank and a national fiscal authority, even under the arrangements of national independent central banks (another requirement for the EU Member States whose currency is the euro). The ECB may but does not have to operate as lender of last resort. The

ECB cannot directly monetize budget deficits but in this regard does not operate differently from many other central banks (e.g. Bank of England). However, it can determine which national government paper it will accept in its open market operations. The underpinning of the debt of a national government comes from a combination of its tax raising abilities, the willingness by its central bank to purchase national government debt and, as a final resort, its willingness to create money. These underpinnings are reliant on the government debt being denominated in the national currency, which cannot be the case within a single currency area.

The focus of attention in the 'convergence criteria' and then in SGP was on the government budget deficit with no attention given to the current account deficit. Yet the current account deficit is a summary measure of what a country has to borrow from outside its borders. There is a further issue which can be seen by reference to the national accounts identity:

> Private savings minus private investment + Government budget surplus + Current account deficit (capital account inflow) is equal to zero

This relationship is a reflection of the fact that when one economic actor has a surplus of income over expenditure (and is saving and lending), another must have a deficit of income over expenditure (and is dissaving and borrowing).

If countries differ (as they do) substantially in terms of their current account position, then seeking to impose a common budget position on all does not make a great deal of sense, unless it is believed that there are compensating differences in the balance of savings and investment intentions. More generally, in seeking to impose a balanced government budget, recognition must be given to the consequences for the balance between savings and investment and the current account position.

Economic Performance of the Euro Area

The economic performance of the euro area countries over the period since the creation of the EMU has been rather lacklustre, even before the 'great recession' struck. Economic growth has been generally sluggish, averaging 1.9 per cent in the period 2002 to 2007, though growth rates varied with countries such as Germany and Italy growing much slower (at 1.2 per cent and 1.1 per cent respectively) and others enjoying much faster growth (notably Ireland at 5.5 per cent and Greece at 4.2 per cent). The rate of unemployment also differs significantly amongst countries and on average remained over 7.5 per cent throughout the 2000s. It has now risen to reach over 11 per cent (2012), though, confounding those who claimed that:

> Employment has risen by almost 15% since the launch of the single currency while unemployment has fallen to about 7% of the labour force, the lowest rate

in more than fifteen years. [...] The bulk of these improvements reflect reforms of both labour markets and social security systems carried out under the Lisbon Strategy for Growth and Jobs and the coordination and surveillance framework of EMU, as well as the wage moderation that has characterised most euro area countries (European Commission, 2008: 6).

Unemployment is into double figures in over half of the EMU countries. Inflation has remained low, though often breaking the 'below but close to 2 per cent' target of the ECB. There have been continuing disparities in economic performance in terms of unemployment and standards of living, which are of course highly significant as measures of economic well-being.[4]

Budget deficits, which under the terms of the SGP should have been less than 3 per cent of GDP and have been broadly in balance over the cycle, averaged 2.2 per cent of GDP (2002–2007), though seven of the original 12 Member States at some point exceeded the 3 per cent limit. The average ratio of public debt to GDP for the euro area was near 70 per cent in 2008 and in that year exceeded the intended 60 per cent limit in seven countries. The 'great recession' pushed deficit levels well beyond the 3 per cent limit with tax revenues falling sharply as economic activity slowed. Whilst in general the southern European countries entered the euro area with significant current account and trade deficits, the northern European countries entered with surpluses (or small deficits). Germany was a major exception in that it entered it with a small deficit, but with low inflation, depressed real wage growth and improving competitiveness that moved into a substantial surplus of around 5 per cent of GDP subsequently. The euro area as a whole has tended to run a current account close to balance, meaning that the current account surpluses of the northern European countries were in broad terms equal to the current account deficits of the southern European countries. Differences in inflation rates and in the evolution of competitiveness were a marked feature of the first decade of the EMU and went in the direction that the current account deficits of the southern European countries widened and the surpluses of the northern also increased (most notably in the case of Germany moving from small deficit to large surplus). There were substantial differences between countries in terms of changes in unit labour costs, which affected competitiveness. In terms of the loss of competitiveness (as measured by unit labour costs), it is estimated to be between 25 per cent and 30 per cent for Greece, Ireland, Portugal and Spain since the creation of the EMU in January 1999. The current account deficits of the southern European countries meant that those countries were borrowing heavily from other countries, mainly from northern European banks as well as British and American ones. In the context of the EMU with its single capital market and with southern euro area countries experiencing

---

4   All the statistics quoted in the text have been calculated from data in OECD *Economic Outlook* (various issues) available at http://www.oecd.org/eco/economicoutlook. htm.

much lower interest rates than previously, debts were rapidly built up by the southern European countries. The debts were mainly, though not exclusively, private sector rather than public sector ones. However, when the 'great recession' hit, the borrowing became increasingly government borrowing. For example, in 2007 Portugal had a current account deficit of 10 per cent of its GDP and a budget deficit of just over 3 per cent of its GDP; by 2010 the figures were 9.7 per cent and 9.2 per cent respectively.

This brief review of the economic performance of the euro area indicates that it was lacklustre in growth terms even before the financial crisis and does not give any support to the notion that the creation of a single currency would stimulate growth. There had been some improvement in the unemployment situation until the crisis, which has been completely reversed by the 'great recession'. Overall, this performance undermines claims that the drive to 'flexible labour markets' has delivered lower unemployment and it highlights the crucial role of aggregate demand in determining the level of unemployment. Targets on the inflation rate were just missed, but more significantly, differential inflation in prices and unit labour costs showed the 'one size fits all' problem of monetary policy that cannot address such differentials and which poses problems for a single currency area, as some countries gain in competitiveness and others lose. The budget deficit targets were frequently missed, which has undermined the 'rules-based' approach to fiscal policy and raises the question (to which we return below) of whether balanced budgets are in general achievable. The current account imbalances tended to increase and the capital flows between Member States (notably the lending flows from northern European countries to southern European countries) built up a debt situation which looks to be unsustainable.

Neoliberalism and the European Social Model

The policy framework governing the euro can be aligned with a more general theoretical framework, which finds its expression in the 'new consensus macroeconomics' (NCM).[5] The essential features of that theoretical framework are as follows:

i.   Politicians in particular, and the democratic process in general, cannot be trusted with economic policy formulation with a tendency to make decisions that have stimulating short-term effects (reducing unemployment), but which are detrimental in the longer term (notably a rise in inflation). In

---

5   The NCM framework, and its implications for monetary policy, was suggested initially by Goodfriend and King (1997), and Clarida, Gali and Gertler (1999). For an extensive theoretical treatment see Woodford (2003). For a critique see Arestis (2007), Arestis and Sawyer (2008) and Angeriz and Arestis (2008). Fontana (2009) critically assesses the role of government and fiscal policy in the NCM framework.

contrast, experts in the form of central bankers are not subject to political pressures to court short-term popularity and can take a longer-term perspective, where it is assumed that there is a conflict between the short term and the long term. Policy makers' scope for using discretion should be curtailed and the possibility of negative spill-overs from irresponsible fiscal policy must be reduced.

ii. There is only one objective of economic policy and this is price stability. This objective can only be achieved through monetary policy, and through manipulating the rate of interest in particular.

iii. Inflation is a monetary phenomenon and can be controlled through monetary policy. The central bank sets the key policy interest rate to influence monetary conditions, which in turn through their short-run effects on aggregate demand affect the future rate of inflation. Central banks have no discernible effects on the level or growth rate of output in the long run, which is determined exclusively by aggregate supply factors like technology, capital, and labour inputs. However, central banks do determine the rate of inflation in the long run.

iv. The level of unemployment fluctuates around a supply-side determined equilibrium rate of unemployment, generally labelled the NAIRU (non-accelerating inflation rate of unemployment). The level of the NAIRU may be favourably affected by a 'flexible' labour market, but is unaffected by the level of aggregate demand or by productive capacity.

v. Fiscal policy is impotent in terms of its impact on real variables (essentially because of beliefs in the Ricardian Equivalence Theorem and 'crowding out' arguments) and it should be subordinate to monetary policy in controlling inflation. There is allowance for the operation of 'automatic stabilizers' as the actual budget surplus or deficit will fluctuate during the course of the business cycle with tax revenues rising in boom and falling in recession and this provides some dampening of the cycle. The budget should be set to average balance over the course of the business cycle, though.

The structure of the ECB clearly conforms to all five points. The sole objective of the ECB is price stability and decisions are made by a governing body composed of bankers and financial experts. There are, and can be, no involvement by any other interest groups or any democratic body. The only EU-level policy form controlling inflation is monetary (interest rate) policy, which presumes that monetary policy is a relevant and effective instrument for the control of inflation. Inflation is in effect targeted by the ECB in the form of pursuit of 'price stability' interpreted as inflation between 0 and 2 per cent per annum. The third point is fully accepted and adopted by the ECB. This can clearly be confirmed by the monthly statements of the Governor of the ECB at his press conferences after the announcement of the decisions on the level of the rate of interest.

The implementation of what is in effect a balanced budget requirement at the national level under the SGP and the absence of fiscal policy at the euro area level has eliminated the use of fiscal policy as an effective instrument for the reduction of unemployment (or indeed of containing inflation pressures). These balanced budget requirements have been re-enforced in the 'fiscal compact' as discussed below.

The ECB is the only EU-level economic institution and it operates with the objective of attaining low inflation. There are three points of note here. First, this key institution is undemocratic in nature (indeed it is barred from taking instructions from democratic organizations) and operates in a secretive and non-transparent way – for example, the minutes of the decision-making process are never published before a great number of years has passed. The ECB decision makers are central bankers and there is no representation of other interests (e.g. industry, trade unions) in the decision-making process. It is only the interests of bankers and the financial sector that are represented.

Second, the only objective addressed through macroeconomic policy (and that is monetary policy) at the EU level is price stability (with inflation of just less than 2 per cent, a target which has been generally missed over the years). Employment targets have been set by the EU, as part of the European Employment Strategy, and are to be achieved through measures such as increased labour market flexibility, life-long learning, etc. and, more generally, adoption of 'flexicurity'. There is no macroeconomic policy, based on fiscal or monetary policy, designed to create high levels of employment. Indeed the general tenor of macroeconomic policy runs counter to the creation of high levels of employment. It is also relevant to note that as the ECB's only objective is that of price stability, there is then no mention of objectives of financial stability or similar.

Third, this policy operates according to the notion that monetary policy is the relevant policy for the control of inflation. Yet monetary policy has become interest rate policy and the linkages between changes in interest rates and changes in inflation are at best weak and at worst controversial (see, for example, Arestis and Sawyer, 2004, 2008).

The term European Social Model (and similar phrases such as Social Europe) does not have a universally accepted meaning and it could be said (whether as something that actually exists or is an aspiration) to have the feature of standing in contrast to the American model (or perhaps the Anglo-Saxon one). However, although the European Social Model is far from being a well-developed analytical concept, in essence it is characterized by three main features: 1) the universalistic character of welfare provision and a high degree of coordination between economic actors, 2) the acknowledgement that workers need special protection and have a right to collective interest representation and 3) widespread public ownership, especially in public services (Hermann, 2009: 88). The main point made here is that the policies advocated within the EMU particularly with regard to the labour market run rather counter to the notions associated with the European Social Model. The ECB has been at the forefront of calling for more 'flexible' labour markets and for changes in the pension arrangements.

The Governing Council [of the ECB] ... urges all euro area governments to decisively and swiftly implement substantial and comprehensive structural reforms. This will help these countries to strengthen competitiveness, increase the flexibility of their economies and enhance their longer-term growth potential. In this respect, labour market reforms are key, with a focus on the removal of rigidities and the implementation of measures which enhance wage flexibility. In particular, there is a need for the elimination of automatic wage indexation clauses and a strengthening of firm-level agreements so that wages and working conditions can be tailored to firms' specific needs. These measures should be accompanied by structural reforms that increase competition in product markets, particularly in services – including the liberalisation of closed professions – and, where appropriate, the privatisation of services currently provided by the public sector, thereby facilitating productivity growth and supporting competitiveness (ECB, 2011: 7).

The European Commission has argued along similar lines.

Member States should design benefits to reward return to work or incentives to go into self-employment for the unemployed through time-limited support, and conditionality linking training and job search more closely to benefits. Member states need to ensure that work pays through greater coherence between the level of income taxes (especially for low incomes) and unemployment benefits. Member States need to adapt their unemployment insurance systems to the economic cycle, so that protection is reinforced in times of economic down-turn. [...] all Member States [...] should keep public expenditure growth firmly below the rate of medium term trend growth (European Commission, 2011).

Second, there are in reality a number of 'social models' and more generally the national economies have different institutional, social and political arrangements. With specific regard to the labour market and its institutions, there are clearly substantial differences between the Member States of EMU.[6]

These differences have two points of significance here. First, these differences between countries and models interact with macroeconomic policies and events. The impact of, say, a downturn in economic activity will have different impacts on unemployment and its consequences across countries depending on, inter alia, 'hire and fire' practices. The determinants of wage inflation may well vary between countries and may help understand the differences in inflationary experience indicated above. The effects of demand and economic activity (and changes therein) will differ. Countries differ in their use of forms of income policy

---

6 For example, van Veen (2006) identifies four distinct models, which he labelled Nordic or social democratic, Continental European conservative corporatist, Mediterranean or tradition rudimentary and Anglo-Saxon or liberalist-individualistic model.

and the more corporatist countries have tended to have lower rates of inflation than the 'traditional' model.

Second, the different models and the different historic traditions have produced different inflation trajectories. There may be underlying differences between the models as to the underlying rate of wage inflation which is generated and the relationship between productivity increases and wage increases. These differences would not be sustainable, but are not addressed by the existing policies on wage and price determination.

One Size Fits All Problems

The EMU has suffered from a number of 'one size fits all' problems, most notably in the operation of monetary policy and the attempts to impose common fiscal policies on all countries under the SGP.

It is in the nature of monetary policy that it suffers from the 'one size fits all' problem – monetary policy has by its nature to be uniform across a currency union. Yet the economic issues and problems, which are being addressed by monetary policy, vary across the currency union, e.g. by region or in the EMU by country and by region. The severity of the 'one size fits all' problem is much reduced if the conditions in the member regions are closely correlated (e.g. over the movements of output, inflation) and if the responses of economic variables of relevance to the policy instruments (interest rate) are similar between member regions.

It is also the case that a numerical target is introduced for budget deficits without any rationale other than to proclaim an overall zero budget deficit. An alternative rationale for the size of a budget deficit, drawing on the 'functional finance' view (for example, Arestis and Sawyer, 2011, Sawyer, 2011) would be to use the budget deficit to ensure a high level of economic activity. Then, the target budget deficit would need to be in line with private savings minus investment plus current account deficit, which would be forthcoming at that high level of economic activity. On that basis, the appropriate scale of the budget deficit depends on a range of factors including the average propensities to save, propensity to invest and to import and the scale of exports. Countries vary in their savings and investment behaviour and in their net export position and hence the appropriate budget deficit would vary from country to country. The SGP fiscal policy then also suffers from a rather severe 'one size fits all' problem.

Although inflation targeting is focused on the interest rate/inflation dimension via demand linkages, it has become widely acknowledged (particularly since the financial crisis) that the interest rate can have effects on asset prices and on exchange rates. The 'one size fits all' issue feeds into aspects of the financial crisis. A relevant example is Spain, where the economy had expanded considerably prior to the 'great recession', as a construction boom developed, which (at least with hindsight) was unsustainable. This construction boom no doubt had a range of causes, but low real interest rates were supportive of such a boom. If the Spanish authorities had wished to dampen down the boom or to have coped with the bust through the use of interest rates and monetary policy more generally, it was completely powerless to do so. Further, the ECB was charged with the price stability objective and paid no regard to financial stability or to dampening credit booms.

The 'Fiscal Compact' as a 'Fiscal Suicide Pact'

The Fiscal Compact

The remedy to the euro-area crisis, which is currently being brought into force, is embodied in the Treaty on Stability, Coordination and Governance in the Economic and Monetary Union (TSCG)[7] of which the 'fiscal compact' is the central part on which we focus here.[8] The argument here is that the 'fiscal compact' cannot work on its own terms and will bring considerable economic damage and could be more accurately labelled a 'fiscal suicide pact'.

The essential features of the 'fiscal compact' and the Treaty are:

1. The imposition of the 'structural budget deficit' rule that the structural deficit may not exceed 0.5 per cent of GDP. Article 3 stipulates that the budgetary position of the general government of a contracting party shall be balanced or in surplus. This is interpreted as the annual structural balance of the general government at its country-specific medium-term objective, as defined in the revised SGP, with a lower limit of a structural deficit of 0.5 per cent of GDP at market prices. Furthermore, Article 3 TSCG requires contracting parties to ensure rapid convergence towards their respective medium-term objective and within a time frame proposed by the European Commission.

2. A stricter policy imposed on countries with a debt ratio exceeding 60 per cent of GDP. The Treaty (following the 'six pack') makes it possible to open an EDP (excessive deficit procedure under Article 126 TFEU) on the basis of the debt criterion (Article 4 TSCG). To avoid being placed under EDP, Member States with government debt ratios in excess of 60 per cent of their

---

7   http://European-council.Europa.eu/media/639235/st00tscg26_en12.pdf [accessed 01/09/2013].

8   There is also the so-called 'six pack' of secondary law measures which entered into force on 13 December 2011 and involved five Regulations and one Directive (hence 'six pack'). It applies to all 27 Member States, with some specific rules for EMU members. The six pack covers not only fiscal surveillance, but also macroeconomic surveillance under the new Macroeconomic Imbalance Procedure. The crucial aspects of the 'six pack' appear in the Treaty and are discussed under that head. For further information see http://ec.Europa.eu/economy_finance/articles/governance/2012-03-14_six_pack_en.htm.

GDP should reduce this ratio in line with a numerical benchmark, which implies a decline of the amount by which their debt exceeds the threshold at a rate in the order of 1/20 per year over three years. The precise impact of this would depend on the rate of nominal growth and the imposition of the EDP is optional rather than mandatory. However, in a slow growth economy with a debt ratio of say 120 per cent of GDP this approach would involve a budget surplus of the order of 3 per cent of GDP (and a primary surplus which was substantially greater when interest payments on debt are considered).

3. The deficit requirement is to be written into a country's national constitution or equivalent (Article 3 (2) TSCG). The same article demands that these rules shall be implemented at the latest one year after the TSCG enters into force. The national implementing rules should be based on common principles to be proposed by the European Commission, while fully respecting national parliamentary prerogatives (Article 3 (2) TSCG). The 'fiscal compact' could be viewed as a development of the SGP in which the intention to balance the budget deficit over the cycle is superseded by a balanced structural deficit rule, with the addition of the stricter policy rule as under (ii). Further, the sanctions for breaking the 'fiscal compact' are re-enforced after the failures under the Stability and Growth Pact for the rules on budget deficits to be followed. The attention to the 60 per cent debt to GDP ratio remains, even though it has been widely disregarded in practice under the SGP. No rationale has been given for the 60 per cent ratio (rather than any other percentage) and any debt ratio is sustainable under the condition that the debt ratio is equal to the deficit ratio divided by growth rate (hence a deficit ratio of 3 per cent of GDP with a nominal growth rate of 5 per cent would lead to a 60 per cent debt ratio). There is an inconsistency between a 60 per cent debt to GDP ratio and a budget on average near balance.

The implementation of rules for economic policy decision-making raises two crucial issues which are particularly relevant to the 'fiscal compact' rule of a balanced structural budget. The first is that economic decision-making of relevance is forward looking and often involves the adjustment of policy variables in response to forecast future economic events. The policy decisions will then depend on forecasts and assessments of the economic future. The second relates to the validity of the policy-making rule which is being set in place – specifically, is the rule feasible and would the operation of the rule achieve the desired end? As an example of the latter problem, we would cite the operation of Taylor's rule in the setting of interest rates[9] and the question as to whether the use of interest rates

---

9   Taylor's rule states that the policy interest rate set by a central bank is based on deviation of inflation from a target level and on the output gap (the difference between actual output and potential output; see, for example, Arestis, 2007).

can indeed lead to effective control of inflation without impacting on other key economic variables such as asset price bubbles and exchange rate. The balanced structural budget rule of the 'fiscal compact' is a case for which we would argue that the achievement of the rule will likely turn out to be impossible (as set out below) and striving to meet the rule would have deflationary effects and increase unemployment.

We have previously argued (Arestis and Sawyer, 2006) that the inclusion of economic policy matters in what was intended to be the European Constitution was inadvisable and the argument carries over to the Treaty of Lisbon. Apart from the concerns expressed above on the nature of the economic policy structures (the 'independence' of the European Central Bank, for example), we would point to the difficulties of making variations to the Treaty, which would require the unanimous approval of national governments. The particular issue with regard to economic policies and institutions is that ideas on economic policies and the role of institutions (the independence of the central bank being a key example) are contentious and ideas on what constitutes the right policy framework change over time. Economic policies are subject to fads and fashions and inclusion in such a Treaty is inadvisable. The TSCG takes this a step further by imposing the achievement of a structural balanced budget into national constitutions or equivalent, which combines, as we argue below, an often unachievable objective which will be difficult to change. But, of course, the reality is that economic policies and institutions are included in the Treaty and serve as a major constraint on making future changes in a sensible direction. It is a folly to incorporate ideas that some, but by no means all, think are appropriate policies into a document that is difficult to change, especially when those ideas are controversial if not mistaken. This has been an underlying problem in the EMU context with the Treaty of Lisbon and its predecessors including independence of the central bank with price stability as an objective: when in our view it should be changed to financial stability, there are many hurdles in changing the Treaty to be surmounted. It can also be seen as an attempt to tie the hands of the electorate and future governments on economic policies – what is the point of a party presenting a manifesto committed to raising public expenditure when the constitutional court would rule the implementation of such a commitment illegal? All tiers of government operate subject to a budget constraint in the sense that expenditure (current and capital) minus revenue has to be covered by borrowing and for many tiers of government, limits are placed on the scale of borrowing (e.g. limited to cover capital expenditure, subject to approval by higher tier of government). The limits on borrowing may be imposed by a 'higher authority' (e.g. national government over local government) or may be self-imposed. Placing such limits on borrowing is not inherently undemocratic and depends on where the effective decision-making lies. The features of the 'fiscal compact', which are troublesome in this regard, are, first, the ways in which policy decisions are being imposed on national governments. Most clearly this has been the case for Greece already, but further the Treaty seeks to impose a specific range of policy decisions ('structural reforms') as a condition of membership to the EMU. Second, the writing of the 'fiscal compact' conditions into national constitutions unnecessarily binds future governments and future prospective governments with regard to issues of taxation and public expenditure. It must be questioned whether economic policies should be embedded into constitutions or quasi-constitutional legislation, which limit the necessary flexibility to change economic policies as conditions and ideas on policies change. The ideas of 'independent central banks' and of 'balanced structural budgets' are not universal panaceas and indeed many of us would argue that the idea of 'independent central banks' is highly problematic. It is also an idea that could be viewed as a current fashion whose attraction is fading. If an economic policy is to be given the force of law, it should be capable of precise definition so that whether the policy has been implemented can be accurately judged. Further, it should be a policy that is capable of being achieved.

Third, the implementation of a balanced structural budget requirement will be made difficult by disputes over the measurement of the structural budget position. The implementation of a requirement that there be a balanced annual budget (as is the case with the European Union itself) does not face such difficulty as the annual budget outcome can be readily measured, though it is the *ex post* annual budget that can be measured but not the *ex ante* budget. The structural budget is 'structural' public expenditure (that is, some 'normal' level of expenditure excluding any one-off forms of expenditure) less the tax revenues, which would be generated from the 'normal' set of tax rates when the economy operates at some 'average' level (which will be described as 'potential output' in line with the economics literature). Each of the elements of the structural budget is a matter of estimates and dispute and, notably, what constitutes 'potential output', as we discuss in a subsection below.

The preamble to the TSCG notes the intention of the European Commission is 'to present further legislative proposals for the euro area concerning, in particular, *ex ante* reporting of debt issuance plans, economic partnership programmes detailing structural reforms for Member States under an excessive deficit procedure as well as the coordination of major economic policy reform plans of Member States'. Article 5 TSCG states that a contracting party that is subject to an excessive deficit procedure 'shall put in place a budgetary and economic partnership programme including a detailed description of the structural reforms which must be put in place and implemented to ensure an effective and durable correction of its excessive deficit'.

Within the Treaty, 'structural reforms' are not defined. But there can be little doubt as to what is in mind. In an interview with the *Wall Street Journal*, Mario Draghi, President of the ECB, stated that amongst the most important structural reforms were 'first [...] the product and services markets reform. And the second is the labour market reform which takes different shapes in different countries. In some of them one has to make labour markets more flexible and also fairer than they are today'.[10] This echoes the sentiments that have been repeatedly expressed

---

10   Available at: http://www.ecb.Europa.eu/press/key/date/2012/html/sp120224.en.
html [accessed 20 March 2012].

by the European Central Bank in their *Monthly Bulletin*. For example, writing in December 2009, the ECB argued that:

> With regard to structural reforms, most estimates indicate that the financial crisis has reduced the productive capacity of the euro area economies, and will continue to do so for some time to come. In order to support sustainable growth and employment, labour market flexibility and more effective incentives to work will be needed. Furthermore, policies that enhance competition and innovation are also urgently needed to speed up restructuring and investment and to create new business opportunities (ECB, 2009: 7).

The nature of the intended 'structural reforms' can be also seen by reference to those imposed on Greece in terms of privatization and labour market 'reforms' (notably, drastic reduction of minimum wage).[11]

There is here the underlying neoliberal assumption that 'structural reforms', which are directed towards labour market de-regulation, reduction of employment and wage protection measures, privatization and product market de-regulation, will have beneficial effects on the economy concerned and serve to reduce the size of budget deficits which is the centre of policy attention. However, that case is far from being established and we would argue along with Glyn, Howell and Schmitt (2006) that the evidence linking various indicators of the implementation of labour market reforms and unemployment is unconvincing. In a similar vein, Whyman *et al.* (2012) conclude in their extensive literature survey that 'there are a large number of studies which have found little or no significant impact arising from labour market deregulation' (p. 229). The effects of labour market reforms may well be to reduce rather than increase employment. For example, Tridico has recently argued that:

> The flexibility agenda of the labour market and the end of wage increases [...] diminished workers' purchasing power. This was partly compensated with increased borrowing opportunities and the boom of credit consumption, all of which helped workers to maintain unstable consumption capacity. However, in the long term, unstable consumption patterns derived from precarious job creation, job instability and poor wages have weakened aggregate demand. Hence, labour market issues such as flexibility, uneven income distribution, poor wages and the financial crisis are two sides of the same coin (Tridico, 2012: 17).

The Ambiguity of the Structural Budget

The structural budget deficit appears to be left without a precise definition in the 'fiscal compact' and, lacking any clear indication of the methodology to be used

---

11   See European Commission (2012) for a discussion of the measures imposed on Greece.

in its estimation, this is a serious omission. However, it can be viewed as the deficit that would result from the application of current tax rates and prevailing public expenditure levels if the economy was operating at some 'normal' level of output which has come to be linked with the level of 'potential output'. We put inverted commas around 'potential output' to signify that this term is used in a specific way in this literature as explained further below and does not correspond to the everyday usage of the term 'potential' which would signify capability and capacity. We use the term structural budget deficit (*SBD*) below though cyclically adjusted budget deficit is also used in the 'fiscal compact' and elsewhere and the two are treated as synonymous. Thus the structural budget deficit (*SBD*) is given by:

(1) $SBD = G^* - t(Y^*)$

Where G^* is underlying the ('structural') level of government consumption and investment, t is tax function relating to prevailing tax rates with income transfers regarded as negative taxation and Y^* 'potential output'. There would generally be some issues over exact measures of G^* as to elements that could be regarded as temporary or discretionary and hence not included. In a similar vein, there would be issues over the tax function to be used to reflect prevailing tax rates – for example, with an income tax system involving tax-free allowances and tax rates that vary with the level of income, what is assumed about the adjustments of the tax-free allowances and levels of taxable income at which tax rates change in the face of inflation and changing aggregate income levels. Here we leave those issues on one side to focus on the more major issues.

There are two key major measurement issues here and the interactions of them (combined with measurement issues over 'potential output') generate considerable ambiguity over the measurement of the structural budget deficit so that it is not a suitable concept to embed in law.

The first is that a structural budget deficit is a hypothetical calculation and the question is as to whether a consistent estimate of the SBD can be made (for some measure of potential output). The difficulty here can be readily seen by reference to the national accounts relationship which is here written as:

(2) $G - T = S - I + M - X$

Where G is government expenditure, T tax revenue, S private savings, I private investment, M imports and X exports (including net income). In terms of outturns, a balanced budget with the left-hand side equal to zero would require the right-hand side to be similarly equal to zero.

Suppose the SBD in conditions appertaining at time t was calculated as equal to α. For reasons of consistency and sustainability this would mean that:

(3) $S_1^* - I_1^* + M_1^* - X_1^* = \alpha$

Where * after a variable signifies the level of the variable which would correspond to 'potential output', e.g. $S*$ is the intended level of savings which would be forthcoming at the potential output.

Now consider the case where the policy intention is to change the *SBD* through changes in tax rates and levels of public expenditure and the target is β. Then not only would $SBD = \beta$, but the following equation would also need to hold:

(4) $S_2* - I_2* + M_2* - X_2* = \beta$

This would be possible if there were relevant changes in 'structural' savings, investment, imports and exports, e.g. if intentions to save diminished between (3) and (4) (in the case of $\alpha > \beta$). This could arise with a strong form of Ricardian equivalence – the intention to reduce a structural budget deficit would be exactly matched by corresponding changes in private expenditure.

The second issue relates to the concept of 'potential output' itself. It must first be said that the term 'potential output' is used in a number of different ways which need to be distinguished and that it is a theoretical notion for which there may not be a counterpart in the real world. Further, any estimation of 'potential output' (for a given definition) is inevitably backward looking in the sense of using past data, but the measure of 'potential output' which is relevant for policy is the current and future levels.

The term 'potential output' is generally linked with the supply side of the economy. In common usage, the term 'potential' would suggest some form of maximum output. When we speak of someone's potential, we are thinking of the most they could achieve or be capable of. In economic terms, 'potential output' can be linked with productive capacity. As such, 'potential output' could be interpreted as the (sustainable) physical capacity output, though more usually some notion of costs would be involved such as the level of production at which costs would start to rise 'sharply'. This approach to 'potential output' is closely related to some upper limit to the level of output. However, the notion of 'potential output', which is common in the current dominant paradigm in macroeconomics – that is, the 'new consensus in macroeconomics' – is more akin to some average level of output around which the economy fluctuates and more recently has tended to be aligned with the level of output at which inflation would be constant (Arestis, 2007).

It is also apparent that the estimation of 'potential output' requires data – that is, the estimation can only be conducted after the event, but to be useful in policy decisions estimates of 'potential output' need to be available prior to the decision. As output tends to grow over time, this would clearly involve not only scaling potential output against actual output, but also deriving estimates of the growth of potential output. This can only be highly speculative in a world of uncertainty where the future cannot be readily foretold from the past.

The more general theoretical framework within which 'potential output' is cast is one of the independence of demand and supply factors (Arestis, 2007, Fontana, 2010). The actual level of output is viewed as determined in the short run by the level of aggregate demand, whereas potential output is set on the supply side of the economy and in general the growth of 'potential output' is unaffected by what happens on the demand side and the level of demand fluctuates around potential output (and hence the output gap tends to average out as zero).

The Impossibility of a Balanced Structural Budget

The question here can be simply posed in terms of the conditions for a structural balanced budget (the argument would apply with minimal adjustment to conditions for a structural budget deficit of, say, 0.5 per cent of GDP). Drawing on the national accounts equations above, the condition for a structural balanced budget would be:

(5) $G - t(Y^*) = S^* - I^* + M^* - X^* = 0$

In other words, the savings, investment and net exports, which would be forthcoming at 'normal' savings, investment rates and when output is at the potential level, are consistent with this equation. The 'fiscal compact' asserts in effect that condition is always fulfilled – at each point in time and for every country (at least those within the Economic and Monetary Union). The actual budget deficit could diverge from this balanced position as privately aggregated demand fluctuates – for example, through a change in the propensity to invest, leading to change in level of output and thereby in tax receipts. But it is asserted that if investment demands were at some 'normal' level (along with savings and net export behaviour correspondingly) then equation (5) would be satisfied.

The key argument here is that there is little reason to think that equation (5) would indeed be satisfied. In Sawyer (2012), the argument is developed at length. One part of the argument is that of historic experience. The occurrence of budget deficits has been the norm in many countries without clear evidence of 'overheating' and the average budget has been in deficit – indeed, government debt levels of the order of 40 to 80 per cent of GDP would not have been the norm within EMU countries without a history of budget deficits. Another part of the argument is the absence of forces which would equate savings and investment at a high level of economic activity. The pace of investment is closely linked with the pace of growth of the economy: in the simple case, the net investment ratio to GDP will be around the capital-output ratio times the growth rate. Savings depend on the desire of households to save, often linked with pension provision and the saving by corporations. The forces at work on investment and those on savings are rather different and there is little reason to think that there will be factors bringing savings and investment into line.

Fiscal Suicide Pact

The 'fiscal compact' seeks to impose the achievement of an ill-defined objective ('structural budget balance') applicable across all countries regardless of their economic conditions. It is for many countries an unachievable objective in that there is little reason to think that a balanced budget and economy operating where output is at potential output are mutually compatible. Each country striving to achieve that objective threatens to create further austerity in not only its own country, but in the other Member States (in light of the extent of trade between Member States). As each country strives to reduce the budget deficit, it makes it more difficult for other countries to do so. The 'fiscal compact' also threatens to impose a programme of neoliberal 'structural reforms', where there is little evidence that those reforms would improve employment and economic performance. As indicated above, EMU countries in general failed to reach the budget deficit requirements of SGP. One interpretation of that would be a lack of political will which can be overcome by a more stringent application of the balanced budget requirements as under the 'fiscal compact'. Our interpretation is more that the balanced budget requirements were unachievable and that countries used, where required, budget deficits to support the level of demand.

Summary and Conclusions

We have argued in this chapter that the present 'euro crisis' arises from the way in which the EMU was constructed, rather than 'bad behaviour' by some Member States, and can only be resolved through major policy changes that permit the combination of the continued existence of the euro with acceptable economic performance.

The chapter has briefly reviewed the economic performance in the EMU in the years of the euro and highlighted the relatively poor economic performance, the degree to which objectives on fiscal deficits and inflation were not met, and the continuing and growing current account imbalances. The policy responses to the euro crisis, which are being brought in through the 'fiscal compact', will do nothing to address either the current account imbalances or the unemployment crisis; indeed, they will fail to achieve their own objectives in terms of a balanced structural budget.

References

Angeriz, A. and Arestis, P. 2008. Assessing Inflation Targeting Through Intervention Analysis, *Oxford Economic Papers*, 60(2), 293–317.

Arestis, P. 2007. What is the New Consensus in Macroeconomics? in *Is There a New Consensus in Macroeconomics?* edited by P. Arestis. Houndmills, Basingstoke: Palgrave Macmillan, 22–42.

Arestis, P. and Sawyer, M. 2004. Can Monetary Policy Affect the Real Economy? *European Review of Economics and Finance*, 3(3), 9–32.

Arestis, P. and Sawyer, M. 2006. Macroeconomic policy and the European constitution in *Alternative Perspectives on Economic Policies in the European Union*, edited by P. Arestis and M. Sawyer. Houndmills, Basingstoke: Palgrave Macmillan, 1–36.

Arestis, P. and Sawyer, M. 2008. A Critical Reconsideration of the Foundations of Monetary Policy in the New Consensus Macroeconomics Framework. *Cambridge Journal of Economics*, 32(5), 761–79.

Arestis, P. and Sawyer, M. 2011. Economic Theory and Policies: New Directions After Neo-Liberalism, in *New Economics as Mainstream Economics*, edited by P. Arestis and M. Sawyer, Basingstoke: Palgrave Macmillan, 1–38.

Arestis, P. and Sawyer, M. 2012. Can the Euro Survive After the European Crisis?, in *The Euro Crisis*, edited by P. Arestis and M. Sawyer, Houndmills, Basingstoke: Palgrave Macmillan, 1–34.

Clarida, R., Galí, J. and Gertler, M. 1999. The Science of Monetary Policy: A New Keynesian Perspective. *Journal of Economic Literature*, 37(4), 1661–707.

European Central Bank (ECB) 2009. *Monthly Bulletin*, December 2009.

European Central Bank (ECB) 2011. *Monthly Bulletin*, September 2011.

European Commission 2008. EMU@10 Successes and challenges after ten years of Economic and Monetary Union. *European Economy* 2.

European Commission 2011. Communication from the Commission to the European Parliament, the Council, the European Economic and Social Committee and the Committee of the Regions: Annual growth survey: advancing the EU's comprehensive response to the crisis COM(2011) 11 final, Brussels: European Commission.

European Commission 2012. The Second Economic Adjustment Programme for Greece. *European Economy*, Occasional Papers 94, March 2012.

Fontana, G. 2009. Whither New Consensus Macroeconomics? The Role of Government and Fiscal Policy in Modern Macroeconomics. In *Macroeconomic Policies on Shaky Foundations – Whither Mainstream Economics?*, edited by E. Hein, T. Niechoj and E. Stockhammer, Marburg: Metropolis Verlag, 187–208.

Fontana, G. 2010. The return of Keynesian Economics: A contribution in the spirit of John Cornwall's work. *Review of Political Economy*, 22(4), 517–33.

Glyn, A., Howell, D. and Schmitt (2006). Labor Market Reforms: The Evidence does not tell the orthodox tale, *The Challenge Magazine*, 49(2), 5–22.

Goodfriend, M. and King, R.G. 1997. The New Neoclassical Synthesis and the Role of Monetary Policy. in *NBER Macroeconomics Annual: 1997*, edited by B.S. Bernanke and J.J. Rotemberg, Cambridge, MA: MIT Press, 231–96.

Hermann, C. 2009. The European Social Models: contours of the discussion in *Privatisation Against the European Social Model*, edited by M. Frangakis, C. Hermann, J. Huffschmid and K. Lóránt, Basingstoke: Palgrave Macmillan, 77–92.

Sawyer, M. 2011. Progressive approaches to budget deficits, in *Stabilising an unequal economy? Public debt, financial regulation, and income distribution,* edited by O. Onaran, T. Niechoj, E. Stockhammer, A. Truger, and T. van Treeck, Marburg: Metropolis Verlag, 143–59.

Sawyer, M. 2012. The contradictions of balanced structural government budgets in *From crisis to growth? The challenge of imbalances and debt*, H. Herr, T. Niechoj, C. Thomasberger, A. Truger, and T.L. van Treeck, Marbur: Metropolis Verlag, 281–98.

Tridico, P. 2012. Financial crisis and global imbalances: its labour market origins and the aftermath. *Cambridge Journal of Economics*, vol. 36(1), 17–42.

Van Veen, T. 2006. Institutions and the labour market: examining the benefits in *Growth and Cohesion in the European Union: The Impact of Macroeconomic Policy*, edited by W. Mitchell, J. Muysken and T.V. Veen (eds), Cheltenham: Edward Elgar Publishing Limited, 109–29.

Whyman, P.B., Baimbridge, M. and Mullen, A. 2012. *The Political Economy of the European Social Model*, London: Routledge.

Woodford, M. 2003. *Interest and Prices: Foundations of a Theory of Monetary Policy.* Princeton, NJ: Princeton University Press.

Chapter 3

The European Currency in Turbulent Times – Austerity Policy Made in Brussels the Only Way Out?

Amy Verdun*

Introduction

Since January 2010 the European Union (EU) has arguably been in the midst of its worst crisis since its inauguration in 1993.[1] The Greek government's announcement of a considerably increased budget deficit in October 2009 is frequently seen as the trigger for the crisis to spiral out of control, since it seemed to indicate gross disregard of the euro area's fiscal governance and potentially more substantial problems elsewhere (Featherstone 2011). Rating agencies and financial markets responded increasingly negatively (Eijffinger 2012). Neither the Member States' government leaders nor EU institutions were able to come up with a timely response that would halt a negative spiral of lack of confidence in the governance of Europe's Economic and Monetary Union (EMU). As the crisis evolved, an increasing number of media commentators and academics forecast that a country such as Greece would leave the euro or that the euro area might collapse completely, if contagion would occur. Some warn that complications related to the Eurocrisis would undermine the entire euro area edifice (Eichengreen 2012b, Feldstein 2012, Krugman 2012; compare the reporting in various newspapers such as *Financial Times* 2011a, b, *The Telegraph* 2011 and even more recently *The Economist* 2013). Demands for austerity are the main proposal for overcoming the sovereign debt crisis, leading to protests in the streets and a concern for a deflationary spiral.

* This chapter forms part of a larger project entitled 'Europe's sovereign debt crisis: lessons for European integration' which has received generous support from the Social Science and Humanities Research Council of Canada (SSHRC), grant number: 410-2011-0405. Related publications are: Verdun 2012a, b and 2013a and b.

1 The formal inauguration of the EU was preceded by the European Communities (the European Coal and Steel Community (ECSC), the European Atomic Energy Community (EURATOM) and the European Economic Community (EEC), founded in 1951, 1957, and 1957 respectively), which also experienced their fair share of crises.

This chapter examines the origins of the current problems, going back to the reasons and purposes for creating EMU and recalling the compromises made at that time. It also reviews whether a solution to current problems should necessarily undermine the EU's social model.

To address these issues, the chapter is structured as follows. The next section reviews the rationale behind creating the EMU and how it related to Europe's social model. Section three reviews the EMU architecture and highlights some of its features, including its asymmetrical nature (Verdun 1996, 2000). It then examines the adjustments made through the Stability and Growth Pact (SGP) and how the crisis exposed the flaws in the EMU governance structure. Section four analyzes how the crisis of 2007–2008, the recession of 2009 and the euro debt crisis that started in 2010 managed to take hold of Europe, launching it into a constitutional and existential crisis, causing many national governments to fall. Section 5 turns to an analysis of the options that lay before European and national governments to deal with the sovereign debt crisis and what some of the trade-offs are.

Economic and Monetary Union: Rationale and Connection to the Social Model

The idea to create a single currency originated in the early days of the European Economic Community (EEC). The goal to fix the exchange rates – indeed, to introduce a single currency – was seen as integral to the prospect of deeper economic integration. The thinking was that full benefits of market integration would presuppose a single currency. Already at the Hague Summit, in December 1969, a decision was made to create an EMU that would ideally lead to the creation of a single currency. The so-called Werner Report (1970) envisaged a staged plan that would see full EMU be obtained by 1980. The benefits would be the elimination of exchange rate volatility, reduction of transaction costs for cross-border trade in the common market and to have an important symbol of deeper European integration. The Werner Report envisaged two Community institutions: a central bank and another institution named a 'Centre for Decision of Economy Policy' (with a goal to coordinate economic policy, responsible to the European Parliament, Werner Report 1970: 12–13). However, due to the oil crisis, rising inflation, recession and different national responses to the crisis of the early 1970s, the plans to create an EMU failed at this time.

A system that focused mostly on exchange rate stability, referred to as currency snake (in the early and mid 1970s), had some success. By 1979 a European Monetary System (EMS) was set up to replace the snake. It contained an Exchange Rate Mechanism (ERM) that stipulated that EEC currencies would stay within agreed bandwidths (for most Member States, no more than plus-or-minus 2.25 per cent of the agreed parity). Throughout the 1980s the EMS and its ERM managed to keep exchange rates of EEC Member States currencies stable, as all countries, except the UK, were part of the ERM.[2] With the Single European Act, agreed to in 1985 and signed in 1986, renewed impetus was given to the idea of creating EMU. Chaired by Commission President Jacques Delors, a committee of 12 central bank presidents, a commissioner and a few experts produced a plan (the so-called 'Delors Report'), published in April 1989, to create EMU in three stages, culminating in the introduction of the euro no later than 1999 (Delors Report 1989). Neither the Werner Report nor the Delors Report had designed a monetary union with extensive integration in the area of fiscal or political union (although the Werner Report went further than the Delors Report in that respect). Instead, coordination on national budgetary deficits and public debt through setting of common goals was seen as sufficient (Tsoukalis 1977, Dyson and Featherstone 1999, Verdun 1999, 2000).

To deal with economic woes, a nation-state government has a number of instruments (taxing and spending) and within a country the government can make transfers from one area to another. Europe's monetary union is called 'Economic' and 'Monetary' Union because for a successful monetary union one needs a fair amount of 'economic' integration. This is necessary to ensure a good policy mix between fiscal and monetary policy (as happens within countries) but also to achieve convergence of macroeconomic performance among Member States. It could also have included a larger centralized European budget to offset any imbalances.

The 1977 MacDougall Report examined the possible need for such a centralized budget to accompany deeper economic and monetary integration within the EEC (Verdun 2013b). The report offered some insights into mature federal states, concluding that public finance could serve many goals such as cushioning the effects of a recession or reducing differences in per capita income among the different regions of a fiscal federation (European Commission, 1977: 12): 'As well as redistributing income regionally on a continuing basis, public finance in existing economic unions plays a major role in cushioning short-term and cyclical fluctuations.' By having a larger budget and by levying taxes, Community public finance could serve as an automatic stabilizer. In fact, the Report deemed it conceivable that the Community could somehow become involved in matters ultimately affecting income differentials (ibid: 14). Furthermore, it called for a Community budget of 2–2.5 per cent of gross domestic product (GDP) for the so-called 'pre-federal stage' and higher percentages for subsequent economic integration scenarios, giving a larger role to Community public finance (ibid: 17).

Yet, due to a combination of unfavourable circumstances existing at that time, the MacDougall Report went unheeded, making EMU unlikely to be achieved in the near future. Instead, the 1980s focused on the European Monetary System

---

2   The UK joined in 1990 but was soon forced to leave when financial speculation forced the pound (and also the Italian lira) out of the ERM in 1992 (see Buiter, Corsetti and Pesenti 1998). During the 1980s the Italian lira had a larger bandwidth (± 6 per cent) (see Ludlow 1982 on the origins of the EMS).

(EMS), the Single European Act and the relaunching of the Internal Market project. Yet once EMU came back onto the agenda, there was no backing for any increase in the Community budget to accompany deeper economic and monetary integration.

In this sense EMU's design was *asymmetric* (Verdun 1996, 2000): although it was understood that a monetary union would benefit from having deep integration of other areas of economic policy (budgets, fiscal, market integration) and possibly more centralized budgetary means to deal with imbalances, it was unclear to those designing EMU how much of that coordination would have to be done centrally. More importantly, there was not the support for such a transfer of funds and responsibilities.

Eventually, the institutional blueprint of EMU was introduced in the Treaty on European Union (the Maastricht Treaty) signed on 7 February 1992 and entered into force on 1 November 1993. There had been insufficient consensus on what deeper economic integration would look like, thus that part of the integration process was left to be determined by Member States at a later date. It was widely understood that this matter was left as 'incomplete' integration (Verdun 1996, 2000, see also De Grauwe 2006 and Boonstra 2010). Yet no one knew what the cost would be of not settling the need to have deeper economic integration in order to make EMU workable. It was also not clear how and when it would emerge that deeper economic integration would become necessary to accommodate monetary union. Some have referred to this 'deeper economic integration' as deeper 'political unification', as a transfer of funds to a centralized level will also require representation at that level (Sargent 2011, De Grauwe 2012).

By the early 1990s and early 2000s the benefits of EMU and the euro that Member States hoped to achieve still included many of the same objectives thought of in the late 1960s: reduced transactions costs, transparency of prices, easier operation of the single market by having a single currency in that market and having a currency that would serve as a reserve and trading currency to replace the usage of the dollar for that purpose in the European context. Also, by this time the institutionalized system of fixed exchange rates had been strongly relying on the Federal Republic of Germany. At the time the German central bank (the *Bundesbank* in Frankfurt) was a policy setter (Kennedy 1991, Kaelberer 1997, Verdun 2000). Many other national central banks closely followed the interest rates determined in Frankfurt. With the creation of the European Central Bank (ECB), this policy-setting role would be assumed by the ECB. In the third stage of EMU, all Member States in the euro area would have a formal say over the setting of European monetary policy for the euro area. Thus, formally speaking, except for Germany, all other EU Member States that joined the euro area with its European System of Central Banks (ESCB) gained influence over monetary policy. Of course, Germany gained in return. During the ERM period, the Deutschmark often appreciated against other European currencies and had to be re-valued (Giavazzi, Micossi and Miller 1988, De Cecco and Giovannini 1989). This situation was challenging for German exporters as they competed against goods made in other

ERM countries whose currencies would frequently devalue. In the 1980s and early 1990s, high-level political negotiations surrounding revaluations were often challenging and jolted financial markets. But to honour the fact that Germany *de facto* dominated the system, the European framework took over many of the German characteristics and best practices (Gros and Thygesen 1992, Dyson 1994, Verdun 2000).

When the euro was introduced, the initial concerns focused on the cost of transition. Consumers noticed increases in prices of day-to-day goods and were concerned over the low inflation credentials of the new currency, as they perceived inflation to be higher than stated in official statistics (Döhring and Mordonu 2007, Verdun 2007, European Commission 2008b: 32). Yet they enjoyed the ease of having a single currency in the euro area, and trade increased among its members, as well as between the euro area countries and the euro-outs (Micco, Stein, and Ordoñez 2003, Flam and Nordström 2006, Bun and Klaassen 2007, De Nardis, De Santis and Vicarelli 2007, Chintrakarn 2008). Furthermore, the project seemed attractive to Member States new to the EU, particularly smaller ones, such as Slovenia, Cyprus and Malta (Verdun 2007, 2009).

In the early years, states' cost of borrowing money decreased, approximating the interest rate to be paid on German government debt and those of other countries, e.g. Greece (European Commission 2008b: 95, Barrios *et al.* 2009, Ardagna and Caselli 2012). This meant that EMU was producing another positive effect for, in particular, those countries that had had a high cost of attracting funds earlier. In the first decade of EMU, these countries experienced a major increase in the availability of cheap credit. Of course, some of these short-term advantages (such as easier access to loans) were a benefit in the short run but contained the risk of long-term costs, as the euro sovereign debt crisis soon made clear (De Grauwe and Ji 2012, Eichengreen 2012a).

While Europe's Economic and Monetary Union was being discussed, its potential impact on any form of social cohesion or Europe's social model[3] was also widely debated (Bolukbasi 2009). In my earlier work (Verdun 2000), I examined the perspectives of trade unions and employers' organizations, central banks and ministries of finance on EMU. Remarkably, although the social dimension did play an important role in the debates preceding EMU, no social dimension

---

3   There is no one single accepted generally held definition of Europe's Social Model. Those upholding the existence of 'Social Europe' (Trubek and Trubek 2005, Scharpf 2002) and 'Europe's Social Model of Society' (Martin and Ross 2004) for instance highlight how, in the European context, considerable consideration is given to social matters, social justice, solidarity with the weak, commitment to redistribution and a major role for the state in obtaining a more equitable division of wealth including developing some minimum guaranteed resources for its inhabitants. There are, however, various different models and preferences within Europe as to how to obtain these more general objectives and how to respond to the challenges facing the various sorts of European welfare states (see, for example, Hemerijck 2002).

was explicitly incorporated into the framework of EMU. Commission President, Jacques Delors himself, had been keen to put the social dimension on the table. Nevertheless, the Delors Report mentioned the word 'social' only six times and often not to discuss explicitly how to ensure social cohesion through EMU. 'Economic cohesion' was also mentioned – meaning that there should be more balance between economic prosperity in all parts of EMU: 'The broad objective of economic policy coordination would be to promote growth employment and external balance in an environment of price stability and economic cohesion' (Delors Report 1989: 24).

My study showed that by the late 1980s and early 1990s the model of wage bargaining and the role for trade unions therein in Western European Member States was deemed in need of reform (Verdun 2000). EMU was to be used to some extent to encourage more competition among Member States and to ensure that wages would reflect productivity. But it was not thought that Europe's social model would or should be deconstructed. Rather, modest competition would ensure better balance in the EU (Verdun 2000).

Architecture of EMU and Adjustments Made Through the Stability and Growth Pact

In order to meet the conditions for entry into EMU, Member States had to meet the so-called 'convergence criteria' that focus on interest rates, exchange rates, inflation rates and budgetary deficits and public debts.[4] The Commission would offer a recommendation on whether Member States met the criteria. Since the criterion for the public debt was 60 per cent of GDP or moving continuously and substantially towards that, all were assumed to be on the right track and those reaching the criterion were deemed to be meeting the criteria. The European Council at a summit meeting in Brussels on 3 May 1998 decided that 11 countries met the criteria and that those 11 were ready to enter stage three of EMU on 1 January 1999. Greece joined the third stage on 1 January 2001 and thus was part of the original 12 countries introducing banknotes and coins on 1 January 2002.

---

4   The convergence criteria stipulate: low inflation (no more than 1.5 per cent difference from the best three performing Member States), a budgetary deficit of no more than 3 per cent of GDP, public debt not exceeding 60 per cent of the GDP, a currency fluctuation within ±15 per cent while the Member States participates in ERM and long-term interest rates within 2 per cent of the best three performing Member States. A Member State could temporarily and exceptionally have a budgetary deficit higher than 3 per cent. Alternatively, it could meet the convergence criteria with a budgetary deficit of more than 3 per cent if it has 'declined substantially and continuously and reached a level that comes close to the reference value'. The 60 per cent norm was similarly flexible. These criteria were first introduced in a protocol annexed to Article 109j EC (Treaty of Maastricht) and have not been changed since. They are now contained in protocol 13 to the Treaty on the Functioning of the European Union.

Earlier already, there were concerns about the post-decision. In fact, by the mid 1990s the Germans put forward a proposal to ensure that compliance with these rules would be ensured well after the countries had qualified to join. Thus, rules were created under the heading 'Stability and Growth Pact' (SGP)[5] that stipulated a continuing commitment to keeping budgetary deficits at 3 per cent of GDP of the Member States.[6] If Member States would not meet the criteria once in EMU, they could eventually be subject to fines (now Articles 126 (9–11), 132 and 139 (2) TFEU). Yet this set of rules became undermined by the very same countries (France and Germany)[7] that had been at the forefront of its creation and could have modified it at that time. Instead, the SGP rules were revised only a few years after euro banknotes and coins started circulating. The reputation loss caused by the flouting of the rules by two leading EU countries put the scheme's credibility in jeopardy. But even those who had created EMU and the SGP realized that it was far from ideal to enforce strict rules instead of achieving integration. It was anticipated that at some point deeper integration could prove to be necessary (Pisani-Ferry 2004, Buti, Eijffinger and Franco 2005, Heipertz and Verdun 2010). With the EU sovereign debt crisis of the past few years, the time has come to revisit this part of EMU design and write that unwritten chapter in European history about the exact form of economic governance and political union to accompany monetary integration and to increase its democratic accountability (see also Trichet 2013).

Enthusiasm about the start of the euro was not universal; some analysts across the globe predicted the euro's collapse from the start. Harvard economist Martin Feldstein famously argued in a 1997 *Foreign Affairs* article that the euro could lead to increased conflict (perhaps even war) within Europe and between Europe and the US (Feldstein, 1997, 1992). Yet during the first ten years the euro appeared to be performing well and the number of such doomsday-sayers warning against the euro's demise or possible destabilizing effects declined rapidly. What were the arguments used? Indeed, as we have seen above, the euro was created without a fully fledged economic and political architecture – some would say it was insufficiently embedded in a federalist framework and thus lacked the necessary institutional structures for the Europeans to deal with difficult times. There was

---

5   Council Regulation (EC) 1466/97 on the strengthening of the surveillance of budgetary positions and the surveillance and coordination of economic policies [1997] OJ L209/1 (as amended by Council Regulation (EC) 1055/2005 [2005] OJ L174/1) and Council Regulation (EC) 1467/97 on speeding up and clarifying the implementation of the excessive deficit procedure [1997] OJ L209/6 (as amended by Council Regulation (EC) 1056/2005 [2005] OJ L174/5).

6   For details on the origins, crisis and reform of the SGP see Heipertz and Verdun 2010. See also Schuknecht *et al.* 2011.

7   In 2003, Germany and France defaulted the budgetary deficit criterion. When the Commission proposed a Council decision spelling out consequences of this excessive budget deficit, the Council did not support this and the Court of Justice subsequently held that the rules contained in what is today Article 129 (9) TFEU were not, indeed, justiciable (case C-27/04 *Commission v Council* [2004] ECR I-6649).

no centralized government or a central budget to deal with potential imbalances among Member State economies.

Barry Eichengreen (2012a: 128–31) sums up the problems with the euro as follows. European leaders had put their confidence in a so-called 'no bailout clause' and in rules that would ensure that budgetary deficits and public debt would be kept at a reasonable level. Many commentators have been focusing on the difficulties of that part of the architecture. In this piece, he also analyzes some of the other, more structural, underpinnings of the difficulties in the euro area. He points to the imbalances in the euro area, in the economy, in areas other than the fiscal domain. For instance, the financial crisis led to problems in the banking sector when the value of assets declined. Financial distress in the banking sector then led to fiscal problems in Member States. Also, in the first years of EMU, cheap credit was abundant, which led to money being invested in the euro area periphery with ample lucrative opportunities, rather than in the countries that had plenty of savings but lower returns on investments. Furthermore, EMU architecture did not include mechanisms to react to changes in productivity throughout EMU. Eichengreen also highlights that it may have been incorrect to assume that countries with a lower GDP per capita would be able to catch up within the euro area, without having access to interest and exchange rate policy. Finally, following Folkerts-Landau and Garber (1992), Eichengreen points to the need for effective oversight of banking and financial systems at the EU level, which had not been part of EMU's original institutional architecture.

In another recent paper, Paul de Grauwe (2011, compare De Grauwe and Ji 2012) explains how one of the problems underlying the sovereign debt crisis is that countries of the monetary union resemble emerging market economies: if there is a sufficiently empowered statistical office able to sound alarm bells when Member States report inaccurately, as happened in Greece with its debt, there is no central bank and no currency to offset some of the costs. Thus, financial markets can freely take money out of the country, leaving the country vulnerable. But without a central bank or independent national currency, nothing changes. In the case of a country outside a monetary union, the currency will devalue because those holding sovereign bonds before, after selling them, will either have to reinvest in the same currency (which serves as a buffer on the performance of the economy) or sell the currency – which in turn has a downward pressure on the currency (De Grauwe 2011). If this situation happens to one country, it can easily affect other countries. As does Eichengreen, De Grauwe (2011) points to matters in the real economy. He shows that countries in the periphery of the euro area have seen real wages go up whereas those in Austria and Germany have come down. Should these periphery countries encounter difficulties, the only strategy left for them is an internal devaluation, which means a downward correction of prices and wages. This situation will make financial markets nervous which feeds into the point made earlier about solvency problems.

The Financial Crisis, the Economic Crisis and the Sovereign Debt Crisis

Indeed, the 2007–2008 financial crisis, followed by the economic crisis of 2009 and the sovereign debt crisis of 2010–2012, has put the euro to the test. The euro edifice showed cracks in its architecture in three stages. In the first stage, in 2007, when the financial crisis took hold of Europe, when there was insufficient money to go around, the ECB made overnight lending easily available. This ECB support was necessary because as the money dried up, banks were increasingly reluctant to lend to one another and these ECB measures facilitated them to park their funds with the ECB (Drudi, Durré and Mongelli 2012). This was a bold and innovative step, on the part of the ECB, that few expected it was prepared to do. One saw the ECB rising to the occasion and it would do so a few more times subsequently when credit was tight or bond markets worried.

The financial crisis brought to the fore the incomplete nature of European integration in economic and monetary affairs. Fiscal policy remained firmly in the hands of national authorities and there was no collective fund or responsibility to come to the aid of Member States in need. Indeed, the crisis exposed not only the weaknesses in fiscal policy architecture; banking supervision was also weak (see Schure 2013). Or as British economist Charles Goodhart (2009: 16) put it: 'a cross-border bank is international in life but national in death' (House of Lords 2009: 30). It meant that in the face of a severe banking crisis and subsequently major downward corrections of the stock exchanges, EU countries found themselves not knowing what strategy the EU would take and national governments turned to domestic solutions. A fortnight after the Lehman collapse,[8] Ireland decided, unilaterally, to secure consumer bank deposits (*Financial Times* 2008a). The German government criticized the Irish government for such unilateral action, but a week later followed suit with a similar unilateral policy (*Financial Times* 2008b). Only by November 2008 had the EU furnished a European response that focused on having the Member States and the EU inject 200 billion euro into the EU economy (1.5 per cent of GDP) and on ways to improve competitiveness (European Commission 2008a). However, the EU central budget did not have access to such large funds. First, it does not have a large budget to spend (the EU manages about 1 per cent of the EU GDP) and the Commission would only have a very small proportion of that amount to allocate to crisis management. Second, by autumn 2008 it only had access to a small amount of loans to deal with crisis management. Thus, what it did in November 2008 was offer to act as 'clearing house', a broker for a coordinated response by Member State governments. In fact, after this decision the proposal still needed to go to national parliaments for approval. This episode exposed the problem that the EU lacked a sufficiently large central budget or other fund to be tapped into at a time of crisis. It also showed the vulnerability of

---

8　Lehman Brothers, the US investment bank, filed for bankruptcy on 15 September 2008 (*The Economist* 2008). This particular event is often seen as having escalated the 2007–2008 financial crisis (for an insightful account of the unfolding of the financial crisis, see Sorkin 2009).

collective action in the EU – it being so reliant on national parliamentary approval. As we will see below, the EU eventually sought to deal with this shortcoming by creating the European Financial Stability Facility (EFSF) (since October 2012: the European Stability Mechanism) and is musing about steps towards deeper economic integration (for instance, the creation of a banking union). Also, the European Central Bank took on an important role throughout the crisis.

After the financial crisis hit in full force, the economic crisis ensued. In 2009 the EU was in recession (European Commission 2012: 43, table 7). Member States of all EU countries sought to combat the crisis by finding domestic solutions. Governments in these countries spent vast amounts of public money to keep the economy going. Fearing a repeat of the recession of the 1930s, which followed the stock exchange crash of 1929 and subsequent banking crisis, the spending of national governments led to a considerable increase in public debt and budgetary deficits in most EU countries (see Trichet 2010). As Figure 3.1 shows, in 2008 the average public debt of the 17 countries of the euro area was below 70 per cent of GDP. By 2009 it was steeply on the rise (see also European Commission 2012: table 78).

The crisis changed its nature in autumn 2009. In October 2009 the newly elected government of Greece under George Papandreou informed the world that

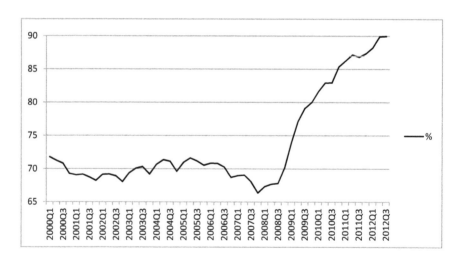

Figure 3.1   General government debt to GDP – 17 Euro Area Member States

Note: Euro area 17 (fixed composition) based on Maastricht assets/liabilities. General government (ESA95) – NCBs. All sectors without general government (consolidation) (ESA95) – NCBs. Financial stocks at nominal value. Neither seasonally nor working day adjusted.

Source: ECB 2013 (http://sdw.ecb.europa.eu/quickview.do?SERIES_KEY=121.GST.Q.I6. N.B0X13.MAL.B1300.SA.Q).

its budgetary deficit was much larger than reported by the previous government, namely 12.8 per cent instead of 3.6 per cent of GDP (see also Featherstone 2011). The result was a chain reaction of responses ranging from rating agencies downgrading Greek debt to an increase in the cost of lending for the Greek government. Member State governments had a hard time deciding what to do in response to this problem. They were facing two possible scenarios. They could decide not to do anything because Article 125 TFEU[9] does not allow the EU to bail out a Member State that is running a large debt and has difficulties refinancing this debt. Alternatively, the EU Member States could decide to help out collectively, as provided for by Article 122 TFEU.[10] Germany, led by Chancellor Angela Merkel, was initially reluctant to help. But by May 2010 it became apparent that the problems were too large. If no help were given, Greece would default with unpredictable but probably disastrous consequences for Greece, the euro area and EU Member States as a group. If the EU wanted to avoid that, Greece would need to be rescued after all (Featherstone 2011). The big problem here is that the options were difficult. To provide Greece with funds meant having to decide the structure and mechanism through which one would provide funds to a country in need, but also dealing with the fallout from that situation. Providing funds to such a country ultimately implies a transfer from one group of people (tax payers in the Member States) to another one (those holding Greek debt). A default would affect not only investors within Greece but also outside Greece, many of them banks in other EU Member States (notably in France and Germany). Yet those contemplating providing loans to Greece demanded assurances that Greece would be able to pay back the loans, alongside a credible commitment to restructuring expenses and revenues. There was also agreement that, if funds were made available to Greece now, funds should be earmarked for other Member States facing major refinance problems in the future. Worried by a perceived breach of Article 125 TFEU, Member States acted in an intergovernmental capacity. A year later, in March 2011, they decided to make a minor change to Article 136 TFEU, which should ensure beyond doubt the legality of setting up a stability mechanism. This amendment should have entered into force on 1 January 2013, provided that all Member States had ratified.[11]

---

9   Under Article 125 (1) TFEU the 'Union shall not be liable for or assume the commitments of central governments, regional, local or other public authorities, other bodies governed by public law, or public undertakings of any Member State, without prejudice to mutual financial guarantees for the joint execution of a specific project'. Also, Member States shall not assume such liability for other Member States, but this is 'without prejudice to mutual financial guarantees for the joint execution of a specific project'.

10   Article 122(2) TFEU enables the EU to provide financial assistance to a Member State 'in difficulties or seriously threatened with severe difficulties caused by natural disasters or exceptional occurrences beyond its control'.

11   European Council Decision (EU) 2011/199 amending Article 136 of the Treaty on the Functioning of the European Union with regard to a stability mechanism for Member States whose currency is the euro [2011] OJ L91/1. The additional text reads as follows:

None of this was planned for in the original architecture of EMU as per the Maastricht Treaty or its reform by the SGP (Heipertz and Verdun 2010). As we saw above, having had France and Germany fail to meet the SGP deficit rules had given the scheme a credibility problem. Yet now with Greece violating the rule so blatantly, the Germans were having difficulties accepting that they might need to step up to the plate and assist Greece. The problem was that with Germany responding so slowly and refusing to send a clear signal that it would act, the sovereign debt crisis quickly escalated. As financial markets were not sure if Greece was going to be assisted, the cost of borrowing for Greece increased sharply.

The yield spreads for Greek government debt rapidly went up, making it increasingly difficult (bordering on impossible) for the Greek government to refinance its debt. Eventually, in May 2010, it came to a climax when EU leaders needed to decide whether they would let Greece default or if they would provide Greece with enough funds that it could renew its loans. They opted for the latter and created a new European Union fund: the European Financial Stability Facility (EFSF). In the first instance the EFSF received 750 billion euro. The Troika of European Commission, European Central Bank and IMF made 110 billion euro available to assist Greece.

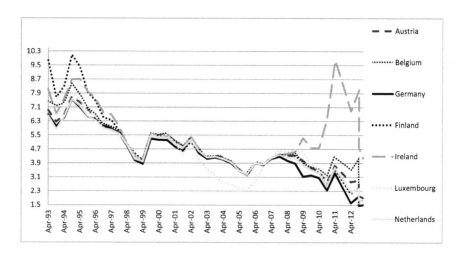

Figure 3.2a   Pre-2004 Euro Area 10-year government bond yields (per cent) – 'northern' countries

Source: ECB 2013 (http://www.ecb.int/stats/money/yc/html/index.en.html).

'The Member States whose currency is the euro may establish a stability mechanism to be activated if indispensable to safeguard the stability of the euro area as a whole. The granting of any required financial assistance under the mechanism will be made subject to strict conditionality.' This article has been ratified by 26 Member States by 31 December 2012 and by the Czech Republic in Spring 2013. It entered into force on 1 May 2013 (see European Parliament 2013).

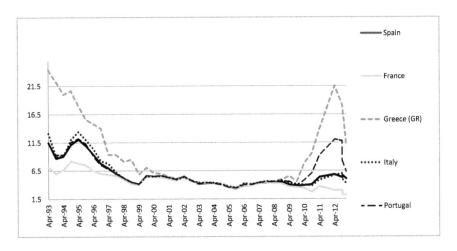

Figure 3.2b   Pre-2004 Euro Area 10-year government bond yields (per cent) – 'southern' countries

Source: ECB 2013 (http://www.ecb.int/stats/money/yc/html/index.en.html).

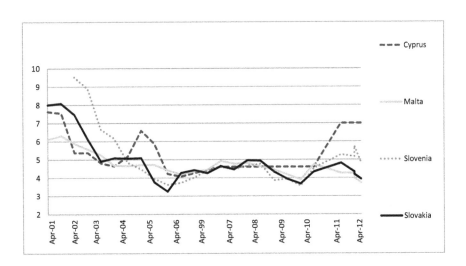

Figure 3.2c   Post-2004 Euro Area 10-year government bond yields (per cent)

Source: ECB 2013 (http://www.ecb.int/stats/money/yc/html/index.en.html).

Unfortunately, however, the sovereign debt crisis continued. The difficulties to refinance debt (attract capital at an affordable rate) also affected other countries in the periphery of Europe. By November 2010 Ireland was given a financial support package of loans for the amount of 85 billion euro with contributions from the euro area Member States through the EFSF, bilateral loans from Denmark, Sweden and the UK (countries not in the euro area), assistance from the IMF and even an Irish contribution (from the national pension fund). In May 2011 Portugal was also provided with a 'financial and economic support package' of 78 billion euro, again a mix of loans or lines of credit from the IMF, the EU and euro area, managed by the IMF, the EFSF and the European Financial Stability Mechanism (EFSM). On 8 October 2012 a new permanent crisis mechanism, the European Stability Mechanism (ESM), was inaugurated.[12] It is an intergovernmental organization set up by the euro area Member States to ensure financial stability in the euro area.

In July 2011 and again in November 2011, the costs of refinancing government debt in Greece and, to a lesser extent, Italy (and to some extent Spain), were making headlines. Financial markets and analysts were worried about the health of the euro area, because the situation in Greece was bad, but if a similar situation happened in Italy or Spain individually, but especially together, these countries would be considered as too big to bail out (*The Economist* 2012). In July 2011 Greece was offered a 109 billion euro rescue package. This time there was some 'restructuring' of debt (meaning that effectively Greece went through a partial default). In July and August 2011, the ECB had been buying up sovereign debt of countries in difficulty in order to provide those countries with the funds they needed. But in order to stabilize the euro, further institutional changes were required. The crises in Greece and Italy in November 2011 quickly entered the political domain, ultimately costing the political life of Prime Minister Berlusconi in the wake of the resignation of Greek Prime Minister Papandreou. Both men were replaced by caretaker Prime Ministers, by 'seasoned eurocrats' – both were economists with ample experience in European institutions (Lucas Papademos of Greece had previously served as the Vice-President of the ECB and Mario Monti of Italy had served for ten years as an EU Commissioner, first of the internal market and then for competition).

Besides the situation in Greece and Italy, in a number of other EU Member States governments either fell over the difficulties related to the sovereign debt crisis or during regular elections. Examples of the former are the Netherlands,

---

12   Article 136 TFEU indicated the need to set up an instrument to ensure financial stability. In the end it materialized in the form of the Treaty Establishing The European Stability Mechanism, concluded between all the Member States whose currency is the euro. This treaty was signed on 2 February 2012 and entered into force on 27 September 2012. The European Stability Mechanism was inaugurated in Luxembourg on 8 October 2012. For the treaty text see: http://www.european-council.europa.eu/media/582311/05-tesm2. en12.pdf; for the information on the completion of the ratification see European Parliament 2013, see also Council of the European Union 2012.

Slovakia and Slovenia – where the crisis, arguably, led to early elections in those countries. Examples of the latter are France and Spain where the ruling candidate or ruling party lost in generally scheduled national elections.

Throughout all of this turmoil, the ECB played an important role in stabilizing markets. As was mentioned above, the ECB made credit readily available in August 2007. In autumn 2008, it collaborated actively with other major central banks to respond to the financial crisis. In the May 2010 period, it was one of the troika to assist countries in need. In December 2011, it enabled long-term refinancing by making nearly 489 billion euros in loans available (at a 1 per cent interest rate) to 500 banks. The ECB made another 530 billion euro available to 800 banks in its second long-term refinancing operation in February 2012 (Wyplosz 2012). In June 2012, Spain requested 100 billion euro in soft loans from the EFSF and later that month Cyprus also requested support. In June 2012, the first steps were taken to devise a so-called banking union and the role of supervisor would be given to the ECB. In summer 2012, when the yield spreads between countries of the periphery and the euro area core were widening too much – due to speculation of a euro area collapse and unsustainable finances – the ECB took another major step. It introduced a programme called OMT (Outright Monetary Transactions). This policy meant that the ECB would buy an unlimited quantity of bonds (less than three years' maturity) from a country that has a debt market that appears not to function because of financial speculation. The ECB announced that it would only make these funds available to those countries that have applied for assistance from the ESM and agreed to the economic conditionality (see Drudi, Durré and Mongelli 2012). In this way, the ECB took numerous bold steps to act during the euro debt crisis. Indeed the many daring decisions made under the leadership of ECB President Mario Draghi earned him the 'person of the year 2012' award of the *Financial Times* (2012).

Institutional Challenges and Solutions

As has been made clear, the original designers of EMU were aware of the asymmetries in the institutional design (Verdun 1996, 2000). Indeed, it was understood that when the shortcomings of the asymmetrical EMU would come to the fore, the European Union would face a crisis. As I have argued based on research conducted in the run-up to the creation of EMU, leaders were aware that once such a crisis happened, the EU would need to take bold and daring steps to deepen integration (Verdun 2000).[13] What is often not mentioned is that this design was meant to leave the door open to the exact expression of what deeper political and economic integration would entail. The reason it was not right away designed as a fully fledged federal state or a larger mandate for EU institutions to borrow,

---

13   For a perspective from the ECB see ECB 2003, 2008, 2011 as well as an interview with Mario Draghi (*Der Spiegel* 2012).

tax and spend or to coordinate budgetary policy through a supranational body was that there had not been the support for such a larger role for the EU at the time. It was also unclear if there would be sufficient support for these steps later or exactly for what level of mandate there would be support.

The crisis has brought to the fore that Europeans are increasingly worried about the well-being of the institutional design of Europe's single currency. Many Europeans consider the euro now as an achievement, a right or entitlement they would be loath to give up. Indeed, for many the euro is the symbol of successful integration, one that gives consumers and citizens a concrete token of the entire European integration process that has brought to the European continent peace and prosperity. They are uneasy with the political struggles around the euro debt crisis; problems few really understand. Yet they feel that the EU is the level at which problems should be solved. A Eurobarometer study, conducted in autumn 2010, found the commonly held view that 'the EU is the best placed to take effective action against the effects of the crisis' (Eurobarometer 2010: 10).[14] In concrete terms, about 70–75 per cent of those interviewed agreed that 'more coordination between countries and an increased role for the EU are considered effective in tackling the crisis' (Eurobarometer 2010: 11). In other words, they anticipated that supervision of banks, coordination of budgetary policies and regulation of financial services, for instance, would be effective at the EU level.

One of the problems facing the euro is that any change to EMU institutional architecture is challenging. In the EU context, the rules that determine the operation of EMU are written down in the Treaty and changes thereof are by no means easy. Treaty changes require unanimity of the European Council (made up of the Heads of States and Governments of all the EU Member States – currently 28) and subsequently these changes require the approval of all EU national parliaments or governments (sometimes also with the help of a popular referendum). Notwithstanding these provisions, there are a few other ways to change EMU governance. For instance, the SGP is secondary law (regulations)[15] and thus can be amended more easily. Other ways are by setting up initiatives that are agreed to by the European Council in principle, but will later be inserted in the Treaty. The EFSF is one such arrangement.

In December 2011 an intergovernmental treaty was agreed to by 25 of the 27 Member States. This agreement is formally called the Treaty on Stability, Coordination and Governance in the Economic and Monetary Union (TSCG). It is commonly referred to as the 'Fiscal Compact'. This treaty entered into force on 1 January 2013 (European Parliament 2013), since a minimum of 12 Member States of the euro area had ratified it. It is only binding upon those Member States whose currency is the euro. The TSCG imposes stricter compliance with the rules in a

---

14   Although Member States that have not adopted the euro trust their national governments more with the task to solve the financial and economic crises (Eurobarometer 2010: 10).

15   See footnote 8 above about the SGP regulations.

number of ways: for instance, the Court of Justice of the EU may impose sanctions of up to 0.1 per cent of the GDP of the Member State in question for not complying with the new budget rules.

What times of crisis should do, as they have done throughout history, is to focus the attention of leaders and their populations on coming up with the next steps to secure the achievements of the past whilst realizing the potential of possible increased benefits of the future. The EU has an opportunity to show great leadership. It needs to draw on the bright minds of many economists, lawyers, political scientists, bureaucrats, politicians and the like to balance out the need to have effective leadership at the helm of the EU – acting effectively and efficiently – whilst having the support of the European citizens for proposed changes. Many citizens are hoping that present-day leaders will 'get on with it' and rescue the euro. The longer the crisis drags on, the more outside investors and the image of the EU in the global economy will suffer. It seems the permissive consensus is there for leaders to come up with packages that will enable all of the EU members to help those in need. Indeed, despite the enormous challenges, leaders of EU Member States to date are determined to save the euro. On many occasions, when presented with the question of whether to let a country 'fall' or pay the price to 'save' it, the leaders of the euro area countries have chosen the 'save' option (for instance, the Council meetings of November/December 2011 and again in June 2012 etc.). Citizens of the Member States that belong to the euro area are equally committed to the EU single currency.[16] The euro symbolizes many different aspects of successful European integration: it reinforces the advantages of the single market, it is something that every citizen can experience first-hand and there is a widespread feeling that, although the problems in the Euro Area were caused in part by poor accounting, poor governance and dishonesty by the Greek governments for their deficit reporting, it is short-sighted to blame only Greece (government and citizens) for the problems. Some of the structural imbalances were insufficiently recognized in advance of the financial crisis. It is challenging to determine who should pay for the cost of the situation and how best to devise a scheme that would spread the burden in an equitable way. The EU is facing an opportunity to redesign its EMU. Despite mammoth challenges to do so, leaders to date are still prepared to give it full support, even though they realize it is difficult to design good solutions.[17]

---

16   Here are some of the findings of Eurobarometer 2012: 4 about perceptions of euro area countries as held by the inhabitants of the euro area Member States interviewed in October 2012. More than half of those living in the euro area think the euro is a good thing for their particular Member State, and two thirds (67 per cent) say that the euro is a good thing for the EU, with the majority of respondents in each country saying this. Those who think that having the euro is a good thing for their country are much more likely to say the same thing about the euro's impact on the EU. Furthermore, roughly one quarter (24 per cent) of respondents say that the euro makes them feel more European.

17   The UK and the Czech Republic were 'outliers' in this regard. The Czech Republic's then President, Vaclav Klaus, was not interested in deeper European integration.

What might be some solutions to the current problems? Some have already been toyed with and will likely be further consolidated in the near future. The EU will become more closely involved in monitoring the budgetary deficit and fiscal debt of Member States; the ECB and the EFSF will remain important institutions in ensuring that credit is made available to Member States that are unable to attract capital at reasonable rates in the financial market – those that, without this support, could easily become subject self-fulfilling prophecies. There are some initiatives that are floating about Eurobonds (von Weizsäcker and Delpla 2011). The idea would be that bonds be drawn on the collective instead of issued by individual Member States. Citizens believe, as do some key observers, that having Eurobonds would reduce the likelihood that financial markets would attack one particular country (Daniele and Geys 2012). Finally, an orderly Greek default would require more funds to be mounted centrally, while the EU still needed to find funders to assist with replenishing the EFSF. It would need to be prepared for the effects of this default in the region and draw up a plan for containing the contagion. It would also need to develop further the rules on budgetary policies, management of government finances and some core macroeconomic indicators. Perhaps this episode will offer the Europeans another opportunity to review the democratic credentials of the EU and ask itself the question of whether the time might be ripe for deeper integration also in political representation so as to include citizens and EU-level politicians more explicitly. The alternative, demise and disintegration, is not something that is supported by many citizens or indeed by politicians. It is a time of opportunity for the European project. It is up to leaders to seize the moment.

Conclusion

At the time of writing, the euro area has faced a period of crisis; the most intense period was 2010–2012 during which time it became increasingly clear that a Greek problem was ultimately an EU problem. The EU has been facing challenges from financial markets, experienced a slow response by leaders of the euro area to the problems – which in part is due to the fact that the matters on the table are complicated. As the sovereign debt crisis continues to pose greater challenges, the blame game is played. Whose responsibility is it to 'rescue' Europe? Who is accountable to whom (so far) for having successfully averted the collapse of the euro area? What about the cost of bringing down public debt and budgetary deficit? Who pays for those austerity measures? How is this new governance structure legitimate? Then there is the so-called moral hazard problem: how can leaders ensure that future government leaders would not take advantage of the situation and simply overborrow and overspend and not worry about collecting

---

Neither Member State has provided reasons other than that they do not want 'too much Europe'. The UK Prime Minister David Cameron made an announcement in January 2013 that he would hold a referendum about the UK position in the EU by 2017.

taxes to pay for it all? The big concern, though, is that to benefit fully from all that the euro and EU have to offer, one needs to work a little harder at trying to solve the current crisis, rather than at every critical junction making minor steps to solve yesterday's problem. The citizens of today are increasingly feeling that they are paying for the problems of the past by having to pay for austerity measures needed to cut back the debt and deficits. They, however, do not feel that the citizens caused the problems in the first place. They perceive the situation as unfair – indeed, profoundly unjust. In fact, governments need not cut back on spending only. They can opt to increase taxes to offset the need to cut the deficit and debt. Clearly, the cost will hit many groups throughout different parts of society.

The governance of the euro and of EMU has to change in response to the sovereign debt crisis. To save the euro area, deeper integration is needed. The EU made major progress towards deeper integration in the past few years by having created the EFSF and the ESM, organized that there be a European semester[18] (whereby the European Commission examines macroeconomic indicators and public finances), signed a Fiscal Compact among 25 Member States, which has since entered into force, and made major steps towards the creation of a banking union. In addition, the ECB has worked hard to maintain liquidity in the markets. All in all, these are major achievements. Yet it does raise questions about how democratic accountability will be safeguarded in this context. That is a next step that has not been dealt with yet.

The fact that EMU was incomplete in and of itself should not have come as a great surprise to those who studied the origins of EMU. The original architects of EMU both in the 1960s and early 1970s, as well as those who were instrumental in relaunching it in the 1980s and 1990s, knew they designed an asymmetrical EMU. In other words, those that drafted the text that created the euro knew they put in the world a 'work in progress'. They foresaw that there would come a moment for change – a time that would demand further, deeper, integration – in order for EMU to succeed. The part that worried people throughout the process is that they felt the crisis and observed the political impasse in the run-up to the governance response. As I concluded in my 2000 study on perceptions of EMU and the reasons behind an asymmetrical EMU, sometimes it is necessary that people observe an external threat before they can gather support to make a leap to deepened integration (Verdun 2000). Of course, the major problem, which was not foreseen by the original architects, is that too many people at this stage are distrustful of the EU, of political leaders in Member States and of leaders at the helm of the EU. As much as they feel that the EU level is the appropriate level to solve the problems, they are still dissatisfied with the fallout of the financial crisis (high unemployment, austerity measures and it seemingly taking a long time to solve the euro debt crisis and questions about democratic accountability).

---

18   The European semester complements the Europe 2020 strategy, as decided by the European Council in its session on 17 June 2010 (Conclusions point 11 – http://www.consilium.europa.eu/uedocs/cms_data/docs/pressdata/en/ec/115346.pdf).

Those in charge of EU institutional design and governance need to balance two tasks. At once they need to be visionary leaders who are crafting the best governance model for EMU whilst at the same time finding ways to convince national parliamentary representatives and the general public that deeper integration is the way to go, whilst garnering support for the cost of doing so. The latter task may well turn out to be the most trying one yet, but one foretold. European leaders: seize the moment!

References

Ardagna, S. and Caselli F. 2012. The Political Economy of the Greek Debt Crisis: A Tale of Two Bailouts. *LSE mimeo*, http://personal.lse.ac.uk/casellif/papers/greece.pdf.

Barrios, S. *et al.* 2009. Determinants of intra-euro area government bond spreads during the financial crisis. *European Communities, European Commission, DG ECFIN, Economic Papers*, ISBN 978-92-79-13363-3 DOI: 10.2765/29413.

Berger, H. and Nitsch V. 2010. The Euro's Effect on Trade Imbalances, *IMF Working Papers* 10/226, International Monetary Fund.

Bolukbasi, H.T. 2009. On consensus, constraint and choice: economic and monetary integration and Europe's welfare states. *Journal of European Public Policy.* 16(4), 527–44.

Boonstra, W. 2010. How EMU can be strengthened by central funding of public deficits. *mimeo*, http://www.feweb.vu.nl/en/Images/paper-boonstra_tcm97-150398.pdf.

Buiter, W.H., Corsetti G.M. and Pesenti C.A. 1998. Interpreting the ERM-crisis. Country-specific and systemic issues. *Princeton Studies in International Finance.* 84 (March).

Bun, M.J.G. and Klaassen F.J.G.M. 2007. The Euro Effect on Trade is not as Large as Commonly Thought. *Oxford Bulletin of Economics and Statistics.* 69, 473–96.

Buti, M. and Giudice G. 2002. Maastricht's Fiscal Rules at Ten: An Assessment. *Journal of Common Market Studies* 40(5), 823–48.

Buti, M., Eijffinger S. and Franco D. 2005. The Stability Pact Pains: A Forward-Looking Assessment of the Reform Debate. *University of Tilburg Discussion Paper*, ISSN 0924-7815.

Buti, M. and Carnot N. 2012. The EMU Debt Crisis: Early Lessons and Reforms. *Journal of Common Market Studies.* 50(6), 899–911.

Chintrakarn, P. 2008. Estimating the Euro Effects on Trade with Propensity Score Matching. *Review of International Economics.* 16(1), 186–98.

Council of the European Union. 2012. The European Stability Mechanism (ESM) inaugurated, http://www.consilium.europa.eu/homepage/highlights/the-european-stability-mechanism-(esm)-inaugurated?lang=en.

Daniele G. and Geys B. 2012. Public Support for Institutionalised Solidarity: Europeans' Reaction to the Establishment of Eurobond. *Wissenschaftszentrum, Berlin. Discussion Paper* SP II 2012–112 December 2012.

De Cecco, M. and Giovannini, A. 1989. *A European Central Bank? Perspectives on Monetary Unification after Ten Years of the EMS*. Cambridge: Cambridge University Press.

De Grauwe, P. 2006. What Have we Learnt about Monetary Integration since the Maastricht Treaty?. *Journal of Common Market Studies*. 44(4), 711–30.

De Grauwe, P. 2011. The Governance of a Fragile Eurozone, *Katholieke Universiteit Leuven Discussion paper* www.econ.kuleuven.be/ew/academic/intecon/Degrauwe/PDG-papers/Discussion_papers/Governance-fragile-eurozone_s.pdf.

De Grauwe, P. 2012. The Eurozone's Design Failures: can they be corrected?, *LSE Public Lecture*, 28 November 2012.

De Grauwe, P. and Ji Y. 2012. Mispricing of Sovereign Risk and Macroeconomic Stability in the Eurozone, *Journal of Common Market Studies*. 50(6), 866–80.

Delors Report. 1989. *Report on Economic and Monetary Union in the European Community*. (Committee for the Study of Economic and Monetary Union) Luxembourg: Office for Official Publications of the E.C.

De Nardis S., De Santis R. and Vicarelli C. 2007. The Euro's Effects on Trade in a Dynamic Setting, *Working paper "Documenti di Lavoro"* of the Istituto di Studi e Analisi Economica 80 (April).

Der Spiegel. 2012. Interview with ECB President Mario Draghi: "We Couldn't Just Sit Back and Do Nothing" 29 October 2012. http://www.spiegel.de/international/europe/spiegel-interview-with-ecb-president-mario-draghi-a-863971.html.

Döhring, B. and Mordonu A. 2007. *What drives inflation perceptions? A dynamic panel data analysis*. Brussels: European Communities.

Drudi, F., Durré A. and Mongelli, F.P. 2012. The Interplay of Economic Reforms and Monetary Policy: The Case of the Eurozone, *Journal of Common Market Studies*, 50(6), 881–98.

Dyson, K. 1994. *Elusive Union: The Process of Economic and Monetary Union in Europe*. London/New York: Longman.

Dyson, K. and Featherstone, K. 1999. *The Road to Maastricht: Negotiating Economic and Monetary Union*, Oxford: Oxford University Press.

ECB. 2003. The relationship between monetary policy and fiscal policies in the euro area, *Monthly Bulletin*. February.

ECB. 2008. One monetary policy and many fiscal policies: ensuring a smooth functioning of EMU. *Monthly Bulletin*. July.

ECB. 2011. European Stability Mechanism. *Monthly Bulletin*. July.

Eichengreen, B. 2012a. European Monetary Integration with Benefit of Hindsight, *Journal of Common Market Studies*, 50(S1), 123–36.

Eichengreen, B. 2012b. When currencies collapse. *Foreign Affairs*. 91(1), 117–34.

Eijffinger, S.C.W. 2012. Rating Agencies: Role and Influence of Their Sovereign Credit Risk Assessment in the Eurozone, *Journal of Common Market Studies*, 50(6), 912–21.

Eurobarometer. 2010. Economic Governance in the EU. *Eurobarometer*. 74 (autumn).

European Commission. 1977. *Report of the study group on the role of public finance in European Integration ('MacDougall Report')* Volumes 1 and 2. Brussels: European Commission.

European Commission. 2008a. Communication from the Commission to the European Council, 'A European Economic Recovery Plan', COM (2008) 800 final.

European Commission. 2008b. *EMU@10: successes and challenges after 10 years of Economic and Monetary Union, European Economy 2*, Luxembourg: Office for Official Publications of the European Communities.

European Commission. 2012. *Autumn Economic Forecast. Statistical Annex of European Economy. European Economy*. Brussels: European Commission.

European Parliament. 2013. Table on the ratification process of amendment of art. 136 TFEU, ESM Treaty and Fiscal Compact. Directorate General for the Presidency Directorate for Relations with National Parliaments Brussels, 21/02/2013 Legislative Dialogue Unit and updated version of 19/07/2013, available at http://www.europarl.europa.eu/webnp/webdav/site/myjahiasite/shared/Publications/Fiscal%20Treaty%20ESM%20Overview%20table/art.%20136,%20ESM,%20Fiscal%20compact%20ratification.pdf.

Featherstone, K. 2011. The Greek Sovereign Debt Crisis and EMU: a Failing State in a Skewed Regime, *Journal of Common Market Studies*, 49(2), 193–217.

Feldstein, M. 1992. The Case Against EMU. *The Economist*, 13 June 1992.

Feldstein, M. 1997. EMU and International Conflict. *Foreign Affairs*, 76(6), 60–74.

Feldstein, M. 2012. The Failure of the Euro: The Little Currency That Couldn't, *Foreign Affairs*. 91(1), 105–16.

Financial Times. 2008a. Ireland guarantees six banks' deposits, By John Murray-Brown and Neil Dennis. 30 September 2008, *Financial Times*, http://www.ft.com/intl/cms/s/0/2124f8f4-8eb9-11dd-946c-0000779fd18c.html#axzz2LZuSQMxX.

Financial Times. 2008b. Germany guarantees savings. By Bertrand Benoit and James Wilson, 6 October 2008, *Financial Times*, http://www.ft.com/intl/cms/s/0/d895ef54-92ef-11dd-98b5-0000779fd18c.html.

Financial Times. 2011a. The eurozone really has only days to avoid collapse. By Wolfgang Münchau, 27 November 2011, *Financial Times*.

Financial Times. 2011b. Ten crucial days in race to save euro, 29 November, 2011, *Financial Times*, http://www.ft.com/intl/cms/s/0/66bc845c-1aae-11e1-bc34-00144feabdc0.html#axzz1fdU82ufv.

Financial Times. 2012. FT Person of the Year: Mario Draghi (By Lionel Barber and Michael Steen), 13 December 2012, *Financial Times*.

Flam, H. and Nordström H. 2006. Trade Volume Effects of the Euro: Aggregates and Sector Aggregates, *Stockholm University: Institute for International Economic Studies, Seminar Paper* 746.

Folkerts-Landau, D. and Garber P. 1992. The ECB: A Bank or a Monetary Policy Rule, in *Establishing a Central Bank. Issues in Europe and Lessons from the U.S.* edited by M. Canzoneri, V. Grilli and P. Masson. Cambridge: Cambridge University Press, 86–124.

Giavazzi, F., Micossi S. and Miller M. 1988. *The European Monetary System.* Cambridge: Cambridge University Press.

Goodhart, C.A.E. 2009. Procyclicality and financial regulation, *Banco de España, Estabilidad Financiera* 16.

Gros, D. and Thygesen, N. 1992. *European Monetary Integration*, Longman, London.

Havranek, T. 2010. Rose effect and the euro: is the magic gone? *Review World Economy*, 146, 241–61.

Heipertz, M. and Verdun, A. 2010. *Ruling Europe: The Politics of the Stability and Growth Pact.* Cambridge: Cambridge University Press.

Hemerijck, A. 2002. The Self-transformation of the European Social Model(s), in *Why we need a new welfare state*, edited by Gøsta Esping-Anderson. Oxford: Oxford University Press, 173–214.

House of Lords, European Union Committee. 2009. The Future of EU Financial Regulation and Supervision. *14th report of session 2008–2009*. Vol II Evidence. London: UK Stationary Office.

Kaelberer, M. 1997. Hegemony, Dominance or Leadership? Explaining Germany's Role in European Monetary Cooperation, *European Journal of International Relations* 3(1): 35–60.

Kennedy, E. 1991. *The Bundesbank: Germany's Central Bank in the International Monetary System.* New York City: Council on Foreign Relations Press.

Krugman, P. 2012. Greece and the Euro: Is the End Near? *Truthout*, 24 May 2012 http://truth-out.org/opinion/item/9358-greece-and-the-euro-is-the-end-near.

Ludlow, P. 1982. *The Making of the European Monetary System.* London: Butterworth.

Martin A. and Ross G. 2004. *Euros and Europeans: Monetary Integration and the European Model of Society.* Cambridge: Cambridge University Press.

Micco, A., Stein, E. and Ordoñez, G. 2003. The currency union effect on trade: early evidence from EMU. *Economic Policy*, 18, 315–56.

Pisani-Ferry, J. 2004. Reforming the SGP: Does it matter? What should be done? in *Economic Reform in Europe – Priorities for the Next Five Years*, edited by R. Liddle and M.J. Rodrigues. Policy Network.

Sargent, T. 2011. *United States Then, Europe Now.* Nobel Prize speech 2011.

Scharpf, F.W. 2002. The European social model: coping with the challenges of diversity. *Journal of Common Market Studies* 40(4), 645–70.

Schuknecht, L. *et al.* 2011. The Stability and Growth Pact, Crisis and Reform, *ECB Occasional Paper Series*, 129 (September).

Schure, P. 2013. European Financial Market Integration, in *Mapping European Economic Integration*, edited by A. Verdun and A. Tovias. Houndmills, Basingstoke: Palgrave Macmillan, chapter 6, 105–24.

Sorkin, A.R. 2009. *Too Big To Fail: Inside the Battle to Save Wall Street*. London/ New York/Toronto: Allen Lane (Penguin Group).

The Economist. 2008. Nightmare on Wallstreet: A weekend of high drama reshapes American finance. *The Economist*.15 September 2008. http://www.economist. com/node/12231236.

The Economist. 2011. The euro area's flagging economy: The shadow of recession, *The Economist*, 24–30 September 2011 400(8752), 89.

The Economist. 2012. The Spanish bail-out. Going to extra time, *The Economist*, 16–22 June 2012. 403(8789), 26–8.

The Economist. 2013. The Eurocrisis: So many ways to fail, *The Economist*, 4 February 2013. http://www.economist.com/blogs/freeexchange/2013/02/euro-crisis.

The Telegraph. 2011. Whatever Germany does, the euro as we know it is dead, *The Telegraph*, 29 August 2011, http://www.telegraph.co.uk/finance/comment/ jeffrandall/7746806/Whatever-Germany-does-the-euro-as-we-know-it-is-dead.html.

Trichet, J.-C. 2010. *Shaping a new world: The crisis and global economic governance*. Speech by Jean-Claude Trichet, President of the ECB, Lecture at Bocconi University, Aula Magna, Milano, 9 April.

Trichet, J.-C. 2013. The euro zone and the global crisis. *International Herald Tribune*, 16–17 March 2013, 6.

Trubek D.M. and Trubek L.G. 2005. Hard and Soft Law in the Construction of Social Europe: the Role of the Open Method of Co-ordination. *European Law Journal* 11(3), 343–64.

Tsoukalis, L. 1977. *The Politics and Economics of European Monetary Integration*, London: George Allen and Unwin.

Verdun, A. 1996. An 'Asymmetrical' Economic and Monetary Union in the EU: perceptions of monetary authorities and social partners, *Journal of European Integration*, 20(1), 59–81.

Verdun, A. 1999. The Role of the Delors Committee in the Creation of EMU: An Epistemic Community? *Journal of European Public Policy* 6(2), 308–28.

Verdun, A. 2000. *European Responses to Globalization and Financial Market Integration, Perceptions of EMU in Britain, France and Germany*, Basingstoke/ New York: St. Martin's Press, Macmillan.

Verdun, A. 2007. Economic Developments in the Euro Area. *Journal of Common Market Studies*, 45(Annual Review), 213–30.

Verdun, A. 2009. The Adoption of the Euro by Cyprus, in *Understanding and Evaluating the European Union: Theoretical and Empirical Approaches*, edited by Stelios Stavridis, Nicosia: University of Nicosia Press, 293–310.

Verdun, A. 2012a. The Euro Has a Future, in *Key Controversies in European Integration*, edited by H. Zimmermann and A. Dür, Houndmills, Basingstoke: Palgrave Macmillan, 113–20.

Verdun, A. 2012b. Introduction to the Symposium: Economic and Monetary Union and the Crisis of the Eurozone, *Journal of Common Market Studies*, 50(6): 863–5.

Verdun, A. 2013a. Small States and the Global Economic Crisis: An Assessment *European Political Science*, 12(1), 276–93, advance online publication, 26 October 2012; doi:10.1057/eps.2012.34.

Verdun, A. 2013b. The building of economic governance in the European Union, *European Review of Labour and Research* 19(1), 23–35.

von Weizsäcker, J. and Delpla, J. 2011. *Eurobonds: The blue bond concept and its implications*, 21 March 2011 Bruegel, www.bruegel.org/publications/ publication-detail/publication/509-eurobonds-the-blue-bond-concept-and-its-implications/.

Werner Report. 1970. Report to the Council and the Commission on the realisation by stages of Economic and Monetary Union in the Community – "Werner Report" – (definitive text) [8 October 1970]. *Bulletin of the European Communities*, Supplement 11/1970.

Wyplosz, C. 2012. The ECB's trillion euro bet, *VoxEU*, 13 February 2012.

Chapter 4

The Contested Scope of Labour Law Requirements in Public Procurement – a Multi-Level Analysis

Julia Vinterskog*

Introduction

In line with the discussions on reconciliation of social and economic policies within the European Union (EU), this chapter suggests that public procurement may constitute an important instrument to implement labour law standards. It explores how different levels of socio-economic governance interact in negotiating tensions between economic integration and social values in this field. In doing so, it focuses on the legal orders of the International Labour Organization (ILO) as an international organization, the EU as a supranational organization and Sweden as a Member State of both. Public procurement is used as an example where labour law requirements are employed to protect a social dimension within a framework geared to maintain transnational competition for services required by the public sector. After the controversial rulings of the Court of Justice in *Rüffert*[1] and *Commission v Germany*,[2] the question remains whether Member States still have scope to effectively implement ILO Convention 94 on imposing labour law requirements on public contractors. Within this frame, the chapter examines whether a balance between the economic and the social can be achieved.

Initially, the European Economic Community (EEC) aimed to pursue a common market of free internal trade of goods, services, labour and capital. European integration has thus been characterized by an unbalanced relationship between economic and social policies. Whereas the former have been subject to Europeanization at a supranational level, the latter have essentially been left to protection at national levels. This 'decoupling' of the social and the economic spheres has constrained welfare states in their attempts to promote a national

* This chapter is based on the author's master's thesis. Special thanks go to Mia Rönnmar for unfailing encouragement and support and to Dagmar Schiek and Ida Otken Eriksson for indispensable feedback. The usual disclaimer applies.
1 Case C-346/06 *Dirk Rüffert v Land Niedersachsen* [2008] ECR I-1989.
2 Case C-271/08 *Commission v Germany* [2010] ECR I-7091.

social dimension (Scharpf 2002: 665 *et seq.*), which again has been said to further deepen the EU's social deficit (Joerges 2004: 16 *et seq.*).

The entering into force of the new legal order on 1 December 2009 marked a new milestone in the history of European integration. According to the Treaty on the European Union (Lisbon), hereinafter TEU, Article 3(3), the internal market shall partially be founded on 'a highly competitive social market economy, aiming at full employment and social progress', which implies a need for coherence between economic and social interests. Article 4(2) TEU promotes the EU's respect for the Member States' political and constitutional fundamental structures, indicating respect for national identity and particularism (see further Lenaerts and Guiéterrez-Fons 2010). Furthermore, fundamental rights have been given a prominent position due to the heightened status of the Charter of Fundamental Rights of the European Union as primary law (Article 6(1) TEU). Following these changes, the EU is under an obligation to remedy its social deficit resulting from the decoupling of economic integration at EU levels and social policies at national levels. This chapter suggests that this mandate calls for the acceptance of diversity of national social policies and judicial deference in cases where fundamental economic freedoms and labour law requirements conflict (Joerges and Rödl 2009: 8–9).

For the purposes of this chapter, labour law requirements may comprise health and safety conditions, non-discrimination provisions, working and employment conditions including pay and the observance of collective agreements. 'Social policies' or 'social considerations' will be used in a broader sense to explain the pursuit of different aspects of social justice, and within the framework of public procurement, it encompasses the allocation of means to operate labour market policies and welfare payments (McCrudden 2007: 2 *et seq.*).

This chapter is based on the position that the substance of national labour law is determined through the interaction of different actors, either public or private bodies, operating at supranational (e.g. the EU), national and subnational levels (regional or local), representing different interests (Marginson and Keune 2012: 5). The notion of multi-level governance also entails coordinated action, with the joint participation of different tiers of government regarding formulation of EU policies and legislation.[3] This chapter also addresses levels beyond the supranational level, as illustrated by the ILO as an international organization.

The first part of this overview consists of three sections, providing a description of the legal frameworks determining the scope of labour law requirements in public procurement at ILO (section 2), EU (section 3) and Swedish level (section 4). At the ILO level, the focus will be on ILO Labour Clauses (Public Contracts) Convention 1949 (No. 94). At the EU level,[4] the procurement Directives adopted in 2004 and

---

3   See the Committee of Regions' (CoR) White Paper on Multilevel Governance, CONST-IV-020. Available in all of the EU official languages at: http://cor.europa.eu/en/activities/governance/Pages/white-pape-on-multilevel-governance.aspx.

4   The term Union law will be used predominantly in this chapter. However, where appropriate, references will be made to Community law.

currently in force, namely Directive 2004/17[5] and Directive 2004/18[6] as well as the jurisprudence of the European Court of Justice (CJEU), will be assessed to identify the scope of labour law requirements.[7] At the Swedish level, the Swedish Act on Public Procurement, which is the general legislation governing public procurement in Sweden, is used to exemplify the scope and margin of discretion left to the EU Member States. In section 5, these frameworks and the relationship between these multi-levels of governance will be assessed in terms of parallel application and/or collision between the economic and the social, as represented by the term 'social market economy' in Article 3(3) TEU. In section 6, some concluding remarks will be presented with a view to highlighting the social objectives of the Lisbon Treaty in the context of the 'decoupling' of social and economic integration.

The ILO Level

Core Features of the Organization

The ILO is a United Nations organization responsible for drawing up and overseeing international labour standards. It was established in 1919 by the signatory states of the Treaty of Versailles, in recognition of the need to regulate a globalized economy in order to guarantee that economic progress would emerge alongside social justice, prosperity and peace for all.[8] The ILO has ever since promoted international labour standards by means of Conventions and Recommendations. In 1998, the ILO attempted to reinforce its position in the context of a globalized economy context by distilling international labour standards to a set of core labour

---

5   Directive of the European Parliament and of the Council (EC) 2004/17 coordinating the procurement procedures of entities operating in the water, energy, transport and postal services sectors [2004] OJ L134/1.

6   Directive of the European Parliament and of the Council (EC) 2004/18 on the coordination of procedures for the award of public works contracts, public supply contracts and public service contracts [2004] OJ L134/114.

7   It is worthy of note that the Commission has presented a proposal for a new public procurement Directive (Commission Proposal for a directive of the European Parliament and of the Council on public procurement (COM(2011) 896 final, 20.12.2011)), as part of the realization of the Single Market Act. The new directive will include rules on subcontracting and guarantee respect for labour laws and collective agreements. According to the European Parliament report presented in January 2013, social considerations were not enough covered by the Commission proposal. Also, a new recital was inserted stating that 'the Directive should not prevent Member States from comlying with the ILO Convention 94' (European Parliament report (COM(2011) 896-C7-0006/2012-2011/0438(COD)). In June 2013, the European Parliament and the Council reached a provisional agreement on the reform of the EU public procurement Directives. The text still needs to be formally approved by the Council and the Parliament's Internal Market Committee, which will lead the way to a plenary vote.

8   See for further elaboration on this ILO 2009.

standards in the Declaration on Fundamental Principles and Rights at Work and its Follow-up (Macklem 2005: 65).[9] These standards are binding for all members of the ILO, regardless of whether the state at issue ratified a particular Convention the standard (para 2 of 1998 Declaration).

The ILO is characterized by its tripartite decision-making structure where representatives of worker and employers' organizations are able to vote on the adoption of ILO Conventions alongside national governments as well as participate in determining the agenda of the International Labour Conference through the ILO Governing Body.[10] The prerequisite of consensus for the adoption of any regulatory measures provides the instruments of the ILO with greater legitimacy and facilitates and consolidates its implementation (Novitz, 2005: 224).

The ILO and the EU

The relationship between the ILO and the EU has been characterized as a reciprocal link where the formulation of EU social policies may draw inspiration from the ILO and the treatment of international labour law standards, whilst contributing to the further determination and enforcement of such standards (Novitz 2005: 215). Novitz identifies two ways for the EU to recognize the ILO's core standards: either by internal regulatory action targeting the conduct of the Member States by means of legal regulation and through the jurisprudence of the Court on fundamental rights or by external relations, e.g. by making trade and aid agreements conditional on compliance with such standards (Novitz 2005).

By means of soft law, the EU is committed to encouraging its Member States to increase their financial support for the ILO (European Commission 2001). Even though the internal implementation of ILO normative provisions within the EU's social field has increased, certain key areas of social policy are still excluded from EU competence.[11] Since even existing labour standards are to be justified in both economic and social terms, dialogue between the EU and the ILO with a view to promoting international labour standards is far from complete (Novitz 2005: 216 *et seq.*).

As regards normative conflicts, Article 351(1)–(2) of the Treaty of the Functioning of the European Union (TFEU) stipulates that international agreements concluded between Member States before their accession and third countries shall not be affected by the Treaty provisions. However, should such agreements be

---

9   The Core Labour Standards Conventions are: Convention No. 87 (Freedom of Association and Protection of the Right to Organise), Convention No. 98 (Right to Organise and Collective Bargaining), Convention No. 29 (Forced labour), Convention No. 105 (Abolition of Forced labour), Convention No. 138 (Minimum Age), Convention No. 182 (Worst Forms of Child Labour), Convention No. 100 (Equal Remuneration) and Convention No. 111 (Discrimination, Occupation and Employment).

10   ILO Constitution, Articles 3, 7, 14 and 19.

11   See in this respect, Article 153(5) TFEU.

found incompatible with the Treaties, the Member State 'shall take all appropriate steps to eliminate the incompatibilities established'.

Accordingly, certain bilateral agreements between a Member State and another state or organization shall not be affected by the requirements stemming from the Treaties inasmuch as they are compatible with the Treaties. Since the competences in the field of social policy is shared between the Member States and the EU, the Treaty allows the Member States to implement more stringent measures as complete uniformity is not the primary objective pursued. The *Levy*[12] case concerned ILO Convention No. 89 which prohibits night work for women. The Court found that it is for the national courts to determine to what extent national legislation prohibiting night work for women was in breach of Union law. Should the national provision be found in conflict with Union law, national courts shall refrain from applying such conflciting legislation, unless such legislation stems from a prior agreement with a non-member country (paras 21–2). In Bercusson's view, should the ILO Conventions remain in force as earlier international agreements, this would result in a division among the EU Member States with respect to the ability to impose clauses in public contract, making collective agreements mandatory labour standards. Bercusson contends that there is no apparent conflict between the full application of Convention No. 94 and Union law, including the procurement Directives (Bercusson 2009: 448–9).

Convention No. 94
Convention No. 94 was adopted by the ILO in 1949, addressing the issue of labour law requirements in public procurement. The Convention is founded on the idea that the state should act as a model employer offering the most advantageous conditions to workers remunerated directly or indirectly by public funds (ILO 2008: paras 174–7). The objective is described as dual. Firstly, the Convention aspires to eliminate labour costs as being used as competitive advantages among tenderers. Secondly, it aims to guarantee that public contracts are not exercised in a manner that could have a downward effect on wages and working conditions. This plain social objective leads to a well-defined scope of labour law requirements in public procurement. Local, regional or national collective agreements are to be observed according to Convention No. 94, safeguarding the prevailing working conditions in the locality where the work is to be performed. The Convention further stipulates that the awarding authority is responsible for guaranteeing that the working conditions in force are regulated in the contract. In the absence of such protective provisions, the awarding authority is responsible for ensuring that workers enjoy fair and reasonable conditions of health, safety and welfare (Article 3 Convention No. 94, see also ILO 2008: para 122). In order to ensure proper implementation in practice as regards protection of prevailing working conditions, Convention No. 94 is also applicable to subcontractors (ILO 2008: paras 80–81).

---

12   Case C-158/91 *Criminal proceedings against Jean-Claude Levy* [1993] ECR-4287.

According to Article 1 of the Convention, the scope of application concerns services and works where at least one of the contracting parties is a public authority, the execution of the contract involves the expenditure of public funds and the other contracting party employs the workers. The Convention requires the competent authorities of the ratifying states to ensure that the public contracts include clauses on wages, including allowances, hours of work and other working conditions that may not be less favourable *vis-à-vis* the conditions established by collective agreement, arbitration award or by national laws or regulations for work of the same character in the district where the work is carried out.

The Convention does not contain any substantive minimum standards: it merely demands that the national, regional or local conditions shall be respected. Requiring that labour clauses shall be set after consultation between the competent authority and the employers' and workers' organizations, the Convention explicitly promotes the tripartite structure of the organization as a whole (see Article 2). The overall purpose of the Convention and the attempt to reinforce its rules shows the distinctive ambition of eradicating the risks of using public procurement as grounds for unhealthy competition (ILO 2008: paras 174–7).

The EU Level

Secondary EU Law on Public Procurement

The EU Public Procurement Directives 2004/17 and 2004/18 aim to secure that the procedure of awarding contracts does not cause any distortion of competition (recital 4 of Directive 2004/18). To this end, and to avoid unjustified restrictions of the fundamental freedoms,[13] public authorities are required not to favour national economic operators to the detriment of foreign economic operators when awarding public contracts and to safeguard the principle of non-discrimination (Bercusson 2009: 432).

Nevertheless, demands for simplified rules and the integration of considerations relating to political ambitions have been raised (Ahlberg and Bruun 2011: 89). As indicated by the Monti Report (Monti 2010: 68 *et seq.*), there may be scope for a more extensive use of public procurement as a tool for achieving certain policy objectives at the EU level, where the adoption of mandatory requirements linked to such objectives would promote social cohesion. Frictions between market integration at supranational level and protection at national level are liable to cause impediments to the proper functioning of the single market (Monti 2010).

Public procurement is subject to two arrays of provisions. The main provisions governing public procurement contracts meeting certain thresholds are subject to

---

13   See, as one example, the ruling in case C-234/03 *Contse SA, Vivisol Srl and Oxigen Salud SA v Instituto Nacional de Gestión Sanitaria (Ingesa), formerly Instituto Nacional de la Salud (Insalud)* [2005] ECR I-9315 on public services contracts.

the procedures formalized by the Directives.[14] Procurements not subject to the Directives are nevertheless subject to the provisions of free movement, i.e. the freedom of goods in Article 34 and 35, freedom of establishment in Article 49 and freedom of services in Article 56 TFEU and the principles derived therefrom; the principles of equal treatment and non-discrimination, mutual recognition, proportionality and transparency, provided that the procurement at issue is of transnational interest. Contracts lacking transnational interest will not have an impact on the internal market and do not fall within the ambit of the Treaty.[15]

A report to the European Parliament (Zappalà 2001) suggested that obligations on both foreign and domestic contractors as regards employment and working conditions during the performance of the contract should be integrated into the main body of the Directive, aimed at ensuring that the provisions were consistent with ILO Convention No. 94 and Directive 96/71[16] (Zappalà 2001: 38). The rapporteur proposed that violations of the core ILO Conventions and of the main EU social policy legislation should constitute grave misconduct, which could lead to exclusion from the tender process (Zappalà 2001: 62 *et seq.*). The obligation on contractors to comply with employment protection and working conditions is placed in the preamble of Directive 2004/18 (recital 34). As for the definition of grave misconduct, the remnant in recital 43 lacks reference to compliance with core ILO Conventions. Kilpatrick argues that the placement of social considerations in the recitals reflects the conflict between the EU institutions during the legislative process, resulting 'in a variegated set of relationships between the social recitals and the main body of the Directive' (Kilpatrick 2011: 11).

The public procurement Directives specifying the procedural provisions are Directive 2004/17 governing the contracts in specific sectors and Directive 2004/18 covering most major public contracts. In the area of defence and security, Directive 2009/81[17] was adopted in 2009. Additionally, there are two directives governing the legal remedies of EU public procurement law, namely Council Directive 89/665[18] and Council Directive 92/13,[19] seeking to guarantee restitution

---

14   Procurement of certain services may only be partly covered by the Directive or exempted altogether (Ahlberg and Bruun, 2011).

15   For indications on what factors may constitute a transnational interest, see Case C-507/03 *Commission v Ireland* [2007] ECR I-9777, para 33.

16   Directive of the European Parliament and of the Council (EC) 96/71 concerning the posting of workers in the framework of the provision of services [1997] OJ L18/1.

17   Directive of the European Parliament and of the Council (EC) 2009/81 on the coordination of procedures for the award of certain works contracts, supply contracts and service contracts by contracting authorities or entities in the fields of defence and security, and amending Directives 2004/17/EC and 2004/18/EC OJ L216/76.

18   Council Directive (EEC) 89/665 on the coordination of the laws, regulations and administrative provisions relating to the application of review procedures to the award of public supply and public works contracts [1989] OJ L395/33.

19   Council Directive (EEC) 92/13 coordinating the laws, regulations and administrative provisions relating to the application of Community rules on the procurement

for tenderers where the awarding authorities have failed to observe the procedural provisions.[20]

Directive 2004/18 codifies the case law of the Court of Justice and especially the case law on award criteria, clarifying the possibilities to meet the needs of the public concerned. The Directive recognizes that such needs may include environmental and/or social criteria (recital 1) provided that such criteria are linked to the subject matter of the contract. Further, the use of such criteria cannot confer an unrestricted freedom of choice on the contracting authority, the needs must be expressly indicated, and lastly, they must comply with the general principles governing EU public procurement law. Criteria linked to the performance of the contract may be used to attain certain social objectives supporting, *inter alia*, vocational training, training measures for unemployed or young people, recruitment of disabled persons and the realization of the basic ILO Conventions (recital 33).

The Public Procurement Procedure under Directive 2004/18

The scope for different social concerns may vary depending on the phase of the procurement procedure (Alhberg and Bruun 2011: 92). In the following, a brief summary of the different phases of public procurement set out in Directive 2004/18 and the potential scope for integrating labour law requirements is presented.

Qualification criteria
Should a tender not fulfil the requirements for participation in the tender process, it may be excluded. Qualification criteria may relate to the tenderer's personal suitability (Article 45), the financial standing of the tenderer (Article 47) and the fulfilment of technical specifications (Article 48). As regards financial standing and technical suitability, the criteria imposed must relate and be proportionate to the subject matter of the contract (Article 44). Social considerations can be integrated at this stage as grave professional misconduct, a ground for exclusion, may relate to non-compliance with labour law requirements (Ahlberg and Bruun, 2011: 93).

Award criteria
During the awarding phase, the contracting authority selects among the candidates who have passed the initial stage of participation (Bercusson and Bruun 2005: 113 *et seq.*). The authority may base its decision on two grounds; either the lowest price (Article 53(1)(b)) or the most economically advantageous tender (Article 53(1)(a)). The relative weighting of award criteria must be clearly indicated in

---

procedures of entities operating in the water, energy, transport and telecommunications sectors [1992] OJ L76/14.

20   Those two directives have been amended by Directive of the European Parliament and of the Council (EC) 2007/66 amending Council Directives 89/665/EEC and 92/13/EEC with regard to improving the effectiveness of review procedures concerning the award of public contracts [2007] OJ L335/31.

the contract and linked to the subject matter of the contract (Article 53(1)(a)). According to Arrowsmith, this constitutes a significant restriction as to the possibility to take into account social considerations (Arrowsmith 2009: 242).

Through its jurisprudence, the Court of Justice has developed indicators limiting the scope of using social considerations as awarding criteria, stipulating that award criteria must not give unrestricted discretion to the awarding authority.[21] The criteria must be objective and quantifiable[22] and the application of such must be verifiable.[23] In *Beentjes*, the Court stated that Member States enjoy a broad margin of discretion when weighting the award criteria and confirmed that additional criteria promoting social objectives, in this case an obligation to employ long-term unemployed, may be legitimate given that such criteria are not directly or indirectly discriminatory and indicated in the contract notice (paras 24 and 36).

Abnormally low tenders (Article 55) may additionally constitute a ground for exclusion. Before rejecting an abnormally low tender, the awarding authority is required to request the tenderer for details of the constituent elements. Such elements may in particular include compliance with provisions relating to employment and working conditions in force where the work, service or supply is carried out (Article 55(1)(d)). The term 'particular' implies that the list set out in Article 55(1) is illustrative, rather than exhaustive (Bruun and Ahlberg 2010: 44).

Contract performance criteria
An awarding authority may demand the awarded contractor to comply with certain requirements during the performance of the contract, given that such requirements are in compliance with Union law and explicitly indicated in the contract notice. Article 26 of Directive 2004/18 stipulates that such requirements can comprise social considerations, specified in recital 33. Contract performance criteria can thus be used to combat unemployment and to fulfil requirements stemming from the core ILO Conventions, provided that the criteria are not directly or indirectly discriminatory (recital 33).

Prior to the adoption of the current Directives in 2004, the performance phase was not regulated in public procurement Directives. Kilpatrick contends that Article 26 is essential for clarifying the scope of integrating conditions since the rationale underpinning the provision allows for additional obligations on public contractors, which in turn may ensure higher worker protection than those obligations that generally apply (Kilpatrick 2011: 10).

Arrowsmith argues that a broad interpretation of measures related to the 'subject matter of the contract' (in the context of award criteria) and to the 'performance

---

21   Case 31/87 *Gebroeders Beentjes BV v State of the Netherlands* [1998] ECR 4635 para 26. See also, for further elaboration, Arrowsmith 2009: 242.

22   Case C-513/99 *Concordia Bus Finland Oy Ab, formerly Stagecoach Finland Oy Ab v Helsingin kaupunki and HKL-Bussiliikenne* [2002] ECR I-7213, para 66.

23   Case C-448/01 *EVN AG and Wienstrom GmbH v Republik Österreich* [2003] ECR I-14527, paras 51–2.

of the contract' (in the context of permitted contract terms) would allow Member States to implement different kinds of measures, including requirements connected with workforce matters (Arrowsmith 2009: 244 *et seq*.).

Whereas a narrow interpretation supports a market-oriented approach seemingly governing EU public procurement law, a broader interpretation approach would not only provide the EU Member States with wider abilities to integrate labour law requirements into their public contracts: it would also reflect that the EU is sincere in its attempts to strengthen and protect measures relating to social policy.

EU Internal Market Law Regarding Labour Requirements in Public Procurement

The significance of the case law of the Court of Justice for the fate of fundamental social rights must not be underestimated, in particular with regards to the scope of social considerations and labour law requirements in public procurement. In the following, two important rulings dealing with labour law requirements and the integration of the internal market will be addressed.

Case law by the Court of Justice

To which extent may an awarding authority set the employment conditions and rates of pay to be met by the awarded contractor and potential subcontractors? In transnational procurements, the issue may occur whether Directive 96/71 is applicable to the services offered. According to Ahlberg and Bruun, the starting point is to indicate in the public contract which labour law requirements should apply (Ahlberg and Bruun, 2011). However, following the rulings of the Court of Justice in *Laval*,[24] *Commission v Luxembourg*[25] and *Rüffert*, Member States are constrained as it is now open to doubt whether they can require foreign undertakings to pay wages in accordance with the collective agreement in force to workers posted from the country of establishment to the Member State in question. This occurs, in particular, if those collective agreements do not meet the requirements set out in Directive 96/71 and the cases referred to. To Sweden, this is especially a problem for the national labour law model of Sweden, where there are no statutory minimum wages or a system declaring collective agreement universal.

The *Rüffert* case concerned legislation of the German state *Niedersachsen* on public procurement stipulating that contracts for building services should be awarded only to undertakings that agree to pay their employees at least the remuneration prescribed by collective agreement at the place where those services are performed. The awarded contractor was also responsible for the compliance of those requirements by all subcontractors engaged in the performance of the contract. The legislation aimed to counteract distortion of competition resulting from the

---

24   Case C-341/05 *Laval un Partneri Ltd v Svenska Byggnadsarbetareförbundet, Svenska Byggnadsarbetareförbundets avdelning 1, Byggettan and Svenska Elektrikerförbundet* [2007] ECR I-11767.

25   Case C-319/06 *Commission v Luxembourg* [2008] ECR I-04323.

use of cheap labour. A building contract was awarded to a German company, *Objekt und Bauregie*, who had engaged a Polish company as subcontractor in the performance of the contract. After investigations had shown that the Polish workers were paid half of the minimum wage laid down in the building and work collective agreement in force, the contract was terminated (paras 5–11). This was challenged before the national court, which in turn referred questions to the Court of Justice concerning the potential conflict of the Niedersachsen legislation with Directive 96/71 and the freedom to provide services (Article 56 TFEU).

The Court of Justice found a violation of EU law. It considered that Directive 96/71 did apply to the case, although the Niedersachsen legislation was not intended govern posting of workers. The Directive stipulates that posted workers shall enjoy the same conditions of employment and that such conditions may be prescribed by collective agreements that are universally applicable or by agreements generally applicable to the industry concerned or agreements concluded by the most representative employers' and labour organizations, applied nationwide (paras 20–22). The Court found that the Niedersachsen work and building collective agreement did not meet the requirements laid down in Articles 3(1) and 3(8) of Directive 96/71 and that its wages could thus not be applied to foreign undertakings. The Court also rejected the view that the collective agreement constituted more favourable conditions of employment (Article 3(7) of Directive 96/71). The Court stated that the Niedersachsen legislation was liable of constituting a restriction to the freedom to provide services in Article 49 EC (now Article 56 TFEU) as it imposed an economic burden on foreign undertakings that may render less attractive the provision of their services (paras 31, 32 and 37). Since the rate of pay was only partly applicable to the construction sector and no evidence showed that the rate was necessary for a worker only when employed under a public works contract, the restriction could not be justified due to an overriding reason of public interest. The Court did not accept the contentions made by the German government that the legislation was necessary to ensure independent collective bargaining or the financial balance of social security systems. Consequently, the Niedersachsen legislation was found to be in breach of Union law (paras 40–43).

In *Commission v Germany*,[26] the Court considered whether federal German legislation regulating old-age pension schemes fell within the scope of public procurement law and thus had to be subject to the procedure laid out therein. The legislation provided that an employee had a right to designate a share of his future earnings to contribute to a private old-age pension scheme and allowed for such schemes to be established by means of collective agreements. A collective agreement was concluded between the Federation of Local Authority Employer Association and United Service Sector Union, stating that the conversion should be delegated to public bodies offering supplementary pension schemes or savings banks or local authority insurance companies.

---

26   Case C-271/08 *Commission v Germany* [2010] ECR I-7087.

The EU Commission raised an infringement action against Germany, contending that the omission by the German local authorities to call for tenders at the European level instead of directly awarding insurance contracts to the bodies indicated in the collective agreement constituted an infringement of former Council Directive 92/50[27] or at least a violation of the fundamental freedoms. This was disputed by Germany who claimed that the contracts were excluded from the application of the Directive 92/50 and Directive 2004/18, as they constituted part of the employment relationship. Neither should local authorities be seen as contracting authorities when functioning as employers. Ultimately, the application of public procurement law would be contrary to the autonomy of management and labour in the German basic law (paras 30–31).

The Court noted that collective bargaining is a fundamental right, enshrined in Article 28 of the Charter of Fundamental Rights of the European Union and Article 152 TFEU. However, it considered that this did not imply that local authority employers were automatically excluded from complying with requirements stemming from the Directives at issue (paras 38, 39 and 41). With reference to *Viking*[28] and *Laval*, the Court stated that the right of collective bargaining is not absolute. Even though collective agreements are not *per se* regarded as restrictions to the internal market,[29] directives implementing the fundamental freedoms cannot be automatically prejudiced (paras 43–8). Unlike the objective of enhancing the level of the pensions of local authority employees, the designation of bodies and undertakings in a collective agreement such as that at issue here docs not affect the essence of the right to bargain collectively (para 49). Compliance with the Directives cannot be regarded as irreconcilable with the attainment of the objective pursued by the collective agreement parties, i.e. the objective of participation, the commitments to the principle of solidarity and to financial security (paras 55 *et seq.*, Syrpis 2011: 224). The Court further rejected that the exemption of employment contracts from the scope of the Directives should be extended to any provisions based on such contracts or collective agreements forming an integral part thereof (Article 16(e)). Any derogation from the scope should be interpreted narrowly and can therefore not be extended to a contract concluded between an employer and an undertaking, which provides the authority with insurance services and does not relate to any of the concerns laid down in recital 28 of Directive 2004/18 (paras 81–2). As the total value of the contract was equal to or exceeded the relevant threshold, the Directive was applicable (paras 93 and 105).

---

27   Council Directive (EEC) 92/50 relating to the coordination of procedures for the award of public service contracts, [1992] OJ L209/1.

28   Case C-438/05 *International Transport Workers' Federation and Finnish Seamen's Union v Viking Line ABP and OÜ Viking Line Eesti* [2007] ECR I-10779.

29   See Article 101(1) TFEU and Case C-67/96 *Albany International BV v Stichting Bedrijfspensioenfonds Textielindustrie* [1999] ECR I-5751, para 60 and Case C-222/98 *Hendrik van der Woude v Stichting Beatrixoord* [2000] ECR I-7111.

Implications of the Court's case law

The case of *Rüffert* has had several implications with respect to the principle of equal treatment and the social framework of the public procurement Directives. Directive 96/71 is used to limit the scope of labour law requirements in public procurement.[30] The requirements imposed by the German authority went beyond the provisions laid down in Article 3(1) of Directive 96/71 and deprived foreign undertakings of their competitive advantage of lower working costs. The Court's ruling seemingly suggests that the principle of equal treatment only works one way, in favour of the fundamental freedoms as domestic undertakings are still required to comply with applicable collective agreements (see Kilpatrick 2011: 15). This position clashes with the aim of Convention No. 94, i.e. to counteract the use of labour costs as a competitive element among tenderers, and reveals the difficulty of reconciling the aims pursued by public procurement law at the ILO level and at the EU level.

Even though the Lisbon Treaty had not entered into force at the time of the disputes in both *Rüffert* and *Commission v Germany*, the Court's reasoning in *Rüffert* must be questioned in the light of the ambitions of combating the social deficit of the EU, as identified by the 'decoupling' theory. The Court relies on the promotion of the internal market, where national labour law requirements are viewed as restrictions to the fundamental freedoms, in need of justification. According to Davies, this approach risks leaving the host state workforces quite exposed (Davies 2008: 295).

However, with respect to the attempts at EU level to promote a social agenda through, *inter alia*, Article 3(3) TEU, the reinforcement of fundamental rights and the increased emphasis on the notion of subsidiarity (Article 4(2) TEU), the *Rüffert* outcome confirms the pre-existing social deficit of the EU. Nevertheless, the EU institutions now enjoy the legal means to realize social objectives. The integration of mandatory requirements related to EU social policy objectives in public procurement constitute important tools to achieve a 'social market economy'.

The dispute in *Commission v Germany*, concerned the running of occupational pension schemes and whether such schemes were covered by public procurement law. Interestingly, the Court used the term 'reconciliation' between the objectives of the Directives and those pursued by the social partners, possibly suggesting an advancement with regards to balancing the competing interests. According to Syrpis, the ruling essentially suggests that the public procurement Directives apply as a result of the fact that it is possible to accommodate the social objectives proposed with the Directives. In the interest of fair balancing, the reconciliation of economic freedoms and social rights should have focused not only on whether the objectives of the national schemes could be accommodated with the Directives, but also on whether the objectives of the Directives may be

---

30   See Davies and Kilpatrick on the constraints imposed on host Member States (Davies 2008: 295; Kilpatrick 2011: 15).

'accommodated in a way which more fully respects fundamental rights' (Syrpis 2011: 224).

Ultimately, the Lisbon Treaty reflects the urge of the Member States to protect and advance the fundamental social rights. Therefore, a clear shift of orientation from the market-oriented approach as demonstrated in *Rüffert* and *Commission v Germany* to a reconciliation of these seemingly conflicting interests is needed in order to strengthen confidence in the EU as a protector and advocator of fundamental social rights.

The Swedish Level

Swedish Public Procurement Law

Chapter 1 section 9 of the Swedish Public Procurement Act (lag 2007: 1091 om offentlig upphandling (LOU)) lays down the principles governing public procurement procedures. The awarding authorities shall treat all tenderers in an equal and non-discriminatory manner. They are further required to carry out the procurements openly and to respect the principles of mutual recognition and proportionality. In 2010, a provision was implemented stipulating that an awarding authority should consider environmental and social considerations during a public procurement procedure, provided that the nature of the procurement implies such incentives. Due to the increased emphasis on environmental and social considerations within the Union and Sweden's advanced approach on such issues, the Swedish government held the position that there were strong motives for encouraging awarding authorities to use the possibility to integrate such aspects in their contracts.[31]

Following the adoption of Directives 2004/17 and 2004/18, a Public Procurement Committee was established to give suggestions on the implementation. The Committee presented its findings in the Governmental Inquiry Report,[32] stipulating that the downside of a non-mandatory rule is that it cannot be relied upon either by the awarding authorities or by the tenderers. Also, the Committee questioned whether public procurement legislation should be used as an instrument to integrate political ambitions.[33] Although some consultative bodies supported the implementation of a provision making incorporation of environmental and social considerations mandatory, the Swedish government insisted on keeping it facultative. On this note, the Swedish government referred

---

31   Prop. 2009/10: 180 [Governmental Bill], p. 271 *et seq.*

32   Statens Offentliga Utredningar (SOU) [Governmental Inquiry Report] 2006: 28, p. 23 *et seq.*

33   See for further elaboration on this in SOU 2006: 28, as first referenced in preceding footnote, p. 23 *et seq.* and p. 230.

to the case law of the Court of Justice,[34] stressing that only verifiable award criteria are considered in compliance with the principle of equal treatment and that any requirements imposed shall be controlled. The government concluded that it is for the awarding authority to ascertain that any environmental or social requirements imposed are in compliance with general principles of public procurement and relevant for the procurement at issue.[35]

In essence, the Swedish implementation is characterized by a strict and noteworthy literal interpretation of the Public Procurement Directives (Bruun and Ahlberg 2010: 49). In principle, the scope of labour law requirements at the Swedish level could be regarded as more narrowly construed than the scope allowed for at the EU level, as the Union legislator leaves room for the Member States to impose social requirements of a mandatory nature.[36] Bruun and Ahlberg argue that the Swedish implementation was governed by a precautionary principle combined with the absence of political motivation to enforce social considerations in public procurement. Where EU law allows for possibilities to implement mandatory rules as regards the integration of social considerations, the Swedish legislator has kept a consistent cautious profile by using the non-binding alternative (Bruun and Ahlberg 2010: 12 and 46 *et seq.*).

Accession to the ILO Convention No. 94

The Public Procurement Committee also addressed the possible accession of Sweden to Convention No. 94, scrutinizing the potential legal impediments for a ratification and application of the Convention. The Committee noted that the aim of the Convention is to protect the workers, which has been recognized as a legitimate public interest by the Court of Justice. However, this does not imply that such an objective automatically justifies restrictions to the fundamental freedoms. The principle of mutual recognition can lead to the conclusion that the public interest has already been satisfied through the legislation of the state of establishment in a situation containing cross-border elements. The Committee observed that in a situation of shared competence, the Member States are obliged to collaborate under the principle of loyal cooperation that and Sweden did not enjoy exclusive competence in the material area covered by the Convention.[37]

---

34   See for further elaboration, *EVN Wienstrom*, cited above, paras 51–2.

35   Prop. 2009/10:180, as first referenced in footnote 33, p. 272 *et seq.*

36   See for further elaboration on this Bruun and Ahlberg, 2010.

37   See further SOU 2006:28, as first referenced in footnote 34, p. 230 and p. 340 *et seq.*

Contrasting the Legal Frameworks – Parallel Application or Collision?

The Dynamics of the ILO and the EU

The ILO has profoundly influenced international labour law. This has been recognized by the EU legislator, exemplified by recital 33 of Directive 2004/18, where the respect of the core ILO Conventions is promoted, albeit not made mandatory. The importance of a strong incorporation of a social dimension to balance the internal market has become more and more of an issue (Ahlberg and Bruun 2011: 89). The placement of the provision regulating the observance of the core ILO Conventions in the preamble and not in the main body of the Directive indicates that the multi-level dialogue between the ILO and the EU still needs to be enforced in practice.[38]

The *Levy* case[39] has been considered to confirm the mandatory nature of the ILO Conventions (Bercusson 2009: 448). However, should a ratified Convention be found not compatible with the Treaties, the Member State in question is obliged to take appropriate steps to eliminate such incompatibilities (Article 351 TFEU). Article 351 TFEU is liable to result in a division between those EU Member States who have ratified Convention No. 94 and those who have not, where the former are under the obligation to impose clauses in public contracts ensuring the observance of collective agreements in force. This could create impediments to the internal market, as access to the market of ratifying states may be rendered less attractive. In its attempt to solve the normative conflicts between different multi-level legal orders, Article 351 TFEU confirms the principle of supremacy and loyal cooperation set out in Article 4(3) TEU, as it requires Member States to set aside any national legislation contrary to Union law, where an incompatibility is established. As Article 351(1) TFEU constitutes an exception and even an encroachment as regards the integrity of the EU legal order, it has been interpreted restrictively (Schütze 2012: 353).[40]

Formally, as there is no apparent conflict between Convention No. 94 and the EU Public Procurement Directives, a Swedish ratification may be achievable and should perhaps rather be considered a political question than a legal one. Nevertheless, the ruling in *Rüffert* (para 43) suggests the contrary:

> Directive 96/71, interpreted in the light of Article 49 EC, precludes an authority of a Member State [...] from adopting a measure of a legislative nature requiring the contracting authority to designate as contractors for public works contracts only those undertakings which, when submitting their tenders, agree in writing

---

38   See for further elaboration on the relationship between the ILO and the EU, Novitz 2005.

39   See above footnote 11.

40   See also Case C-324/93 *The Queen v Secretary of State for Home Department, ex parte Evans Medical Ltd and Macfarlan Smith Ltd* [1995] ECR I-563, para 32.

to pay their employees [...] at least the remuneration prescribed by the collective agreement in force at the place where those services are performed.

The list of award criteria in the EU Public Procurement Directives is not exhaustive, although limitations on what criteria are legitimate have been developed through the case law of the Court, e.g. the requirement of objective and quantifiable criteria, the curb of discretion left to the public authority and the verifiable application of such criteria. These requirements are liable to restrict the scope for social considerations in public procurement (Arrowsmith 2009: 242). The impact of the social framework of the Directives is yet to be determined, partly due to its subordinated position *vis-à-vis* the integration of the internal market. In comparison, Convention No. 94 clearly reflects a social objective. The Convention supports the integration of labour law requirements in public procurement contracts, including those stemming from collective agreements, in order to ensure the objective of the Convention; i.e. the observance of local and regional working conditions and the prevention of using low labour standards as competitive advantages. The Convention thus also serves to protect the preservation of national labour law standards, in line with the principle of subsidiarity.

In conclusion, the absence of an apparent conflict between the Convention and the Public Procurement Directives implies the existence of a scope for Member States to ratify Convention No. 94. However, labour law requirements are viewed as potential restrictions to the economic rather than complementing them, the scope for an effective ratification of Convention No. 94 appears unattainable. The interaction between these two levels of governance with two distinct objectives demonstrates the need of reconciliation rather than the adoption of a supremacy approach (Everson and Joerges 2012: 655). Thus, the Court's jurisprudence is liable to curb national labour law systems and reflects an optimistic belief in the market and its capacity to create social cohesion. However, in the aftermath of the global financial crisis, the need for reconciliation of the economic and the social appears more and more vital.

The EU and Sweden – a Pragmatic and/or Precautious Relationship?

At the EU level, the cross-institutional struggles during the legislative process of adopting the Directives have contributed to an open wording of the scope of labour law requirements in public procurement law (Kilpatrick 2011: 11). Problematically, this vague scope of application of such requirements has effectively been transposed from the supranational level of the EU to the Swedish level through the Swedish implementation. What appears clear is that there is scope at the Swedish level, albeit subject to the obligation to observe the general public procurement principles. The uncertain legal position of integrating labour law requirements in public contracts is thus not solved by the Swedish implementation, but merely conveyed to the awarding authorities and ultimately the courts. This could result in bold moves on behalf of awarding authorities using labour law requirements in their contracts, exposing themselves to the risk of paying considerable compensation costs should the requirements be found to infringe Union law. Alternatively, the vagueness may result in awarding authorities, refraining from using the scope of labour law requirements in their contracts.

The open structure of the wording of the legislation, both at the EU and Swedish level, undermines a consistent interpretation and allows for the imposition of other implications than those originally intended. Thus, the absence of clarity necessitates court action to assess the proportionality of the measures at issue. Indeed, in order to ensure legal certainty, the legislation itself should be governed by a balance of interests rather than simply leaving this to the discretion of the courts. Certainly, the proportionality assessment of an individual case cannot and should not be avoided, as this may be essential for achieving an adequate solution. However, the balancing of competing interests should primarily be incumbent on the legislature. Thus, a more proactive approach on behalf of the national legislature is much sought after, as national law should be founded on a proportional balance of interests in order to avoid sporadic court assessments unsuitable for providing predictability and clarity.

Concluding Remarks

Public procurement is of significant importance for both economic and social reasons due to its financial impact. Therefore, the question of whether public procurement law should be regulated as a purely procedural legislation, leaving political ambitions aside or whether it should be used as a tool to satisfy societal endeavours, is a contested point. The social frameworks of the Directives and of the Treaty expose a strong motivation on behalf of the Union legislature to integrate labour law requirements into public procurement contracts. Labour law requirements may be considered during all phases of the procurement procedure. Nevertheless, as the principal objective of the coordination of public procurement at the EU level is to advance market integration, the scope of such requirements is in substance limited. Even though the Swedish target provision confirms the strive for imposition of politcally motivated social ambitions, as public authorities should integrate social considerations into their public contracts, it also mirrors the view of internal market integration as an assurance for progress, since the provision lacks any legal sanctions to properly realize the integration of social considerations.

The integration of labour law requirements in public contracts may have an adverse effect on the internal market, possibly leading to the exclusion of some competitors. However, not allowing for requirements relating to e.g. employment conditions, which necessitates the observance of national collective agreements or the equivalent of such conditions in public contracts or making such conditions subject to strict scrutiny, could undermine the overall function of collective agreements by atomizing and subverting the fundamental right to collective bargaining. In *Commission v Germany*, the Court stated that the designation of bodies and undertakings by the local authorities did not affect the essence of the right to collective bargaining. Furthermore, in *Rüffert* the use of collective agreements was limited by the stipulation that national authorities cannot require foreign service providers to comply with national collective agreements falling outside the scope of Article 3(1) of Directive 96/71. What are the practical implications of such a position? Noting that the right of collective bargaining is not absolute, one must question the effective protection of a right, which is observed insofar as it does not entail potential or actual restrictions on the internal market or, in case such a restriction is established, the purpose of the measure is justified and does not have a disproportionate impact on the free movement. *Rüffert* risks consolidating an unfavourable position of work from low-wage Member States, as these workers are allowed to be paid less than their host state equivalents. This opens up for competition based on low labour costs which is in full contrast to the objective of the ILO Convention No. 94.

As the introductory part of this chapter suggests, the Lisbon Treaty marked a milestone in the history of the EU integration process, promoting a dialogue between the Union and its Member States characterized by pluralism rather than monism and by interaction rather than hierarchy.[41] The Treaty references, to national identity reflect the acknowledgement of the complications inherent in the creation of a uniform social model within the EU28. By the same token, the limited competence of the Union legislature in the area of social policy, the existing asymmetries between economic and social policies as well as the respect for constitutional pluralism and integrity imply the exercise of judicial deference.[42] In optimistic terms, the new legal order could serve as the beginning of substantive recognition of both international and national labour law standards, as it puts emphasis on the coordination of economic and social objectives, rather than advocating the supremacy of the former. This would allow for a potent dialogue between the ILO and the EU, facilitating an exchange between the international and supranational level. Also, it would serve national welfare ambitions to use public funds aimed at promoting social cohesion.

At the time of the disputes of both *Rüffert* and *Commission v Germany*, the Lisbon Treaty had not entered into force, possibly explaining the Court's approach as regards the balance of economic freedoms on the one hand and fundamental social rights on the other. In these rulings, the historically established hierarchy between the economic and the social has given rise to clashes between the promotion of the internal market and the further development of a social Europe. Such clashes cannot be overcome simply by reducing the scope of labour law requirements in public procurement and, to that extent, allowing for lower labour costs being used as competitive advantages.

---

41   This line of thinking was inspired by MacCormick 1995.

42   This line of thinking was additionally inspired by Lenaerts and Guiéterrez-Fons 2010: 1663.

In conclusion, the new legal order established by the Treaty of Lisbon provides the EU institutions with the legal means of advancing 'social Europe', whilst accepting the significantly diversified socio-economic structures of the Member States. Considering this, the Court's market-oriented jurisprudence clashes with the endeavours expressed in the social frameworks of the Procurement Directives and of the Treaty, as an actual balance between economic efficiency and protection of labour law requirements is not attained by subordinating the latter in favour of the former. Rather, the realization of a 'social market economy' calls for equal observance and coordination of both economic and social interests. Hence, the Lisbon Treaty formally implies the termination of this historic asymmetry, putting an end to the 'decoupling' of the (national) social sphere and EU economic integration. How this can be achieved substantively remains to be determined.

Bibliography

Ahlberg, K. and Bruun, N. 2011. Public Procurement and Labour Law – Friends or Foes?, in *Labour Law, Fundamental Rights and Social Europe*, edited by M. Rönnmar. Oxford: Hart Publishing, 89–112.

Arrowsmith, S. 2009. Application of the EC Treaty and directives to horizontal policies: a critical review, in: *Social and Environmental Policies in EC Procurement Law*, edited by S. Arrowsmith and P. Kunzlik, Cambridge: Cambridge University Press, 147–248.

Bercusson, B. 2009. *European Labour Law*, 2nd edition, New York: Cambridge University Press.

Bercusson, B. and Bruun, N. 2005. Labour Law Aspects of Public Procurement in the EU, in: *The New Public Procurement Directives*, edited by R. Nielsen and S. Treumer. Copenhagen: DJØF Publishing, 97–116.

Bruun, N. and Ahlberg, K. 2010. Upphandling och Arbete i EU, *SIEPS* 3. Available at: http://www.sieps.se/sv/publikationer/upphandling-och-arbete-i-eu-20103 [accessed: 22 August 2012].

Davies, P. 2008. Case C-346/06, *Rüffert v Land Niedersachsen* [2008] IRLR 467 (ECJ), *Industrial Law Journal,* 37(3), 293–5.

European Commission. 2001. Communication from the Commission to the Council, the European Parliament and the Economic and Social Committee, *Promoting Core Labour Standards and Improving Social Governance in the Context of Globalisation*, 18 July 2001 (COM(2001) 416 final).

Everson, M. and Joerges, C. 2012. Reconfiguring the Politics-Law Relationship in the Integration Project through Conflicts-Law Constitutionalism. *European Law Journal*, 18(5), 644–66.

ILO. *Labour Clauses in public contracts*. 2008. International Labour Conference 97th Session, Report III (Part 1B), Geneva.

International Labour Organisation (ILO). 2009. *Rules of the Game: A Brief Introduction International Labour Standards*, Revised Edition, Geneva.

Joerges, C. 2004. What is left of the European Economic Constitution?, *EUI Working Paper LAW* 13. Available at: http://ssrn.com/abstract=635402 [accessed: 22 August 2012].

Joerges, C. and Rödl, F. 2009. Informal Politics, Formalised Law and the Social 'Social Deficit' of European Integration: Reflections after the Judgements in Viking and Laval. *European Law Journal*, 15(1), 1–19.

Kilpatrick, C. 2011. Internal Market Architecture and the Accommodation of Labour Rights: As Good as it Gets? *EUI Working Papers LAW* 4. Available at: http://ssrn.com/abstract=1824234 [accessed: 22 August 2012].

Lenaerts, K. and Guiéterrez-Fons, J.A. 2010. The Constitutional Allocation of Powers and General Principles, *Common Market Law Review*, 47(6), 1629–69.

MacCormick, N. 1995. The Maastricht Urteil: Sovereignty Now, *European Law Journal*, 1(3), 259–66.

Macklem, P. 2005. The Right to Bargain Collectively, in: *Labour Rights as Human Rights*, edited by P. Alston, New York: Oxford University Press, 61–84.

Marginson, P. and Keune, M. 2012. European Social Dialogue as Multi-Level Governance: Towards More Autonomy and New Dependencies. *European Integration Online Papers*, 16(1), Article 4. Available at: http://ssrn.com/abstract=2006420 [accessed: 22 August 2012].

McCrudden, C. 2007. *Buying Social Justice: Equality, Government Procurement, and Legal Change*, Oxford: Oxford University Press.

Monti, M. 2010. *A New Strategy for the Single Market*, Report to the President of the European Commission José Manuel Barroso. Available at: http://ec.europa.eu/internal_market/strategy/docs/monti_report_final_10_05_2010_en.pdf [accessed 22 August 2012].

Novitz, T. 2005. The European Union and International Labour Standards: The Dynamics of the Dialogue between the EU and the ILO, in *Labour Rights as Human Rights*, edited by P. Alston. Oxford: Oxford University Press, Volume XIV/1, 214–41.

Scharpf, F.W. 2002. The European Social model: Coping with the Challenges of Diversity, *Journal of Common Market Studies*, 40(4), 645–70.

Schütze, R. 2012. *European Constitutional Law*, 1st Edition, New York: Cambridge University Press.

Syrpis, P. 2011. Reconciling Economic Freedoms and Social Rights – The Potential of Commission v Germany (Case C-271/08), Judgment of 15 July 2010, *Industrial Law Journal*, 40(2), 222–9.

Zappalà, S. 2001. Report (A5-0378/2001), on behalf of the Committee on Legal Affairs and the Internal Market, on the proposal for a directive of the European Parliament and of the Council on the coordination of procedures for the award of public supply contracts, public service contracts and public works contracts (COM(2000) 275 – C5-0367/2000 – 2000/0115(COD)).

Chapter 5

From Safety Nets and Carrots to Trampolines and Sticks: National Use of the EU as both Menace and Model to Help Neoliberalize Welfare Policy

Charlotte O'Brien*

Introduction

The EU plays two simultaneous, apparently paradoxical, roles in the development of national welfare policy. It is held up – and promotes itself – as an exemplar of (neoliberal) principles for national welfare regimes, while also being brandished as a threat to limited national welfare resources. But both roles have been harnessed to the same end – retrenching and minimizing access to the national welfare state, repurposing it not as offering a counter balance to but as a limb of the logic of the market.

To examine this dynamic, this chapter focuses on the UK as a case study, as it provides a particularly strong contrast between ostensible hostility to the 'interference' of the EU with the national welfare state, and eager receptiveness to neoliberalizing principles. It is therefore an ideal site for exploring the reconciliation of these roles.[1] Hard law rules coordinating welfare policy and softer measures comprising the European employment strategy together create principles that are transposed from the EU to UK welfare reform. But it is

* With thanks to Helen Stalford and Michael Dougan, Liverpool Law School for their ever insightful feedback, and to Kathryn Wright, York Law School for her generous and constructive suggestions. Special thanks are owed to Dagmar Schiek for her thorough, careful, and analytical input at each drafting stage. Of course, the usual disclaimer applies.

1   The UK is in the minority in the Union as regards traditional welfare state typologies, since it embodies a 'liberal' welfare system (e.g. Esping Anderson 1990, Wood and Gough 2006) – making it an ideal case study of the neoliberalizing phenomenon. The liberal model makes UK authorities wary of narratives of solidarity underpinning a European social model, but amenable to policies promoting conditionality and prioritizing the interests of the economically active over the socially excluded and the vulnerable. Kröger (2009) notes an affiliation between the Union's Open Method of Co-ordination-based policies and neoliberal conceptions of welfare – amounting to an 'encouragement [to other Member States] to "un-learn" the traditional continental welfare model'(5).

inappropriate to elide coordination, the dominant mechanism of EU social law, and *allocation* of social rights. The former is a predominantly economic strategy, a corollary of free movement, the latter a matter of social policy – a distinction theoretically upheld thanks to claims of non-interference in national welfare regimes. Such claims can, however, act as a 'veil for extensive and discretionary intervention' (Fine 2004: 226) or at least mask actual, if unintended, impacts upon national welfare policy.

Tapping into the principles underpinning coordination has helped to fuel a zeitgeisty neoliberalism which reconstructs ideas of citizenship and fairness. The coordination framework does, after all, have a specifically economic orientation (provided for in Directive 2004/38[2] and expressed in Regulation 883/2004)[3] that is arguably well suited to the EU, a transnational internal market with limited claims to transnational social solidarity. But these essentially neoliberal principles have been adopted at a national level to determine fair allocation of benefits. Three principles in particular, analyzed in the first section, are held out as models for principles of welfare allocation, aiding the ideological capture of concepts of citizenship and fairness.

Rather than deal with EU and national measures in separate sections, this chapter reflects a standpoint that the European and the national are indivisible, dealing with each of the principles (of both the 'model' and 'menace' approach) in turn, and exploring the interaction between the European and the national within each. The theoretical perspective adopted treats the European social model as meaningful when made manifest at a domestic level – i.e. a level at which rights become actionable, drawing from Dworkin's interpretative theory (2006) and suggesting that the act of interpretation translates law from the abstract into the real. But it is not the CJEU that guards the core interpretive portal, since it creates legal structures *to be interpreted* by national courts and national authorities. Alter (2009: 39–40) has described the various other steps and actors that precede and succeed CJEU intervention, though most of the national-level interpretation happens without a preliminary reference at all (Komarek 2007). This position on the ontology of European rights treats implementation as something broader than transposition of legislation (drawing upon implementation theory – Sindbjerg Martinsen 2007, Pressman and Wildavsky 1992). In this case, implementation also comprises the domestic realization of European policies and judge-made law. Not only are national courts European ones (Maher 1994); European social law is national law – meaning that it cannot be unitary, and must be disaggregated within states according to different authorities and courts (Mattli and Slaughter 1998).

Three EU principles of coordination have percolated into national laws governing welfare allocation in the UK. The first principle is here termed 'active

---

2   On the right of citizens of the Union and their family members to move and reside freely within the territory OJ L158/77-123.

3   On the coordination of social security systems OJ L166/1-123.

citizenship' – an umbrella term to capture the principle that welfare entitlement should be work-based, that recipients should be 'responsibilized' and the inactive penalized. This leads to the second principle – the shift from discourses of vulnerability and social responsibility to that of 'burdens' and targets. Such burdens, it seems, are to be weighed up according to the third borrowed principle – proportionality. This test, imposed on EU migrants, is used in recent welfare reforms, replacing the test of need, pitting individuals against the 'economic well-being of the country'.

Alongside the 'model' role for the EU is the seemingly disjunctive role of threat. By suggesting that the equal treatment of migrants presents a menace to national welfare systems, the UK government has justified a restrictive approach to the material scope of benefits, imposing higher conditionality, and precluding benefit exportation, examples of which are analyzed in the second section. This is a more complex development than the simple use of an EU scapegoat to make changes – these restrictions reduce migrant access to benefits, making migrants superficially appear to be an even better model for nationals, so the government can point approvingly to low welfare uptake and high work levels, glossing over the exclusion of swathes of EU citizens.

The model/menace messages are thus not as paradoxical as they first seem, as both contribute to the redefinition of the core components of welfare. Activation trends reliant upon benefit conditionality and responsibilization policies are not new to EU Member States, and certainly not to the UK. Rhodes (2000: 26, 39) documents the rather 'lean and mean' nature of the UK post-war welfare state and the 'reverse Robin Hood programme' under Thatcher which used responsibilization tactics to redirect wealth from the poor to the rich. Various commentators have noted the incremental 'creep' of conditionality (Dwyer 2004) and pointed to successive waves of conditionality-based reform (Plant 1991, Fitzpatrick 2005). But EU input has allowed the displacing of the social contract with the (neoliberal) economic one – borrowing from a coordination regime to frame citizenship as a set of conditions and exclusions, and fairness as a question for individualist calculations, an approach here termed 'bootstraps citizenship'. The co-opting of EU market principles has helped to strip away any ambiguity attached to the responsibilization paradigm, which hitherto has usually been trammelled with the trappings of collectivist social policy concerns.

The EU 'Model' for Restrictive National Welfare Principles

While various rhetorical legal forays in different policy areas (e.g. Article 3 TEU)[4] encourage the EU institutions to engage with the language of poverty,

_____

4   (The Union) 'shall combat social exclusion and discrimination, and shall promote social justice and protection, equality between women and men, solidarity between generations and protection of the rights of the child'.

social inclusion,[5] and other laudable social objectives, welfare coordination and employment policies have grown around an irreducible core of internal market objectives – primarily promoting economic mobility. That the EU makes no claim to institute poverty-reducing measures is emphasized in the well-worn legislative phrase, that its supporting and complementing competence in the field of social security 'shall not affect the right of Member States to define the fundamental principles of their social security systems and must not significantly affect the financial equilibrium thereof' (Article 153 (4) TFEU).

This non-interference line suggests that the main concerns the EU has with welfare are procedural rather than substantive. Hence coordination is aimed at avoiding excessive detriment to (primarily economically active) persons who move between Member States, rather than imposing harmonized measures.[6] However, procedure cannot help but affect substance, especially when social security coordination rules are combined with employment policy steers as to the very purpose of and the conditions for accessing welfare; a combination that gives rise to three principles of European social law coordination which have been imported into national welfare allocation in Britain.

Model Principle 1: Activation and Active Citizenship

EU citizenship rights remain vested in economic activity, a premise that I have argued in more detail elsewhere (e.g. O'Brien 2008 and 2011a). In spite of the 'fundamental status' promised by EU citizenship,[7] it is still gradated and exclusionary, with attendant rights being heavily qualified and only triggered in certain circumstances. In particular, the right to equal treatment on the grounds of nationality is theoretically available to all EU citizens. However, the conditions and limitations attached to it serve to reward in greater degree those with the closer connection to the labour market, so that equal treatment and free movement become principles essentially invoked to protect traditionally defined economic movement, with little space to consider non-traditional activities of economic and social worth, such as caring and volunteering (O'Brien 2011a). At first blush, allowing the sifting of EU migrants for degrees of economic activity seems like ex ante discrimination on the grounds of nationality. But the CJEU has created something of a 'work around' that allows Member States to continue to apply

---

5   This chapter focuses on the welfare benefit component of the welfare state, since this is the area in which the vulnerable are most explicitly and directly targeted in neoliberal rhetoric, though welfare rights can comprise other non-monetary rights, e.g. associated with health and education in which the effects of neoliberal policy may be more indirect or masked (Flear 2009).

6   Joined cases C-393/99 and C-394/99 *Hervein II* [2002] ECR I-02829 51.

7   Case C-184/99 *Grzelczyk* [2001] ECR I-6193, 31; Case C-135/08 *Rottman* [2010] ECR I-01449, 43; Case C-34/09 *Ruiz Zambrano* [2011] ECR I-01177, 41; see e.g. Dougan 2011, Kochenov 2011, Van Den Brink 2012.

economic criteria to non-nationals – the requirement of a 'real link' with the host society (O'Brien 2008) – typically expressed as a link with the labour market and/ or economy – and more or less automatically fulfilled by nationals.[8]

The alignment of real links with economic activity is reflected in the categories of migrant with a residence right and equal treatment entitlement under Directive 2004/38. Those categories have been treated as exhaustive in UK courts; an EU migrant must fit into one of the approved migrant categories listed in Article 7 of Directive 2004/38[9] before any entitlement to certain solidaristic benefits can even be considered.[10] The difference in treatment this creates between home state nationals and other EU nationals has been held to be justified in the UK Supreme Court.[11] Although the European Commission has begun infringement proceedings regarding some aspects of the test (European Commission 2012), it must be borne in mind that the CJEU has, in *Förster*,[12] endorsed a five-year 'benchmark' (the term the Court of Appeal used in *Kaczmarek*)[13] before some benefit entitlements, so it is plausible that much of the right-to-reside test will survive as EU-law compatible.

Union citizenship does add *something* to *some* claims for *some* people, and as such has been characterized as a form of 'market citizenship' (Nic Shuibhne 2010) or a set of rights dependent on active engagement with the market. The *Ibrahim*[14]/ *Teixeira*[15] cases created a subsidiary right of residence for children of former migrant workers, to continue for potentially years after their parent had ceased working, and also for their non-working, possibly non-EU national primary carers. But even these rights are derived from the past labour market activity of the EU national parent (O'Brien 2011b). Soon after those judgements, the UK curbing mechanisms sprang quickly into action. The Department for Work and Pensions issued a circular that implied greater scrutiny of work records and residence breaks in such claims (DWP 2011).

Ruiz Zambrano[16] could be held up as bucking the active citizenship trend, since it recognized a residence right within the EU for a child who was an EU citizen but had never exercised free movement rights, giving rise to a right for the child's third country national parents to not be deported, where that would mean deportation outside of the EU. In dispensing with the need for cross-border activity, the case

---

8   Case C-224/98 *D'Hoop* [2002] ECR I-06191; Case C-287/05 *Hendrix* [2007] ECR I-06909; joined cases C-523/11 and C-585/11 Prinz and Seeberger, 18 July 2013, nyr.

9   Or have permanent residence under Article 16.

10   The Social Security (Persons from Abroad) Amendment Regulations 2006 SI 2006/1026.

11   *Patmalniece v SSWP* [2011] UKSC 11.

12   Case C-158/07 *Förster* [2008] ECR I-08507.

13   *Kaczmarek v Secretary of State for Work and Pensions* [2008] EWCA Civ 1310 [2009] 2 CMLR 85, 23

14   Case C-310/08 *Ibrahim* [2010] ECR I-01065.

15   Case C-480/08 *Teixeira* [2010] ECR I-01107.

16   Case C-34/09 *Ruiz Zambrano* [2011] ECR I-01177.

crossed 'a crucial conceptual threshold' according to Hailbronner and Thym (2011: 1253). But this judgement might not take us far from an economic citizenship – the main right being claimed was leave to remain in order to work, and much was made of the claimant's work and contribution record. The UK Border Agency has described the result as a single, combined 'right to reside and work' (UKBA 2011) – not as separate residence/work rights, suggesting that were a non-working family to ask to reside and claim benefits, the results might be quite different. In subsequent judgements (*McCarthy*[17] and *Dereci*[18]), the CJEU found respectively that spouses could not make the same last resort claims that were open to children, and that Member States were free to set onerous immigration requirements for the family members of their own nationals. *Zambrano* is likely to be interpreted narrowly and cautiously for some time yet (Nic Shuibhne 2012).

Those who fall between the provisions of Article 7 of Directive 2004/38 might argue that those categories are not meant to be exhaustive, and that EU citizenship creates a residual social safety net for those falling between the gaps. But such lacuna claims have failed to gain traction in UK courts. The one case in which it appears to have given rise to a solidarity-based claim involved a worker who had temporarily given up work to care for her terminally ill partner – rather extreme circumstances.[19] People, we are told, are meant to fall through the gaps.[20] Such gaps include temporarily giving up work on grounds related to pregnancy and childcare, raising questions of sex discrimination within the fabric of the Directive. In *Dias*[21] the UK Court of Appeal described the claimant's having temporarily given up work to care for her infant child as 'perfectly understandable socially but which had nothing whatever to do with her occupational activity'. The same court in *St Prix*[22] rather unconvincingly characterized the refusal to treat a pregnancy gap in a work record like an illness gap as discrimination on the grounds of not having a right to reside, not sex.[23]

Free movement, the core citizenship right, is most easily accessed by the economically active, leading commentators to question whether those unable to

17   Case C-434/09 *McCarthy* [2011] ECR I-03375.

18   Case C-256/11 *Dereci* 29/09/2011 OJ C 25, 20.

19   R(IS)4/09, CIS/408/2006 31.10.2007 Commissioner Mark Rowland. Rowland, M. 2007. *R(IS) 4/09*. [Online]. Available at: http://www.dwp.gov.uk/commdecs/09_10/is_409. pdf [accessed 26 April 2013].

20   *Abdirahman v Secretary of State for Work and Pensions* [2007] EWCA Civ 657; *Kaczmarek v Secretary of State for Work and Pensions* [2008] EWCA Civ 1310 [2009] 2 CMLR 3; *Patmalniece v SSWP* [2011] UKSC 11; *St Prix v Secretary of State for Work & Pensions* [2011] EWCA Civ 806.

21   Secretary of State for Work and Pensions v Dias [2009] EWCA Civ 807.

22   *St Prix v Secretary of State for Work & Pensions* [2011] EWCA Civ 806.

23   This case has been appealed to the UK Supreme Court, which has agreed to seek a preliminary reference on whether Art. 7(3) of Directive 2004/38 should be interpreted to include women who temporarily stop work on grounds of pregnancy/maternity. *Jessy Saint Prix v Secretary of State for Work and Pensions* [2012] UKSC 49.

move freely because of ineligibility for social protection in other Member States are considered 'full' EU citizens (Morgan and Stalford 2005, Currie 2009). The economic profile of EU migrants is of those who can move, excluding the 'vast majority' of EU citizens with 'neither the resources nor the opportunity' (Van Eijken and De Vries 2011: 711). It is thus considerably different to that of 'general' Member States nationals. And yet the 'active' EU migrant has become a model held up to nationals in the current wave of British welfare reform.

It is obviously difficult to trace cause and effect where intertwined policy measures echo each other, but it is possible to see the percolation of the economic activity default from EU citizenship into thinking on national welfare reform, where EU migrants are linked to a rather un-empirical nostalgia for the British work ethic. This thinking glosses over the fact that EU migrants and national benefit claimants are not demographically alike because, thanks to the exclusions outlined above, only the economically active are likely to migrate, whereas national claimants will include those whose employment patterns are affected by incapacity, disability and care responsibilities. However, EU migrants performing low-paid and low-status jobs are thought to flag up the 'unwillingness of British citizens to fill the less coveted positions in the labour market' (Larkin 2011: 15), and media commentators note that immigrants 'are prepared to come here and do the jobs' (BBC Radio Four 2011). *The Telegraph* reported that 'Jobless Britons "lack basic skills and work ethic"' (Porter 2011) as David Frost, the Director General of the British Chambers of Commerce, claimed that 'foreign-born workers were often better qualified, equipped and motivated' than British ones, and that he noted in particular 'there's a stream of able East European migrants who are able to fill those jobs ... [and who] are skilled ... have a very strong work ethic, and ... simply get on with the job' (Porter 2011). The high level of migrant work in the UK was used by Iain Duncan Smith as a trigger for welfare reform to move away from safety nets and towards springing people back into job searching.[24]

The UK parliamentary debates on welfare reform have contrasted the hardworking EU migrant with the greedy laziness of the Brit who weighs up benefit claiming options, and who will, if they can, 'exploit a system that provides hand-downs'.[25] One MP criticized the 'entrenched poverty and worklessness throughout Britain' and told a story of an employer with 52 employees, 40 of whom were Eastern European, because, he said, 'our young people lacked a work ethic'.[26] This migration discourse chimes with the neoliberal story of self-betterment and so has come rather counter-intuitively to be used as a model to justify national welfare reform. Lord Feldman noted that his immigrant great-grandparents came to the

---

24   HC Hansard, 2nd reading of the Bill, Wednesday 9 March 2011 column 919.

25   HC Hansard, 2nd reading of the Bill, Wednesday 9 March 2011 column 964 per Chris Skidmore.

26   HC Hansard, 2nd reading of the Bill, Wednesday 9 March 2011 column 974 per Sajid Javid.

UK with little more than 'values', first among which was 'a strong work ethic ... to lift themselves out of poverty'.[27] He also referred to Lady Warsi's parents as 'immigrants who arrived with nothing and built a successful business',[28] extolling values with which Baroness Margravine claimed many immigrants identify.[29] This conscientious migrant bent on self-improvement has been linked specifically to the European migrant, and in the same debate session, Lord Billamoria expressed shock at the 'huge reluctance' of British nationals 'to move in order to get a job, or even travel to a job' in light of the 'millions of European Union workers in this country who have travelled thousands of miles to get a job'.[30]

Hard law social security coordination and free movement measures instigate a high degree of economic selectivity determining who can avail themselves of EU free movement rights – and so of who can truly claim to be an active EU citizen, resulting in welfare rights primarily for those who do not need them, and frequent loss of such rights at the point when they do. Even so, this selective depiction of the EU migrant has fuelled the national activation and responsibilization programme that applies to those who cannot work (and would not consequently ever become an EU migrant). Such people, if subject to the same expectations as applied to EU migrants, must be treated as burdens. EU soft law employment measures promoting 'flexicurity' reinforce the position, which the UK has adopted with alacrity, that this principle be applied to own nationals.

Model Principle 2: Treating the Economically Inactive as Burdens and Targets

An inevitable flip side of activating citizens is the stigmatizing of the 'inactive'. Just as EU migrants are expected to be economically active or be deemed an 'unreasonable burden' (Directive 2004/38, recital 16), should they make a claim upon the host social security system, so non-working nationals are to be viewed as burdensome, passive and irresponsible. But this principle is not only inferred from hard law social security coordination measures as applied to migrants – it has been explicitly promoted by the Union as appropriately applied to *own state nationals*, through the Union's employment policies on flexicurity. So here we have an overt desire on the part of the Union to influence the purpose and content of national welfare law.

Employment services are exhorted by the EU Public Employment Services Network to target 'the inactive ... like disabled, lone mothers, women at home, early retired, or those on sick leave' (PES 2011: 4). This instruction accepts wholesale the highly politically flavoured assumption that those people can and should be in employed work. The neoliberal rationale is paramount – Member States should withdraw benefits in order to decrease 'the burden for the welfare system'. The

---

27 HL Hansard 2nd reading of the Bill, 13 Sep 2011, 670.
28 HL Hansard 2nd reading of the Bill, 13 Sep 2011.
29 HL Hansard 2nd reading of the Bill, 13 Sep 2011 699.
30 HL Hansard 2nd reading of the Bill, 13 Sep 2011 678.

Council of Ministers adjures each Member State to 'develop its own flexicurity arrangements' (2007: 3). In theory, flexicurity adapts welfare systems and training provision to volatile job markets to ensure seamless coverage of persons between jobs, promoting employment security in recognition of dwindling job security. However, in EU policy, flexicurity is less about plugging welfare gaps between jobs and more about promoting cost saving, activation-based principles of welfare allocation (it is more 'flexi' than 'curity'). Sick and disabled persons fall into the Council's category of inactive targets. The personal responsibility of citizens to join the employment market is repeatedly stressed (European Commission 2007a). In the 2007 Communication from the Commission on 'Common Principles of Flexicurity', there were 36 mentions of active labour market policies (European Commission 2007a). In the Annex to the common principles, the Communication stated that an effective flexicurity system requires 'effective monitoring' – rather than support – 'of job search efforts' – underlining the idea of personal claimant responsibility. This theme is compounded in a report for the Commission containing a section entitled 'From employment to 'activation' and self-responsibility' (European Commission 2009: 37), suggesting that measures to reintegrate marginalized groups into the labour market be 'increasingly based on the strong self-activity and self-responsibility of the job-seeker'.

In making targets of the inactive, there is a risk, noted by Sainsbury (2010: 102), that in times of recession activation may amount to 'an attack on the unemployed at a time when they are least able to do anything about it'. But the European Employment Strategy views an 'intensified' activation stick as the only response to a tough economic climate (Council of Ministers 2011a: 2) – a response with significant implications for the rationale of welfare benefits, which 'should be designed to reward return to work for the unemployed', linking job searching 'more closely' to benefits (Council of Ministers 2011a: 23). The Public Employment Services Working Group also suggests that there needs to be a 'shift from passive to active labour market policies and the mutual obligation approach' (PES 2011: 7). The undercurrent of neoliberalism is evident in the linking of flexicurity not with investment in increasing opportunities, but with reduced state costs (Council of Ministers 2011a: 24).

Pushing people off benefits and into the job market is a very different thing to pushing them into an actual job, bearing in mind the questionable receptiveness of the labour market to the sick, elderly, disabled and caring. Boeri (2005: 389) notes that one group of researchers found that the 'help and hassle' policies of activation had no significant effect on the duration of benefit claims in four experiments in the US. Where people re-entered the job market under some form of administrative duress, they entered at a lower earning point than they might with more 'help' than 'hassle' (Boeri: 382). Van Aerschot (2011) suggests activation does not work as '[m]ost recipients with restricted employability will never get employment' (36). In the UK, commentators are reaching similar conclusions; Larkin (2011) has expressed disquiet in the faith placed in cost-saving activation measures to 'absorb' people into the labour market, since such absorption is 'contingent not only upon the relative buoyancy of the market itself' (which is currently pretty un-buoyant), 'but also upon the resources which government is prepared to invest in back-to-work programmes' (Larkin 2011: 407, such resources will typically be limited: Van Aerschot 2011: 407). Dostal (2008) also doubts the 'workfare illusion', suggesting it is a means of political grandstanding, demonizing the poor.

The EU push from help-to-hassle means that lone parents also form an increasingly legitimate target for benefit withdrawal, as made clear in instructions issued to the UK. The UK has already progressively reduced the age of a child below which a single parent may claim income support and not be in employed work – from 16, to 12, to 10, to 7. Although the Commission has recognized that lack of child care creates an impediment to employment (2011b: 14, 16), in its proposal for a council opinion on the convergence programme, it urged the UK to do more to withdraw benefits from lone parents, suggesting that it is problematic ('a significant issue') to absolve single mothers of children up to age seven of the need to seek employment. This is substantial policy-stirring on the part of an EU institution, speaking to a desire if not to harmonize, then to promote neoliberal convergence in this area.[31]

By the time this proposal had passed through the Council, the emphasis on hassle increased. The Commission had suggested that the UK take 'measures to reduce the high proportion of jobless households by increasing the supply of child care provision' (European Commission 2011a: 736). In the Council's final version, this became measures to 'reduce the number of workless households by targeting those who are inactive because of caring responsibilities, including lone parents' (Council of Ministers 2011b: 4). Thus a supporting measure was displaced by an ominous targeting requirement.

EU social policy has thus given the UK its cues to treat benefit claimants as burdens, and the UK authorities have made clear their amenability to the Union message. Benefit claiming was characterized under the previous Labour government as a 'burden' and as 'distortion' of the market (DWP 2009). The Treasury (2011) submitted a convergence report to the Commission in April 2011 which stated that the UK planned reforms that would promote 'personal responsibility' (4.16) and create a 'fair, simple and efficient' benefits system (4.18). Fairness is thus invoked in the context of restrictions, reductions and conditionality.

In the name of fairness, those who have difficulty finding appropriate employment may face penalties for that very difficulty. In altering the descriptors for Employment and Support Allowance, an out-of-work benefit for the sick and disabled (formerly Incapacity Benefit), the UK government has adopted the cosmetic language of the social model of disability in a somewhat accusatory manner, to argue no health problem or disability should 'automatically be

---

31   Similar developments can be seen in other Member States. Knijn *et al.* (2007) describe the Netherlands as having developed 'a "shock and awe" policy towards lone parents as if it wished to forget its traditional image as a "motherhood-protecting" nation overnight' (2007: 650).

regarded as a barrier to work' (DWP 2010: 1.2). To give some concrete examples, the descriptor on limitations of walking has been revised to 'mobilizing' so being in a wheelchair does not attract ESA points, 'to more accurately reflect the functionality of wheelchair users' (2.5) but without reflecting the reality of many ill-adjusted or non-adapted workplaces. Other switches include replacing 'seeing' with 'navigating safely' (2.11) – though not being able to see will amount to a barrier in many workplaces even for those able to 'navigate' – and being able to hear with 'understanding communication', though again there is a disadvantage in not being able to work in poorly adapted workplaces or where signing is not practised. Admittedly, it would be more socially progressive to head off disadvantage through wide-scale 'universal design' (Wendell 1996: 35) and fully flexible working patterns rather than seek a compensation solution in benefits. But the reforms take no account of how well disabling factors have been dismantled. Making claimants responsible for getting themselves into the workplace or imperilling themselves with poverty endorses an 'attitudinal model of disability'.

The shift away from social protection towards individual culpability echoes attempts to ramp up sanctioning for dereliction of duty (DWP 2007, Shelter 2012)[32] and to 'punish the poor', to borrow Wacquant's term (2009), by moving from welfare to workfare. This process been described as a means of 'controlling and subduing culturally and economically marginalized populations' (Hudson 2010: 594), but the UK Secretary for Work and Pensions has protested that welfare reform 'is not about punishing people; it is about establishing a principle that fairness runs through the whole of the benefit system'. Labelling sanctions, cuts and duties as 'fairness' does not reduce the punitive effects of those measures. But such neoliberal linguistic capture does impact upon perceptions of fairness, justice and a desirable society.

Having established that benefit claimants are burdens, the EU also provides the principle by which those claims are to be determined. The reasonableness of the burden is to be weighed not according to need, but to proportionality, the third principle discussed below, as distilled from Directive 2004/38. The increased indifference to need bolsters Sim's claim that neoliberalism in the western world has allowed those in power to 'reproduce a heartless set of social arrangements that appear to have no moral compass or boundaries in terms of the human waste and destruction generated' (2010: 592).

Model Principle 3: Importing the Proportionality principle from Directive 2004/38 into National Welfare Allocation

In measuring the 'degree of financial solidarity' owed to EU migrants, we accept the idea of reasonable versus unreasonable burdens posed by individuals to the host state. These are to be calculated, following Directive 2004/38, according to

---

32   HB sanctions were proposed in a private members bill by Frank Field between 2003–4; pilot sanction programmes were run between 2007–9 but no sanctions were issued.

'whether it is a case of temporary difficulties and ... the duration of residence, the personal circumstances and the amount of aid granted' (Directive 2004/38, Recital 16). In essence this means the quantity claimed and how deserving the claimant is, since the personal circumstances apart from nationality most likely to weigh in a claimant's favour are evidence of past economic activity; indeed, in *Grzelczyk* much was made of the claimant's past work and contributions.[33] (*Current* workers are not capable of being unreasonable burdens).[34] The driving logic is that regardless of any individuals' needs, some burdens are simply, objectively, too much, i.e. *unreasonable* and easily outweighed by the needs of the public purse. Directive 2004/38 has been treated as establishing a sliding 'scale' of proportionality (Golynker 2005: 118) for determining when claims are reasonable and for limiting the benefit eligibility of EU migrants, in the interests of financial equilibrium (as in *Patmalniece*).[35]

The needs-blind reasonableness ceilings to the quantity and the duration of welfare claims have both been imported into UK welfare allocation for own nationals, in respectively the benefit cap and the introduction of time-limiting for benefits for people too sick to work. The government has presented the reforms as creating a *proportional* relationship between benefits and labour market activity;[36] entitlement should be 'based on the degree to which he or she is participating in society',[37] and be subject to a needs-indifferent 'reasonable maximum amount of benefits'.[38] This maximum is not determined according to need, but according to the 'economic well-being of the country' – a term used four times in the explanatory notes that accompanied the Welfare Reform Bill 2011 before its enactment in 2012,[39] and a term redolent of the financial equilibrium argument deployed in the context of EU migrants.

This cap depends on neoliberal ideals of personal culpability – need is less relevant if self-created. It posits 'biographical solutions' (Borghi 2011: 326) to social problems. But biographies can be subject to a little engineering, and Clarke (2008: 203) has pointed out that welfare can be a 'key site for the construction and management of populations'; hence according to Lord Freud, the cap is meant to influence 'responsible life choices', since claimants must 'take responsibility for their decisions in light of what they can afford'.[40] As the benefit cap only affects those living in parts of the country where social housing is more expensive, and

---

33   Case C-184/99 *Grzelczyk* [2001] ECR I-6193 11; AG Opinion 67.

34   Case 542/09 European Commission v Kingdom of the Netherlands judgement 14.06.2012, nyr, para 63.

35   *Patmalniece v SSWP* [2011] UKSC 11.

36   Welfare Reform Bill explanatory notes as brought from the House of Commons on 16th June 2011 [HL Bill 75] 744.

37   Lords Hansard, 15th sitting 21 Nov, Lord Freud Column GC318.

38   Lords Hansard, 15th sitting 21 Nov, Lord Freud Column GC350.

39   Welfare Reform Bill Explanatory Notes, 744, 761, 764, 765.

40   Lords Hansard, 15th sitting 21 Nov, Lord Freud Column GC345, GC350.

people with a certain amount of children, the implied neoliberal, and slightly Malthusian, steer being given is that survival above the poverty line may require people to make 'choices' to move residence and to refrain from procreation.

Another aspect of the Directive's proportionality principle – a temporal ceiling to benefit claims – has been imported into UK welfare, through time-limiting benefits for those who remain not capable of employed work. Currently, before Universal Credit kicks in, sick and disabled claimants not capable of work are divided into those who might with support be integrated into the workplace and so directed at Employment and Support Allowance (ESA) (Work-Related Activity Group – the WRAG), and those who are incapable of participating in work-related activity, directed at Employment and Support Allowance (Support Group). The vast majority of those found eligible for ESA go into the WRAG. If they have been working, they will get it as a contributory benefit. However, contributory ESA will now run out after one year, 'to recognize [according to Iain Duncan Smith] that unemployment, for those who fall unemployed, is probably a temporary condition'.[41] The fact that some people are incapacitated for much longer was reflected in the previous rules, which allowed for eligibility to continue so long as the condition did. Now, at the end of one year, those who are still not capable of work may be eligible for income-related ESA, but this will not be the case for most claimants with working partners. So they will be left without benefit.

This represents a significant departure from the logic for which the descriptors exist – i.e. awarding the benefit on the grounds of sickness/disability. This needs-indifferent maximum duration of sickness/incapacity benefit seems potentially unfair for those who have made contributions for decades and may not live to claim a pension. Such people are, as Baroness Meacher put it in the House of Lords debate on the Bill, 'a terrific bargain to the state'[42] as their benefit yield will likely not repay decades of contributions, potentially infringing rights to property under Article 1 Protocol 1 of the European Convention on Human Rights.[43] The equality impact assessment of the time limit predicted a disproportionate effect upon persons with disabilities and a disproportionate effect on people in the highest age group,[44] persons likely to receive a frosty reception in the labour market. They may be sprung off, or deflected from, benefits and be allowed to fall below the poverty line.

---

41 HC Hansard: 3rd reading of the Bill – 15 Jun 2011 879.

42 HL Hansard: 8 Nov 2011 Column GC18.

43 The UK government justified its policy as compatible with protocol one of the ECHR by arguing that the measures would be 'proportionate' in light of the 'economic well-being of the country'. WRB Explanatory notes 744.

44 'Nearly 49 per cent of contributory only ESA customers in the WRAG are of aged 50 to 64' (DWP 2011b).

Interim conclusion

In Britain, EU migrants have been used as inappropriate models for national benefit claimants, and the principles governing migrant eligibility have been imported into national welfare allocation. In this way, the EU is a mechanism and site of neoliberal convergence. While O'Connell has gathered together evidence from Ireland, Canada, India and South Africa to suggest that there is some degree of global convergence of judicial norms (2011: 534), it is submitted that the momentum for ideological convergence is even stronger in an EU context. Rather than a nebulous, implicit judicial sphere, the EU is a concrete joint economic, political and judicial project. The 'ulterior' motive of harnessing the European project to a national neoliberal programme explains the UK authorities' ease with contradictory constructions of EU migrants as model citizens and as menaces. The rhetoric seamlessly segues from one to the other; the next section will explore 'menacing' constructions of EU migration, and show that in restricting migrant access to benefits they make EU migrants more of a 'model' for a national programme of curbing societal responsibility and reshaping/resizing the welfare state.

The EU 'Menace' Inspiring Restrictive National Welfare Principles

While EU migrants are supposedly models of active citizenship for the purposes of UK welfare reform, EU migration is also framed as a threat in itself. The government has cited key hard law principles of EU social security law – exportation, aggregation and equal treatment – as causes for adopting more restrictive welfare rules. These restrictions mean migrants have reduced access to benefits, and so are even more of a model to be presented to nationals. EU welfare coordination has thus been used as part of the rationale for UK welfare retrenchment. This section will consider three examples illustrating this general trend: the scrapping of the UK ESA in youth benefit (ESAiy); proposed restrictions on equal access of EU migrants to Universal Credit; and exportation restrictions on disability benefits.

The UK government has claimed that the effects of social security coordination have forced the scrapping of a whole benefit, ESAiy (formerly incapacity benefit in youth). The CJEU's *Stewart* ruling[45] confirmed that it should be exportable to other Member States where an 'effective degree of connection' between the claimant and Great Britain was established. The condition of residence in Great Britain for a period of 26 weeks in the 52 weeks immediately preceding the date of the claim was found to be too 'exclusive in nature', as it 'unduly favours an element which is not necessarily representative of the real and effective degree of connection between the claimant' and the state. As a consequence, Chris Grayling has claimed that 'we could end up paying this benefit, on a long term unconditional

---

45   Case C-503/09 *Stewart* 21 July 2011 nyr.

basis, to more people who have never lived in the United Kingdom but who can simply demonstrate a link to it'.[46] However, this claim does not logically follow from the judgement. Under social security coordination rules, the UK would not be the competent state in such cases.[47] The claimant in *Stewart* was a UK national and the dependent daughter of UK pensioners who had worked in the UK and were still insured there, receiving UK state pensions. The UK was already the acknowledged competent state, crediting her with national insurance contributions and allowing her claim for Disability Living Allowance (DLA).

Moreover, the CJEU has made clear that Member States are entitled to test for links with their social security systems, and in *Stewart* suggested that a requirement of actual prior residence of a reasonable period would be acceptable. Thus those 'who have never lived in the UK' could be excluded. Any other link test would be expected to look for genuine and not remote links.[48] Hence the ruling simply confirmed that of *Tas Hagen*[49] by requiring that a real link test should avoid excluding those with strong connections to the competent state. This does not mean totally discretionary case-by-case decisions, but only excludes one-stroke decisions.[50] The facts establishing the strong connections of a non-resident dependent UK national to the UK in *Stewart* are relatively rare (at the time of writing I know of only two other ongoing claims in the UK for exporting ESAiy). Nevertheless, the government has claimed that there is nothing to be done 'short of abolition'[51] to avoid 'opening our doors wide to current and future dangers of this kind of benefit exportability'.[52] The 'menacing' discourse was in full flow in Lord Freud's declaration that his 'blood was chilled' reading *Stewart*.[53]

Territoriality and resistance to exportation requirements have also been at the heart of the back and forth exchanges between the UK and the CJEU with regard to DLA.[54] The UK's rather grudging and minimalist implementation of exportation provisions for DLA betrays a reluctance to pay the benefit across borders, further evident in deliberations over the DLA replacement benefit, Personal Independence Payment (PIP). The Welfare Reform Act 2012 states that a claimant 'is not entitled to Personal Independence Payment unless the person meets prescribed conditions relating to residence and presence in Great Britain'.[55] The DWP originally planned

---

46   HL Hansard 1 Feb 2012 Column 831–2.

47   Reg 883/2004, Art 11(3)(e).

48   Case C-138/02 *Collins* [2004] ECR I-02703.

49   Case C-192/05 *Tas Hagen & Tas* [2006] ECR I-10451.

50   In the *Geven* case, the Member State in question had discharged national discretion by only allowing two routes to eligibility (Case C-213/05 [2007] ECR I-06347).

51   HL Hansard 14 Feb 2012 Column 729.

52   HL Hansard 11 Jan 2012 Column 144.

53   HL Hansard 14 Feb 2012 Column 733.

54   Case C-299/05 *Commission v Parliament (action for* annulment*)* [2007] ECR-I 08695; Case C-537/09 *Bartlett* [2011] ECR I-03417.

55   s77(3).

for the PIP to only be 'available to people who are resident in Great Britain' (DWP, 2011a). The actual PIP regulations[56] partly allow exportation of the daily living component, but not of the mobility component, thus treating mobility, but not care as an issue with national financial borders.[57] Such a territorial approach is congruent with a neoliberal preference for restricting claims and granting benefits containing a social assistance element only if the costs of refusal would redound upon Britain because the claimant lives there.

Future welfare reform plans also invoke the menace of EU migrant claims, in attempts to restrict equal access of EU work seekers to Universal Credit. The draft regulations provide that EU work seekers will be subject to a different conditionality regime as compared to UK nationals, even work seekers who should be treated as workers – migrant workers who become unemployed and register as work seekers, so retain worker status through Article 7 (3)(b–c) of Directive 2004/38.[58] This work seeker exception effectively removes Art 7(3) (b–c) from the retention of worker status category. Former EU-worker work seekers will not be entitled to fall within sections 19, 20 or 21 of the Welfare Reform Act. This means that they cannot be deemed, on the grounds of disability or caring responsibilities, to be subject to 'no work-related requirements', 'work-focussed interview requirements only' or 'work preparation requirements'. Instead, they must, regardless of disability and caring responsibilities, be subject to all work-related requirements, so that EU migrants are subject to an activation-plus regime. Not only do the measures discriminate on the grounds of nationality, they have a disproportionate impact upon migrants with disabilities, migrants associated with disabled persons, and migrants taking on responsibility for care of children, who will be predominantly women.

Subjecting such persons to all the work search requirements will inevitably create insuperable hurdles. For example, one condition requires claimants to be willing to work in any location up to one and a half hours away from home.[59] For a lone parent EU migrant who has been working and become unemployed, this could necessitate an extra three unpaid hours during which child care must be paid for, and place the migrant at an uncomfortable distance from the child. This draft regulation does make an exception where 'a claimant has a physical or mental impairment that has a substantial adverse effect on the claimant's ability to carry out work of a particular nature, or in particular locations'. But this does not help the lone parent as it relates only to impairment, not caring responsibilities, nor impairment of the child. Nor is it clear that it would help a disabled migrant who has problems with the distance or with the transport options, as opposed

---

56   The Social Security (Personal Independence Payment) Regulations 2013 SI No. 337: Reg. 23.

57   The Court of Justice has accepted this in case C-537/09 Bartlett [2011] ECR I-3417.

58   Draft Regs 83(2).

59   Reg 88(3)(a–b).

to the 'particular nature' or 'particular location' of work. This activationist-plus regime therefore excludes EU migrants from a number of avenues to Universal Credit, and may also serve to exclude them from components of Universal Credit. The DWP is 'currently considering whether EU work seekers ... should also be eligible for all elements, or just the standard allowance' (DWP 2010b: 17).

Extolling the praised migrant worker model while execrating the menace posed by EU migration to the welfare state, the UK authorities seem mired in a contradictory discourse jumble. But somehow, just as Williams noted that the welfare subject can be characterized as both 'knightish and knavish' (1999: 672), there is no tense clash between these positions. The explanation seems to lie in the same policy 'ends' reached by both the model/menace roles. The messages are complementary tools – not oppositional ones – for altering the framework and mechanics of the welfare state. As the next section shows, the more that welfare is tightened by the 'menace' construct, the more that benefit-restricted EU migrants become 'models' of autonomy for UK nationals, feeding a new individualist construct of bootstraps citizenship.

Reconciling the Roles: Life Choices and Bootstraps Citizenship

The welfare reform outcomes from both the model and menace roles of the EU (restrictions of benefits and in an extreme case the scrapping of a benefit) suggest that the EU is both a vehicle and a site for neoliberal convergence, aligning neoliberalism with rationality itself. Conditionality – the approach forcefully pushed by the EU – offers the conceptual justification for restriction. The effect is to displace generalized reciprocity, and the assumption that society has an interest in protecting those in need, with the individual-state balance of interests – represented in an individual-state contract – or the 'mutual obligations' and cost-saving approach required by the Union's flexicurity strategy.

This language has significant consequences for our understanding of the relationship between individual and society at a domestic level. Benefit withdrawal effectively disclaims pre-existing state responsibility. Conditionality, promoted indirectly by comparison of nationals and EU migrants, and directly through EU employment and flexicurity policies, relocates that responsibility upon the claimant and redefines a number of structural or societal problems as life choices – choices to not become employed, to succumb to an attitude of disability, to lose a job, whether to get pregnant, to have a certain number of children, to migrate from the home state (even as a dependent upon your parents), or to migrate to a host state knowing oneself not to be a home national.

Life choices are thought not only to determine the situations claimants find themselves in, but also determine desert, as only 'those who "take charge" of their own lives are deemed to be responsible "active" citizens' (Dwyer 2004b: 138). This 'life choices' approach reflects the individualist, or anti-collectivist, ethos of neoliberalism, which Somek suggests shifts the burden of proof onto benefit claimants to show why their disadvantage merits state intervention – proof now required in the form of individual benefit contracts. Such onus-shifting alters our conceptions of social rights, suggesting an institutional indifference to disadvantage or poverty. Such indifference must be rationalized, and Somek points to Weber's prediction that 'responsibility'[60] would come to do just that since it 'serves consistently the interest of those who are too avaricious to give' (2011: 87).

EU migrants can present an epitome of autonomy – exerting life choices to migrate and to find work – so prove useful models for personal responsibility, in spite of their non-comparability to non-working nationals. The exclusionary principles underpinning coordination are premised on autonomy – no guarantees are to be given to migrants because migrating, and falling out of economic activity, are life choices. Those principles – of active citizenship, of weighing burdens, and of discounting need in favour of proportionality tests against the 'economic well-being of the country' – therefore chime with a domestic responsibilization programme. The 'menace' messages fortify this approach – in scrapping benefits, introducing greater conditions for migrants, and restricting exportability, they reduce the protections offered to EU migrants, who can then be pointed to as even greater exercisers of autonomy. The more the 'menace' approach reduces support for EU migrants, the more those migrants become 'models' for national welfare allocation along more responsibilized lines.

Turning to our case study, this individual, rather than social, contract is strengthened by the menace-model cycle and has crystallized rather literally in UK law. Duncan Smith has declared that UK welfare reforms represent 'a whole new concept: a contract with people who are in need of support'.[61] The individual contract idea permeates the Welfare Reform Act, with claimant 'commitments' peppered throughout.[62] Active citizenship turns the social upside-down, as Borghi claims of 'European welfare capitalism' (2011: 334). The life choices rationale gives rise to an intriguing, oxymoronic incarnation of citizenship, expressed not in terms of society, community, belonging, or the 'values of care' that Williams claims must inform citizenship ('civic virtues of responsibility, tolerance and an awareness of "otherness", of diversity and competing claims' 1999: 678), but in atomistic, individual terms, and in one's capacity to rely upon one's own solitary resources – 'bootstraps citizenship'.

Conclusion

The treatment within the EU of welfare policy as a subset of economic policy forms a significant backdrop to UK national welfare reform. The exclusions created by the gaps in the coordination framework and the activationist steers given by softer

---

60   There are 21 mentions in the WRB explanatory notes of claimant responsibilities with regard to benefits (and controlling for other types of responsibility).

61   HC Hansard 3rd reading of the Bill, Iain Duncan Smith column 920.

62   Welfare Reform Act 2012, s. 14, 44, 54, 59.

law measures have been used to help alter the character, and fundamental principles of, welfare allocation. The global phenomenon of neoliberal convergence as documented by O'Connell (2011) is more explicit in the context of EU Member State relations – thanks to hard law commitments and judicial obligations that go beyond anything shared between the states in O'Connell's study, and also thanks to the effects of the softer adoption of shared economic and political norms.

Neoliberalism is famously self-perpetuating, described by Read (2009: 32) as 'a restoration of capitalism as synonymous with rationality'. In assuming its rationalizer role, it has come to redefine citizenship and fairness as non-collectivist, highly individualist ideals; as expressions and fatalistic consequences of life choices. While Somek (2011: 85) argues that neoliberalism causes market-based reasons to be 'counted as motivationally *stronger* than reasons of morality', it may be possible to go further, and suggest that within neoliberalism, market reasons become the only moral ones.

The coordination of social law within the EU – through hard law coordination of social security and softer policy convergence on employment and flexicurity – has given rise to three influential, neoliberal principles: the promotion, through conditionality, of 'active' citizenship as a prerequisite for socio-economic inclusion; the treatment of the inactive as burdens; and the proportionality-based measurement of eligibility to social support that disregards need.

The parallel role has at the same time reactively strengthened principles of territoriality and indirect nationality discrimination, to scale down or withhold rights from free movers. EU migrants then become more of a model of high conditionality and help exemplify a 'life choices' approach to social problems – even an attitudinal model of disability. Inactivity is redefined as a life choice and activity a precondition for the anti-collectivist bootstraps citizenship, which arguably has very little to do with the *citizenry.*

The UK case study here used shows that the promotion of an anti-collectivist fairness and citizenship means that we may not just be seeing the demise of the socio-economic right (O'Connell 2011), but also of the social contract. Hypothetical generalized reciprocity is replaced with individual contractual agreements imposing commitments upon 'isolated persons who stand as claimants on an administrative or benevolent largesse' (Rawls 1958: 192). The language of responsibility absolves society from duties of protection, or duties of making amends. The sticks of activation are real, but the trampoline into the workplace is deceptive, thanks to the absence of support (and of jobs). It simply deflects claimants – wherever and however they land being their choice and fault.

References

Alter, K. 2009. *The European Court's Political Power.* Oxford: Oxford University Press.

BBC Radio Four: Iain Martin former *Scotsman* editor and current *Telegraph* blogger on *Any Questions?* Friday 19 November 2011.

Boeri, T. 2005. An Activating Social Security System, *De Economist,* 153(4), 375–97.

Borghi, V. 2011. One way Europe? Institutional guidelines, emerging regimes of justification and paradoxical turns in European welfare capitalism, *European Journal of Social Theory,* 14(3), 321–41.

Clarke, J. 2008. Reconstructing nation, state and welfare: the transformation of welfare states in *Welfare state transformations: comparative perspectives,* edited by M. Seeleif Kaiser. Basingstoke: Palgrave Macmillan, 197–209.

Council of Ministers of the European Union. 2007. The Working Party on Social Questions: 'Towards Common Principles of Flexicurity – Draft Council Conclusions' SOC 476 ECOFIN 483, Annex, Common Principles.

Council of Ministers of the European Union (EPSCO). 2011a. Joint Employment Report 7396/11.

Council of Ministers of the European Union. 2011b. Recommendation of 12 July 2011 on the National Reform Programme 2011 of the United Kingdom and delivering a Council opinion on the updated Convergence Programme of the United Kingdom, 2011–14 (2011/C 217/04).

Currie, S. 2009. The transformation of Union citizenship in *50 years of the European Treaties: Looking Back and Thinking Forward* edited by M. Dougan and S. Currie. Oxford: Hart, 365–92.

DWP (Department of Work and Pensions). 2011a. *Personal Independence Payment – Policy Briefing Note* 09.05.2011. [Online]. Available at: http://www.dwp. gov.uk/docs/pip-briefing-introduction.pdf [accessed 2 October 2012].

DWP. 2011b. *Equality Impact Assessment Time limiting contributory Employment and Support Allowance to one year for those in the work-related activity group. October 2011.* [Online]. Available at: http://www.parliament.uk/documents/ impact-assessments/IA11-022AY.pdf [accessed 26 April 2013].

DWP. 2010a. *Housing Benefit and Council Tax Benefit Circular HB/CTB A10/2010.* [Online]. Available at: http://www.dwp.gov.uk/docs/a10-2010.pdf [accessed 2 October 2012].

DWP. 2010b. 'ESA explanatory memorandum to the social security advisory committee' (August 2010).

DWP. 2009. *Summary: Intervention & Options DWP Impact Assessment of Welfare Reform Bill 2009 Primary Legislation Version: 3.* [Online]. Available at: http://www.dwp.gov.uk/docs/welfarereform-bill09-ia-intro.pdf [accessed 2 October 2012].

DWP. 2007. *HB sanction in relation to anti-social behaviour.* [Online]. Available at: http://www.dwp.gov.uk/local-authority-staff/housing-benefit/claims-process ing/claims-guidance/anti-social-behaviour/ [accessed 2 October 2012].

Dostal, M. 2008. The Workfare Illusion: Re-examining the Concept and the British Case, *Social Policy and Administration,* 42(1), 19–42.

Dougan, M. 2011. Some comments on Rottmann and the 'personal circumstances' assessment in the Union citizenship case law in *Has the European Court of Justice challenged Member State sovereignty in nationality law?* edited by J. Shaw. Florence: Robert Schuman Centre for Advanced Studies, 17–18.

Dworkin, R. 2006. *Justice in robes.* Cambridge, MA: Harvard University Press.

Dwyer, P. 2004a. Creeping Conditionality in the UK: From Welfare Rights to Conditional Entitlements? *The Canadian Journal of Sociology: Special Issue on Social Policy: Canadian and International Perspectives,* 29(2), 265–87.

Dwyer, P. 2004b. Agency, dependency and welfare: beyond issues of claim and contribution? In *The ethics of welfare: human rights, dependency and responsibility* edited by H. Dean. Bristol: Policy Press, 135–54.

Esping-Andersen, G. 1990. *The Three Worlds of Welfare Capitalism.* Cambridge: Polity Press.

European Commission. 2007a. Communication from the Commission to the European Parliament, the Council, the European Economic and Social Committee and the Committee of the Regions – *Towards Common Principles of Flexicurity: More and better jobs through flexibility and security* SEC(2007) 861-2 COM/2007/0359 final.

European Commission. 2009. Report for the Commission *The role of the Public Employment Services related to 'Flexicurity' in the European Labour Markets* VC/2007/0927 Final report (March 2009, Policy and Business Analysis).

European Commission. 2011a. *Commission Recommendation for a Council Recommendation on the National Reform Programme 2011 of the United Kingdom and delivering a Council opinion on the updated Convergence Programme of the United Kingdom 2011–2014* SEC(2011) 736.

European Commission. 2011b. *Commission Staff Working Paper* Assessment of the 2011 national reform programme and convergence programme for the United Kingdom, accompanying the document *Recommendation for a Council Recommendation on the National Reform Programme 2011 of the United Kingdom and delivering a Council Opinion on the updated convergence programme of the United Kingdom 2011–2014* SEC(2011) 827 final.

European Commission. 2012. Free movement: Commission asks UK to uphold citizens' rights *European Commission Press Release* IP/12/417 26 April 2012.

Fine, A. 2004. Examining the Ideas of Globalisation and Development Critically: What Role for Political Economy? *New Political Economy,* 9(2), 213–31.

Fitzpatrick, T. 2005. The fourth attempt to construct a politics of welfare obligations, *Policy and Politics,* 33(1), 15–32.

Flear, M. 2009. The Open Method of Coordination on health care after the Lisbon Strategy II: Towards a neoliberal framing? *European Integration Online Papers,* 13(1), Art. 12.

Golynker, O. 2005. Jobseekers' rights in the European Union: challenges of changing the paradigm of social solidarity *European Law Review,* 30(1), 111–22.

Hailbronner, K. and Thym, D. 2011. Case C-34/09 Gerardo Ruiz Zambrano v. Office national de l'emploi, *Common Market Law Review*, 48(4), 1253–70.

HM Treasury. 2011. *Convergence Programme for the United Kingdom April 2011 submitted in line with the Stability and Growth Pact.* [Online]. Available at: http://ec.europa.eu/europe2020/pdf/nrp/cp_uk_en.pdf [accessed 28 April 2013].

Hudson, B. 2010. Review symposium: Punishing the Poor: The Neoliberal Government of Social Insecurity, *British Journal of Criminology*, 50(3), 593–5.

Knijn, T., Martin, C. and Millar, J. 2007. Activation as a Common Framework for Social Policies towards Lone Parents, *Social Policy and Administration*, 41(6), 638–52.

Kochenov, D. 2011. Two Sovereign States vs. a Human Being: CJEU as a Guardian of Arbitrariness in Citizenship Matters in *Has the European Court of Justice challenged Member State sovereignty in nationality law?* Edited by J. Shaw. Florence: Robert Schuman Centre for Advanced Studies, 11–16.

Komarek, J. 2007. In the court(s) we trust? On the need for hierarchy and differentiation in the preliminary ruling procedure, *European Law Review*, 32(4), 467–91.

Kröger, S. 2009. The Open Method of Coordination: Underconceptualisation, overdetermination, de-politicisation and beyond, *European Integration Online Papers*, 13(1), Art. 5.

Larkin, P. 2011. Incapacity, the Labour Market and Social Security: Coercion into Positive Citizenship. *Modern Law Review*. 74(3), 385–409.

Maher, I. 1994. National Courts as European Community Courts, *Legal Studies*, 14(2), 226–43.

Mattli, W. and Slaughter, A. 1998. The Role of national courts in the process of European integration; Accounting for judicial preferences and constraints in *The European Courts and National Courts – Doctrine and Jurisprudence* edited by A. Slaughter, A. Stone Sweet and J.H.H. Weiler. Oxford: Hart, 253–76.

Morgan, H. and Stalford, H. (2005) Disabled people and the European Union: equal citizens? in *The Social Model of Disability: Europe and the Majority World* edited by C. Barnes and G. Mercer. Leeds: The Disability Press, 98–114.

Nic Shuibhne, N. 2010. The Resilience of EU market citizenship, *Common Market Law Review*, 47(6), 1597–28.

Nic Shuibhne, N. 2012. (Some of) the kids are alright: Comment on McCarthy and Derici, *Common Market Law Review*, 49(1), 349–79.

O'Brien, C. 2008. Real links, abstract rights and false alarms: The relationship between the ECJ's 'real link' case law and national solidarity, *European Law Review*, 33(5), 643–65.

O'Brien, C. 2011a. Drudges, dupes and do-gooders? Competing notions of 'value' in the Union's approach to volunteers, *European Journal of Social Law*, 1(1), 49–75.

O'Brien, C. 2011b. Case note: Case C-310/08 Ibrahim, Case C-480/08 Teixiera, *Common Market Law Review*, 48(1), 203–25.

O'Connell, P. 2011. The Death of socio-economic rights, *Modern Law Review*, 74(4), 532–54.

PES (Public Employment Services 2020 Working Group). 2011. *PES and EU 2020: making the employment guidelines work* Adopted by Heads of PES in Budapest, Hungary on 23–24 June 2011.

Plant, R. 1991. Social Rights and the Reconstruction of Welfare in *Citizenship* edited by G. Andrews. London: Lawrence and Wishart, 50–64.

Porter, A. 2 July 2011. *Jobless Britons lack basic skills and work ethic. The Telegraph*. [Online]. Available at: http://www.telegraph.co.uk/finance/jobs/8612055/Jobless-Britons-lack-basic-skills-and-work-ethic.html [accessed 2 October 2012].

Pressman, J. and Wildavsky, A. 1992. *Implementation: How Great Expectations in Washington are Dashed in Oakland*, 3rd ed. Berkeley: University of California Press.

Rawls, J. 1958. Justice as fairness, *The Philosophical Review*, 67(2), 164–94.

Read, J. 2009. A Genealogy of Homo-Economicus: Neoliberalism and the production of subjectivity, *Foucault Studies*, 6, 25–36.

Rhodes, M. 2000. Restructuring the British welfare state: Between domestic constraints and global imperatives in *Welfare and Work in the Open Economy Volume II: Diverse Responses to Common Challenges in Twelve Countries* edited by Fritz W. Scharpf and Vivien A. Schmidt. Oxford and New York: Oxford University Press, 19–69.

Sainsbury, R. 2010. 21st Century Welfare – getting closer to radical benefit reform? *Public Policy Research*, 17(2), 102–7.

Shelter. 2012. *Guidance: Eviction for Anti-social or criminal behaviour Get Advice*. [Online]. Available at: http://england.shelter.org.uk/get_advice/neighbourhood_issues/antisocial_behaviour/eviction_for_antisocial_behaviour [accessed 2 October 2012].

Sim, J. 2010. Review symposium: Punishing the Poor: The Neoliberal Government of Social Insecurity, *British Journal of Criminology*, 50(3), 592–3.

Sindbjerg Martinsen, D. 2007. The Europeanization of gender equality – who controls the scope of non-discrimination? *Journal of European Public Policy*, 14(4), 544–62.

Somek, A. 2011. *Engineering Equality*. Oxford: Oxford University Press.

UK Border Agency. 2011. *Judgment on Carers of British Citizens UKBA Latest News and Updates*. [Online]. Available at: http://www.ukba.homeoffice.gov.uk/sitecontent/newsarticles/2011/september/48-british-carers [accessed: 2 October 2012].

Van Aerschot, P. 2011. Administrative justice and the implementation of activation legislation in Denmark, Finland and Sweden, *Journal of Social Security Law*, 18(1), 33–57.

Van Den Brink, M.J. 2012. EU Citizenship and EU Fundamental Rights: Taking EU Citizenship Rights Seriously? *Legal Issues of Economic Integration*, 39 (2), 273–89.

Van Eijken, H. and de Vries, S.A. 2011. A new route into the promised land? Being a European citizen after Ruiz Zambrano, *European Law Review*, 36(5), 704–21.

Wacquant, L. 2009. *Punishing the Poor: the Neoliberal Government of Social Insecurity*. Michigan: Duke University Press.

Wendell, S. 1996. *The Rejected Body: Feminist Philosophical Reflections on Disability*. London: Routledge.

Williams, F. 1999. Good-enough principles for welfare, *Journal of Social Policy*, 28 (4), 667–87.

Wood, G. and Gough, I. 2006. A comparative welfare regime approach to global and social policy, *World Development*, 34 (10), 1696–712.

Chapter 6

Empowering Consumer-Citizens: Changing Rights or Merely Discourse?

Katalin Cseres and Annette Schrauwen

Introduction

Throughout its evolution in distinct periods (Gormley 2006), the internal market had maintained its role as an instrument to enhance social welfare, rather than being an objective in its own right. The reform package leading up to the Single Market Act of 2011 (European Commission 2011a, 2007a, 2007b, 2007c), however, suggests a re-orientation of its role: in the past the single market aimed at economic growth through removing trade barriers because this would contribute to the overall welfare of the Union. The 21st century's vision of the internal market[1] seems to be more impact driven, guided by the demand-side of the market. It starts from consumers' and citizens' needs beyond economic perspectives of more products at better quality for lower prices encompassing citizenship norms and values such as solidarity, inclusion and sustainability. The re-orientation envisages a changed new role for consumers and citizens through their empowerment as active participants in designing and enforcing economic regulation. It uses an empowerment discourse that moves from the single social (or political) concept of citizenship and the economic concept of consumer to a compound concept of the consumer-citizen. This chapter tests the claims of the empowerment discourse and, to that end, examines whether legal tools and strategies in the citizenship and consumer law field are likely to increase citizen and consumer empowerment. Our examination leads us to conclude that policy initiatives indicate that empowerment lies more with the European Commission than with the citizen or the consumer. This questions the legitimacy of the discourse.

The chapter proceeds as follows. First, we provide a short discourse analysis of policy documents using terms such as 'empowerment' and 'active citizens and consumers' aiming to distil some definitions. Second, we turn to instruments for citizens' participation in agenda setting and designing legislation for the establishment and functioning of the single market with a view to evaluating their capacity to empower. Next, we examine the Electricity Directive as an example of legislation encapsulating empowerment tools for consumers. And fourth, we

---

1   'Internal market' is the term included in the relevant Treaty provisions. The Commission documents all refer to 'single market'.

will scrutinize consumer empowerment through new ways of enforcement of legislation. We attempt to conclude with some remarks on the validity of and flaws in the empowerment discourse.

Active Citizens, Active Consumers and Empowerment

In the EU context, the concept of Active Citizenship was developed as 'a way of empowering citizens to have their voices heard within their communities, to have a sense of belonging and a stake in the society in which they live, to appreciate the value of democracy, equality, and understanding different cultures and different opinions' when developing proposals for the Lisbon 2010 Strategy (Hoskins and D'Hombres 2008: 389). Hoskins (2009: 5) formulates it as follows:

> Although Active Citizenship is specified on the individual level in terms of actions and values, the emphasis in this concept is not on the benefit to the individual but on what these individual actions and values contribute to the wider society in terms of ensuring the continuation of democracy, good governance and social cohesion.

The Lisbon Strategy mainstreams empowerment of active citizens in EU consumer policy and, along the way, the citizen and the consumer are merged into the consumer-citizen model.

While the Commission's Consumer Policy Strategy 2007–2013 (European Commission 2007d, Davies 2011: 52–8) does not explicitly mention the 'active consumer', it stresses consumers' responsibility for managing their own affairs (p. 3), has as one of its objectives to put 'consumers in the driving seat' (p. 5) and views 'equipping the consumer with the skills and tools to fulfil their role in modern economy' as a response to the challenges of growth, jobs and the need to re-connect with the citizens the EU is currently facing (p. 2). The Commission has emphasized that confident, informed and empowered consumers are the motor of economic change as their choices drive innovation and efficiency. In the long-term growth strategy Europe 2020 (European Commission 2010a), the Commission stated likewise that citizens must be empowered in order to play a full part in the single market, which requires strengthening their ability and confidence to buy goods and services cross-border. Thus, the citizen is addressed as market agent and the consumer is addressed as both a chooser and a citizen who is capable of individual and collective political and economic action. Both are conflated in a consumer-citizenship model (Davies 2011: 13). The place of the empowered consumer-citizen is at the heart of the next phase of the single market. Several actions outlined in the Consumer Policy Strategy 2007–2013 can be linked to this empowerment: on a collective level, the 'Consumer Policy Network of senior consumer policy officials will provide a forum for policy coordination and development' and, on a more individual level, information and education of consumers who can make changes in lifestyle and consumption patterns will contribute to public interests such as protection of the environment. Furthermore, effective mechanisms to seek redress must make consumers confident in shopping outside their own Member State and contribute to their active attitude.

These actions correspond to what we see as the formal and the substantive side of consumer-citizenship: active participation in policy-making on the one hand and consumption motivated by public interest at the other. The formal and substantive side are present in the definition of consumer-citizenship that can be found in consumer education projects within the context of the Socrates scheme:

> Consumer citizenship is when the individual, in his/her role as a consumer, actively participates in developing and improving society by considering ethical issues, diversity of perspectives, global processes and future conditions. It involves taking responsibility on a global as well as regional, national, local and family scale when securing one's own personal needs and well-being (Thoresen 2002: 22).

Involvement in policy-making through a forum for policy coordination and development turns (representatives of) consumers into active participants in policy-making and this seems to correspond to the citizen who by his actions contributes to the wider society in terms of ensuring the continuation of democracy, good governance and social cohesion. These governance structures turn the instrumental market citizen depicted by Michelle Everson (Everson 1995) into an active participant.

Again, a similar discourse can be found in the Europe 2020 Strategy for smart, sustainable and inclusive growth (European Commission 2010a). The Strategy at several instances indicates that a more active role is expected from citizens (European Commission 2010a: 4, 12) and that citizens 'must be empowered to play a full part in the single market' (European Commission 2010a: 19).

The proposed Regulation on a consumer programme 2014–2020 (European Commission 2011b) describes empowerment as follows:

> Empowerment is not only a question of consumer rights but of building an overall environment that enables consumers to make use of those rights and benefit from them. It means building a framework wherein consumers can rely on the basic premise that safety is assured and that tools are in place to detect failings in standards and practices and to address them effectively across Europe. It means building an environment where consumers through education, information and awareness know how to navigate the Single Market to benefit from the best offers on products and services. Finally empowerment requires that consumers can confidently exercise their EU rights across Europe and that, when something goes wrong, they can count both on the effective enforcement of those rights and on easy access to efficient redress.

In brief, the EU is providing individuals in their role as consumer-citizens with instruments to participate actively in the establishment and functioning of the European market in order to obtain smart, sustainable and inclusive growth. Thus, we can distil the following definitions from the discourse: active citizens and consumers are individuals who participate in the development of rights and are practising and enforcing their rights; empowerment is the act of providing tools to citizens and consumers with the purpose that they participate in the development, exercise and enforcement of their rights. Empowerment supposes that individuals will use the tools they have been given.

A Eurobarometer survey on consumer empowerment (Eurobarometer 2011) examined 'knowledge, capacities and assertiveness' of consumers to measure to what extent they are empowered consumers. The survey identified the most vulnerable consumers as those who have no computer skills, those with a low social status and retired persons. Unsurprisingly, the survey concludes they show least empowered consumer behaviour. It is something to keep in mind during an examination of the empowerment tools given to consumer-citizens for their participation in design, exercise and enforcement of their rights.

Empowering Consumers and Citizens: Agenda Setting and Designing of Legislation

The Lisbon Treaty has provided a new instrument of empowering citizens to make their voices heard, notably the citizens' initiative (article 11–4 TEU). Furthermore, Article 11 TEU obliges the institutions to give citizens and representative organizations the opportunity to make known and publicly exchange their views in all areas of Union action and makes public consultations a compulsory part of the Commission's work. The listing of these instruments under the 'Provisions on Democratic Principles' in the Treaty suggests that these instruments imply equality and accountability.

Below, we will briefly analyze the capacity of the citizens' initiative and public consultations as empowerment mechanisms. Although they are not limited to consumer issues, these new forms of public participation in Union policy shaping can clearly be used in that field.

Citizens' Initiative

In February 2011, a Regulation was issued on the basis of Article 24 TFEU that gives conditions and procedure for a citizens' initiative.[2] The Regulation puts the Commission at the centre of the procedure, as it registers initiatives (Article 4) and decides to act upon them (Article 10). Organizers and signatories must

---

2   Regulation (EU) No. 211/2011 of the European Parliament and of the Council of 16 February 2011 on the citizens' initiative [2011] L65/1.

fulfil certain requirements (Article 3). Registration is dependent on a number of substantive conditions (Article 4). After registration, the organizers can start to collect signatures. They have one year to collect one million signatures from at least one quarter of the Member States, with a minimum number of signatures per Member State in order to guarantee the 'Union interest'. The procedural and practical thresholds for registering and submitting favour organization by civil society rather than by individual citizens (Dougan 2011: 1847; Bouza García and Del Río Villar 2012). Once submitted, the Commission, after a procedure for examination, shall 'set out in a communication its legal and political conclusions on the citizens' initiative, the action it intends to take, if any, and its reasons for taking or not taking that action' (Article 10–1 (c)). The Commission is the gatekeeper of citizens' initiatives. However, there are no clear guidelines in the Regulation according to which the Commission should act (Emmanouilidis and Stratulat 2010).

Monaghan identifies three democratic contributions the citizens' initiative is supposed to bring according to discussions surrounding the adoption of the Regulation. It can enhance quality, relevance and effectiveness of policy outcomes, it can contribute to the formation of a European public sphere and it benefits individual citizens by challenging feelings of low political efficacy and better realizing the ideal of free and equal citizens (Monaghan, 2012: 292). The benefit for the individual citizen presents especially the perspective of the citizens' initiative as an empowerment tool. The explanatory memorandum of the proposal of the Regulation neglects these benefits for individual citizens. It presents the citizens' initiative as an opportunity to foster greater cross-border debate about EU policy issues and as enhancing output legitimacy by obliging 'the Commission, as a college, to give serious consideration to the requests made by citizens' initiatives' (European Commission 2010b: 2).

The citizens' initiative provisions establish a direct link between citizens and the Commission, whereas according to Article 14–2 TEU, the European Parliament is composed of representatives of the Union's citizens. As a result, and even though the citizens' initiative is supposed to be a complement to the existing representative system (Szeligowska and Mincheva 2012: 271), two institutions might be competing for securing the public's favours, albeit in a distinct way. The Commission will have to look at single issues brought to it by citizens' initiatives, whereas the MEPs will more generally try to steer decision-making in the directions as promised to their voters. The relationship between institution and the public differs between these two settings: the Commission has to react to demands from citizens – probably organized by civil society and emphasizing functional representation (Monaghan 2012: 296), while the MEPs are elected on the basis of election programmes proposed by the political parties. Furthermore, with the citizens' initiative one million citizens are in the driver's seat, which in the traditional decision-making process is occupied by the political parties.

The link between citizens and the Commission might influence the inter-institutional relations. It can be problematic whenever a citizens' initiative touches upon an issue that has been the subject of a political compromise between Council and European Parliament. How can the Commission give 'serious consideration' to the initiative without harming a compromise that has been reached and which the European Parliament supported, probably because it was in the best interest of the voters? Whose claim is more important? That of one million citizens who actively signed an initiative or that of the EP, which represents 500 million citizens even though quite a large number of them choose not to actively vote in European elections? The citizens' initiative could also affect the position of the Commission in relation to the Council, if the Commission is able to use the support of a citizens' initiative on a topic that encounters opposition in the Council (Szeligowska and Mincheva 2012: 282).

How much empowerment is there in the citizens' initiative? Is it providing the citizens with a true possibility to act? Is it, as Dougan has argued, a relatively weak instrument, more in the character of a popular petition (Dougan 2011: 1844), or does it partially empower citizens (Trzaskowski: 2010)? The Commission feels the decision not to act on a citizens' initiative and, in particular, the political analysis on the substance of the initiative cannot be subject to an appeal procedure.[3] The General Court in the end will have to decide on admissibility of an appeal (De Witte *et al.* 2010: 30). Because the decision whether and how to act upon a submitted initiative gives a significant margin of appreciation to the Commission, it is likely that judicial review will only consider procedural obligations and not legal and political reasons (Szeligowska and Mincheva 2012: 280). Supposedly there could be a role for either the European Parliament or the European Ombudsman to act as a watchdog and guard against arbitrary decisions of the Commission (De Witte *et al.* 2010: 30).

The citizens' initiative has limited potential to empower citizens and has less representative value and accountability mechanisms than traditional policy-making by Parliament and Council has. Once the initiative is submitted, decisions are beyond the reach of the active citizens that signed a citizens' initiative, they are forced back into a passive role. The first proposal of the Regulation for the Citizens' Initiative gave rise to the qualification of a misleading instrument, 'paradoxically contributing to the suspicion of the European Union's non-willingness to truly enable citizens to take part in the decision making process at European level' (De Witte *et al.* 2010: 31).

The Citizens' Initiative enhances the link between the citizens and the executive, thereby giving more leverage to the executive, at the expense of the European Parliament. The citizens' initiative needs political support from the Commission who is the main player (Szeligowska and Mincheva 2012: 281, 282). The executive is the gatekeeper and, in the end, determines who has influence and who has not. This is problematic for a 'democratic' empowerment instrument

---

3   See answer 42 on the 'frequently asked questions' page of the Commissions' website: http://europa.eu/rapid/pressReleasesAction.do?reference=MEMO/10/683&format=HTML&aged=0&language=EN&guiLanguage=en [accessed 26 August 2010].

that is supposed to imply equality and accountability. Even if citizens are the addressees of the instrument, in the end it empowers the Commission.

Public Consultation

Public consultation can be considered to be part of new governance structures, like representative and expert network structures which empower consumers to influence and change law and policy (Davies 2011: 90). The Commission refers to consultation procedures in the explanatory memorandums that accompany the proposals for Union acts. Several problems have been identified in respect to transparency and representativeness of such consultations, as well as in relation to weighing of different contributions (Kohler-Koch 2010, Dawson 2011).

The consultation on the 2013 EU citizenship report, open from 9 May till 9 September 2012, may serve as an example.[4] The category 'Your daily life as a citizen' ranges questions on free movement, justice and political rights. A relatively large part of them ask whether the participant to the consultation experienced obstacles, difficulties and problems in exercising free movement rights. Clearly, the questions are designed in support of the idea that citizens still face problems in cross-border activity and that something must be done about that. To put it differently, the consultation is looking for support of the Europe 2020 Strategy without questioning how citizens value both that Strategy and the emphasis on cross-border economic activity in itself. As a result, the citizen is not in the driver's seat or at the heart of the Strategy, but citizens' responses can be used to provide more legitimacy to already decided policies and programmes.

Also, the number of responses seems to suggest a lack of representativeness: There were 329 responses, of which 160 originated from individual citizens, 133 from organizations and 36 from public authorities. The Commission qualified this as 'satisfactory' and 'comparable to that received of other Green Papers' (Sauron 2011). Indeed, responses to consultation on more technical issues are even less numerous. For example, the consultation leading to the Mutual Recognition Regulation received 135 responses, of which 30 per cent originated from individual citizens (European Commission 2007e: 2). In either case, the Commission refers to responses without specifying the numbers in order to lend legitimacy to its proposals, for example by using phrases such as 'the consultation showed that [...]' or 'contacts with interested circles show that [...]' (European Commission 2002: 15, 68; Bouza García and del Río Villar 2012: 315). Nor does it explain the relative weight of the response from an individual participant compared to that of a civil society organization or an organization representing the affected industry. Furthermore, accountability is problematic. Stakeholders signal that the Commission seems to be at liberty to reject, use partially or accept answers that come out of the public consultations (DG SANCO 2007: 9, 10).

---

4   See http://ec.europa.eu/justice/newsroom/citizen/opinion/120509_en.htm (last accessed 7 November 2012). The consultation website itself is no longer available.

The lack of accountability and of clarity who is represented make it in our view questionable whether consultations may be presented as an instrument to translate public participation in the establishment of the single market and as an empowerment instrument. As long as it is not clear who is actually participating and how responses are considered, consultations do not guarantee all citizens equal and efficient opportunities to participate in policy-making. Accordingly, the discourse that presents consultation as a participatory mechanism for citizens and consumers is misleading. Even though consultation is about having a voice, but not a vote, the presentation and selection of these voices as providing legitimacy to policies and proposals should respond to criteria of representativeness and accountability. Arbitrary use of public consultations is empowering the Commission more than it empowers citizens and consumers.

Empowerment in Union Legislation: the Electricity Directive

In general, consumer-citizens are 'empowered' to influence the functioning of the market through knowing and using their rights, complaining, switching and ethical buying. The Electricity Directive 2009/72 may serve as a concrete example of how empowerment tools are integrated in a legislative act.

The objective of the Electricity Directive is the establishment of a competitive, secure and environmentally sustainable market. The Directive lays down common rules for generation, transmission, distribution and supply of electricity. The Directive also contains provisions on universal service obligations which, though a universal service obligation is important from a social model perspective, it is not specifically linked to the empowerment of consumers and citizens this chapter focuses upon. The rights of electricity consumers and provisions on consumer protection are more important from a consumer-citizenship perspective. The directive obliges Member States to set up single points of contact that must give consumers information on their rights, on applicable legislation and on dispute settlement mechanisms. Annex I to the Directive further specifies the rights consumers have and what sort of information energy suppliers should give to them. In the annex, there is one provision that stimulates a more active role of the consumer. Indeed, the consumers must be properly and frequently informed about their energy consumption in order 'to enable them to regulate their own energy consumption'. Furthermore, according to Article 3, paragraph 9 of the Directive, electricity suppliers must specify to final consumers the contribution of each energy source of the overall fuel mix and must give information on the environmental impact. As a result, the consumer is able to take environmental values such as the use of renewable energy into consideration when 'regulating his own energy consumption'. Thus, the directive is an empowerment instrument in giving energy consumers the tools to take public concerns – environmental protection, climate change – into account when consuming. The consumer becomes consumer-citizen. Or, as

Micklitz (2012: 21) writes, the circumspect consumer who opts for the lowest price should become a responsible consumer who also considers ecological, social and political values.

The empowerment of the consumer-citizen relies heavily on providing sufficient information, which should enable consumer-citizens to act responsibly. However, this is not the 'acting together' characteristic for citizenship that is referred to, but still a rights and benefits-based conception of the individual. The discourse of empowerment of consumer-citizens promises a more positive and active picture of individuals acting together – when compared to that of the passive market citizen or consumer. But the instruments provided focus foremost on the individual benefit that can be gained from informed choices and looking for the best opportunities. These are instruments that nowhere take into account the more vulnerable, less informed and less educated individuals. They should be taken into account, if the empowerment tools are to contribute to what the Single Market Act presents as the human dimension of the 'social' market economy that is supposed to put Europeans at the heart of the internal market and restore confidence. It is questionable whether empowerment tools can help vulnerable consumers as well as protection guaranteed through law can. Meanwhile, the 2012 Commission Staff Working Document on the State of Play of the Single Market Act (European Commission 2012) still emphasizes the opportunities for individuals and the importance of access to information. Whether enforcement mechanisms related to the empowerment discourse equally favour individual rights and benefits over a more protective attitude towards consumer-citizens is one of the questions dealt with in the next paragraph.

Empowering consumers and citizens through law enforcement

In the EU's consumer empowerment policy, enforcement receives a distinctive role in realizing the goals of competitive and innovative markets: '[E]mpowered consumers who complain and assert their rights are the most effective consultants in helping businesses to innovate and improve' (European Commission 2011c: 2). Consumer redress is, in fact, perceived as one of the preconditions of consumer empowerment, which is to be realized through legislation on alternative dispute resolution (ADR) and by establishing simple, fast and affordable out-of-court procedures (European Commission 2011c: 3). The Commission's definition of consumer empowerment also relies on effective institutions: consumer organizations and public authorities are seen as intermediaries helping consumers to make better decisions.

What kind of procedural rules and institutional arrangements form the basis of the EU's empowerment model? Besides the general industry neutral rules, we also look at liberalized network industries because sector-specific regulation well illustrates the role of successful law enforcement in empowering consumers. Moreover, the most recent legislative packages (electricity, gas, telecoms) address enforcement of consumer law in a more pronounced way than the earlier legislation.

The aim of this analysis is to understand whether these empowerment tools could be more effective than traditional tools of consumer law enforcement. After mapping out recent EU legislation on consumer law enforcement, the new empowerment tools will be tested with the help of three recent cases of the Court of Justice of the European Union (CJEU).

Consumer Empowerment through Procedures

Consumers' access to justice and consumer redress has been part of the Union's policies since 1975 but it has only been reinforced in soft law documents. A specific legal basis for consumer redress is absent in the EU Treaties (Article 169 TFEU = ex Article 153 EC). Although the Treaty establishes EU consumer protection as an independent field, the Member States retain almost exclusive competence in enforcing EU consumer rights, in accordance with the so-called national procedural autonomy. This autonomy means that the private law consequences of European law infringements fall within the competence of the Member States.[5] Hence, the enforcement of EU consumer law is fragmented by the separation of harmonized substantive rules from decentralized procedures, remedies and institutional design. Moreover, it is challenged by a multi-level system composed of vertical (European and national law) and horizontal (general and sector-specific rules) layers of legal sources.

This competence allocation has changed considerably. While the influence of EU law on national procedures and remedies of law enforcement has been gradually growing since 1992 (de Moor-van Vugt 2011), the institutional autonomy of the Member States has remained largely untouched.

Consequently, there was no guidance from the EU on how to enforce EU law and what kind of institutional design is optimal for law enforcement. This changed with the adoption of Directive 98/27 on injunctions,[6] Regulation 2006/2004 on consumer protection cooperation[7] and the process of enlargement. Since 2007 the enforcement of consumer law has become one of the key priorities of the Commission (European Commission 2007d).

With regard to judicial enforcement, the Commission has launched two proposals: on voluntary dispute resolutions schemes and collective actions

---

5   Case 33/76, *Rewe-Zentralfinanz eG and Rewe-Zentral AG v Landwirtschaftskammer für das Saarland (Rewe I)* [1976] ECR 1989, para 5, Case C-261/95 *Palmisani* [1997] ECR I-4025, para 27, Case C-453/99 *Courage and Crehan* [2001] ECR I-06297, para 29.

6   Directive of the European Parliament and of the Council (EC) 98/27 on injunctions for the protection of consumers' interests [1998] OJ L166/51.

7   Regulation of the European Parliament and of the Council (EC) 2006/2004 on cooperation between national authorities responsible for the enforcement of consumer protection laws (the Regulation on consumer protection cooperation) [2004] OJ L364/1.

and it has also briefly addressed the combination of these two models. The Commission has promoted the development of ADR schemes by adopting two recommendations on minimum quality criteria for the establishment and operation of ADR schemes.[8] Finally, the European Consumer Centres Network (ECC-Net) provides consumers with information and assistance in accessing an appropriate ADR scheme in another Member State.

In 2009 the Consumer Enforcement Package (European Commission 2009) raised two core issues of consumer law enforcement: finding effective means of collective redress and the deterrent effect of available remedies and sanctions. The question was whether, besides injunctive relief[9] and fines, remedies should be extended to damages claims.

In 2008 a Green Paper on collective redress has been published, which addressed compensation through damages claims and offered options for consumer empowerment such as collective ADR schemes and enabling public consumer authorities to require traders to compensate consumers or to skim off the profit of the traders.[10] In 2011 a new public consultation was published presenting a coherent EU approach on collective actions aiming to identify common legal principles among the Member States on injunctions and damages claims (European Commission 2011d). It also re-launched the discussion to resolve consumer disputes via collective consensual dispute resolution.

Simultaneously a public consultation was opened on ADR (European Commission 2011e) with similar questions on extending its coverage, involvement of business and suppliers, awareness of consumers, online dispute resolution and funding.

Beyond these general economy-wide instruments, the Commission has been extending its influence on law enforcement in the liberalized sectors, such as financial services, telecommunications and energy. Besides laying down obligations for the Member States to establish independent regulatory authorities to monitor markets and compliance with consumer laws, the EU Directives, such as the E-commerce Directive,[11] the Postal Services Directive[12] and the Markets in

---

8 Commission Recommendation (EC) 98/257 on the principles applicable to the bodies responsible for out-of-court settlement of consumer disputes [1998] OJ L115/31, Commission Recommendation (EC) 2001/310 on the principles for out-of-court bodies involved in the consensual resolution of consumer disputes [2001] OJ L109/56.

9 Directive 98/27 has been substantially modified several times, for example new Directives have been added to the annex; now Directive 2009/22 (Directive of the European Parliament and the Council (EC) 2009/22 on injunctions for the protection of consumers' interests [2009] OJ L 110/30) codified version.

10 European Commission 2008a:11.

11 Directive of the European Parliament and of the Council (EC) 2000/31 on certain legal aspects of information society services, in particular electronic commerce, in the Internal Market [2000] OJ L178/1.

12 Directive of the European Parliament and of the Council (EC) 2008/6 amending Directive 97/67/EC with regard to the full accomplishment of the internal market of Community postal services [2008] OJ L52/3.

Financial Instruments Directive (MiFID),[13] *encourage* Member States to establish ADR schemes. The EU legislative frameworks regarding the telecom sector[14] and the energy sector,[15] the Consumer Credit Directive[16] and the Payment Services Directive[17] *require* that adequate and effective ADR schemes are put in place.

While sector-specific regulation granted fundamental economic rights to individuals in order to actively participate in these markets, sufficient enforcement of those rights was late coming. This is why the most recent legislative packages addressed enforcement in a more pronounced way than the earlier legislation.

As already noted, in the electricity market the so-called third legislative package established an Agency for the Cooperation of Energy Regulators and Directive 2009/72/EC concerning common rules for the internal market in electricity[18] obliges Member States to create so-called single points of contact to provide information concerning consumer rights, legislation and dispute settlements as well as creating an independent mechanism (energy ombudsman or consumer body) to deal with consumer complaints and out-of-court dispute settlements.[19] Annex I includes among others the obligation for electricity providers to set up transparent, simple and inexpensive procedures for dealing with their complaints. In particular, all consumers shall have the right to a good standard of service and complaint handling by their electricity service provider.

This brief overview shows that consumer empowerment through law enforcement is characterized by a noticeable shift from the state to individual

---

13   Directive of the European Parliament and of the Council (EC) 2004/39 on markets in financial instruments amending Council Directives 85/611/EEC and 93/6/EEC and Directive 2000/12/EC of the European Parliament and of the Council and repealing Council Directive 93/22/EEC [2004] OJ L145/1.

14   Directive of the European Parliament and of the Council (EC) 2009/136 amending Directive 2002/22/EC on universal service and users' rights relating to electronic communications networks and services, Directive 2002/58/EC concerning the processing of personal data and the protection of privacy in the electronic communications sector and Regulation (EC) No. 2006/2004 on cooperation between national authorities responsible for the enforcement of consumer protection laws [2009] OJ L337/37.

15   Directive of the European Parliament and of the Council (EC) 2009/72 concerning common rules for the internal market in electricity [2009] OJ L211/94.

16   Directive of the European Parliament and of the Council (EC) 2008/48 on credit agreements for consumers and repealing Council Directive 87/102/EEC [2008] OJ L133/66.

17   Directive of the European Parliament and of the Council (EC) 2007/64 on payment services in the internal market amending Directives 97/7/EC, 2002/65/EC, 2005/60/EC and 2006/48/EC [2007] OJ L319/1.

18   Regulation of the European Parliament and of the Council (EC) 713/2009 establishing an Agency for the Cooperation of Energy Regulators [2009] OJ L211/1, Directive of the European Parliament and of the Council (EC) 2009/72 concerning common rules for the internal market in electricity and repealing Directive 2003/54/EC [2009] OJ L211/55.

19   Directive 2009/72 Article 3, paras 12–13.

consumers and their collectives to enforce the rules. There has also been a shift from traditional judicial (private) enforcement to less traditional forms of soft enforcement such as the voluntary dispute resolutions and a shift from judicial enforcement to administrative enforcement. With regard to institutions of law enforcement, this concerns a shift from the courts to regulatory agencies but also from the courts to alternative dispute resolution bodies.

Consumer Empowerment through Institutions

The fact that effective law enforcement also depends on its institutional setting has been analyzed by several scholars (Stiglitz 2002: 164, Klein 2000, Coase 1937, 1960).[20] In practice regulators have come to realize that a body of economic regulation is only as good as the institutions (i.e. the structures, processes and procedures of law enforcement) entrusted with their implementation (OECD 2008, ICN 2012). Establishing new regulatory authorities and re-designing old ones served as a significant opportunity to consider the institutional prerequisites for the effective implementation of economic laws. The respective institutional contexts will each shape decisions in their own ways and these will often lead to very different roles for legal rules (Gerber 2009).

There is presently a wide diversity of institutions enforcing EU consumer law: some Member States, such as the Netherlands, predominantly rely on private enforcement, while others, such as the Scandinavian or the Eastern European countries, prefer enforcement by public bodies. There has been no specific EU obligation for the Member States to establish independent consumer authorities. This is in accordance with the principles of national procedural and institutional autonomy. Institutional autonomy is the Member States' competence to design their own institutional infrastructure and allocate regulatory powers to public administrative agencies that enforce EU law[21] (Verhoeven 2010). Accordingly, the Member States were free to entrust public agencies or private organizations with the enforcement of consumer laws as well as to decide on the internal organization, legal competences and powers of public agencies.

However, Regulation 2006/2004 on trans-border cooperation between consumer authorities indirectly intervened with national institutional arrangements by imposing conditions under which national authorities responsible for enforcing consumer rules must cooperate with each other. The regulation prioritized public enforcement, changing the national institutional framework

---

20 New institutional economics which incorporates a theory of institutions into economics has developed as a movement within the social sciences, especially economics and political science, that unites theoretical and empirical research examining the role of institutions in furthering or preventing economic growth. It includes work in transaction costs, political economy, property rights, hierarchy and organization and public choice. Most scholars view the work of Ronald Coase as a central inspiration for the field.

21 Joined cases 51-54/71 *International Fruit Company II* [1971] ECR 1107, para 4.

accordingly (Bakardjieva-Engelbrekt 2006: 3).[22] Similarly, in the liberalized network industries the EU gradually extended the EU principles of *effective*, *dissuasive* and *proportionate sanctions* as formulated in the European courts' case-law[23] to a broader set of obligations and criteria for national supervision of EU legislation. This process of Europeanization of supervision (Ottow 2012) obliged Member States to establish independent national regulatory agencies with core responsibilities for monitoring markets and safeguarding consumers' interests (Micklitz, 2009) through ensuring effective consumer law enforcement and complaints processes (Davies and Szyszczak 2010).

Regulation 2006/2004 on consumer protection cooperation has set up an EU-wide network of national enforcement authorities enabling them to take co-ordinated action for the enforcement of the laws that protect consumers' interests and to ensure compliance with those laws.[24] The Regulation requires public enforcement mechanisms for a set of 15 directives that mostly concern private law rules. The Regulation imposes public enforcement for the consumer *acquis*; however, it does not regulate sanctions. While the Regulation was to coordinate at EU level the enforcement activities of the Member States in cross-border infringements and to raise the standard and consistency of enforcement, it also had a major impact on the domestic institutional structure of consumer protection in the Member States. This can be illustrated by the establishment of the Netherlands Consumer Authority.[25] As mentioned above, the Commission has acknowledged the essential role consumer organizations play in the enforcement of consumer law, but it has not involved them in the process of achieving effective and uniform enforcement EU wide.

The way the public-private divide of consumer law enforcement is steered from the EU raises a relevant question: is the empowerment of administrative authorities the solution to effective consumer law enforcement? There are strong indications that empowering consumers through individual or collective mechanisms of private enforcement has had limited success (Van den Bergh and Visscher, 2008). This is why the European Commission has adopted an explicit policy aimed at strengthening the role of administrative authorities in the Member States. In the following we will tentatively answer this question by relying on law and economics literature, empirical evidence and relevant CJEU cases.

The law and economics literature argues that public agencies with investigative powers can better detect law violations as final consumers may not optimally

---

22   See Article 3c on the definition of a competent authority: '"competent authority" means any public authority established either at national, regional or local level with specific responsibilities to enforce the laws that protect consumers' interests'.

23   Case C-68/88 *Greek Maize* [1989] ECR 2965.

24   On the basis of Article 4 each Member State was obliged to designate the competent authorities and a single liaison office responsible for the application of the Regulation.

25   Wet handhaving consumentenbescherming. 18 Memorie van Toelichting Whc, Kamerstukken II 2005/06, 30 411, nr. 3.

enforce the law due to lack of information, rational apathy and free-riding (Polinsky and Shavell, 2000, Van den Bergh and Visscher, 2008). However, not all parts of consumer law are fit to be enforced by a public agency as most of the consumer rules are private law rules and thus drafted for private enforcement (Scott and Black, 2000). In the law and economics literature, information asymmetries form the most valid economic reasons to intervene in markets and serve as a rationale for regulation in order to protect consumers. Transaction costs, information deficits and cognitive dissonances are accepted arguments to justify intervention in the otherwise unrestricted market processes (Van den Bergh, 2007). Consumer protection is regarded merely as a subsidiary solution to market failures in case the private law system of individual enforcement fails (Ramsay, 1985).

Accordingly, public enforcement is justified when there is serious risk of adverse selection in the marketplace, when consumers face difficulties to discover the infringements and when the size of the total harm significantly exceeds the individual damage suffered (Van den Bergh, 2007). When consumers do not have information about the quality of products, like in the markets of experience and credence goods, intervention is justified.

For example, standard contract terms (de Geest, 2002), unfair commercial practices or financial services involve the risk of adverse selection and thus consumers lack the incentives to take action. But a large part of consumer law is private law and as such it was intended to assist consumers to make use of their rights by way of complaining or by initiating other actions. For example, in the case of package travel, timesharing or price indications, consumers have better information about the law violations and eventual harm occurred. Rational apathy to complain and take action also seems less of a problem. Doorstep selling and distance contracts are parts of consumer law where cooling-off periods apply and thus consumers have enough time to avail themselves of the necessary information to conclude the deal or refrain from it. Accordingly, the Regulation makes public enforcement unnecessary in areas such as doorstep selling, package travel and timesharing where private enforcement can be effective. Furthermore, empirical evidence shows that most of the consumers make a complaint directly to the traders and try to resolve the dispute through direct negotiation instead of turning to a third party (Eurobarometer 2011: 40). This shows that consumers are in the first place interested in actual solutions such as apology, repair, replacement or refund. However, while EU consumers appear to be willing to complain, in fact only 16 per cent turn to public authorities or consumer organizations (Eurobarometer 2011: 41). This confirms earlier research results that claim consumer complaints are the most frequent and most important means of problem solving (Stuyck *et al.* 2007: 27–8, 44, 46, Eurobarometer 2004: 9).

The barriers of consumers' access to justice are well known. Litigation before courts takes excessive time and money when compared to the small value of the dispute at stake. Moreover, civil procedures are often not geared to the institution of mass procedures and in the courts adjudication rather than mediation is arrived at. Further, there are also psychological barriers like unfamiliarity with the legal language and lack of information about the actual infringement combined with the lack of investigatory tools to detect these. Consumers discover harm when it has already taken place and thus are not interested in avoiding the future harm. When individual consumers face substantial costs that are disproportionate to the amount of their complaint, they will decline to seek redress and resolve disputes (Van den Bergh and Visscher, 2008).

There are two acknowledged roads to empower consumers to bring claims: alternative dispute resolution and aggregate or collective consumer actions. The well-known Italian motor car insurance cartel case *Manfredi*[26] illustrated that when claims are small and there is no possibility to aggregate the separate claims, consumers prefer small claims judges where procedures are less formal and less demanding in terms of evidence and burden of proof. This is also acknowledged by the European Commission in its Staff Working Paper accompanying the White Paper, where collective ADR is put forward as a means for early resolution of disputes to encourage settlements (European Commission, 2008b). The Member States have also been experimenting with legislative solutions that would simplify consumers' use of collective actions; for example, by introducing rules of thumb to make proving evidence easier[27] or involving public authorities by filing collective actions on behalf of consumers.[28]

At the same time, ADR as a way to guarantee consumers' effective judicial protection and its interplay with access of consumers to courts and consumer authorities has been questioned in two recent preliminary rulings of the CJEU. In *Alassini*[29] the CJEU ruled on the procedural question whether Article 34 of the Universal Service Directive[30] requiring Member States to ensure transparent, simple and inexpensive procedures for users' complaints and the general principle of effective judicial protection were compromised by the Italian law, which made mandatory an initial out-of-court dispute resolution procedure before a dispute was admissible in the ordinary court process. The

---

26   Joined cases C-295/04 to C-298/04 *Manfredi v Lloyd Adriatico Assicurazioni SpA and Others* [2006] ECR I-6619.

27   In Hungary a legal presumption of 10 per cent overcharge when calculating damages for hard-core cartels has been laid down in competition law. In Bulgaria a flexible procedural rule has been implemented providing that all legal and natural persons to whom damages have been caused are entitled to compensation even where the infringement has not been aimed directly against them.

28   See Article 39 of the Hungarian Consumer Protection Act Law CLV of 1997 and the Swedish Market Act that both provide the Consumer Agencies with standing to file individual or collective actions on behalf of consumers.

29   Joined cases C-317/08, C-318/08, C-319/08 and C-320/08 *Rosalba Alassini v Telecom Italia SpA, Filomena Califano v Wind SpA, Lucia Anna Giorgia Iacono v Telecom Italia SpA and Multiservice Srl v Telecom Italia SpA* [2010] ECR I-02213.

30   Directive of the European Parliament and of the Council (EC) 2002/22 on universal service and users' rights relating to electronic communications networks and services (Universal Service Directive) [2002] OJ L108/51.

Court ruled that the principles of effectiveness, legality, representation and the principle of liberty from the preamble of Recommendation 98/257 did not limit the power of the Member States to create mandatory out-of-court procedures for the settlement of telecoms disputes between consumers and providers.[31] On the question of satisfying the principle of effectiveness, the Court accepted that making the admissibility of legal proceedings conditional upon prior implementation of a mandatory out-of-court settlement procedure affects the exercise of rights which derive from the Universal Service Directive (USD), but various factors revealed that the mandatory procedure did not in practice make the exercise of individual rights impossible or excessively difficult.[32] The Court's line of reasoning is in sharp contrast with the general argument that ADR is effective to solve consumer disputes. For example, the fact that ADR decisions are not binding was always considered a drawback of this procedure while here the Court accepts it as an advantage. While in *Alassini* the Court has set out the conditions prescribing how ADR *may* be used to settle disputes on EU law, the Court has not mentioned the advantages of these procedures for consumer disputes.

In *Volksbank Romania*[33] the Court was asked among others to interpret the Consumer Credit Directive regarding the interplay between ADR schemes and consumers' direct access to consumer authorities. The Court ruled that the Member States' discretionary power under the Directive allows them to implement national law that provides consumers direct recourse to a consumer protection authority without having to use beforehand the out-of-court resolution procedures.[34] Again, the Court's judgment does not reflect the view that ADR can be a significant way to empower consumers to resolve their disputes. In fact, ADR has now been considered as a relevant preliminary step in judicial enforcement of consumer interests and especially before collective actions for compensation is opted for. In other words, the Court's judgement contrasts with the Commission's discourse that considers ADR as a significant enforcement tool to achieve consumer empowerment.

Public authorities' role in the public-private divide of consumer law enforcement is thus more nuanced than the Commission has acknowledged so far. Their role in judicial enforcement through lodging collective or public interest actions can grow into an important contribution to consumer empowerment. Similarly, their

---

31   See paras 37–42.

32   This was because the outcome of the settlement procedure is not binding on the parties and does not prejudice their right to bring legal proceedings; the settlement procedure does not normally result in substantial delay for the parties to bring legal proceedings; for the duration of the settlement procedure, the limitation period for bringing claims based upon the USD was suspended; there were no fees or costs involved. See paras 54–7.

33   Case C-602/10 *Volksbank Romania v Autoritatea Națională pentru Protecția Consumatorilor*, judgement of 12 July 2012 [nyr].

34   See paras 98–9.

role with regard to ADR schemes, either as operators or merely as advocating such schemes, can be relevant tools to increase consumer empowerment.

The Commission's policy shift from judicial enforcement to administrative enforcement should thus be reassessed, also because this shifts competences from the Member States to the EU Commission, who gradually develops European-wide enforcement strategies. This new institutional architecture carries the risk of disregarding the institutional autonomy of the Member States and questions whether the EU's policy on consumer law enforcement is an effective way to ensure compliance with consumer laws in the Member States.

Conclusions

Our analysis leads us to conclude that there are serious gaps between the empowerment discourse and its translation into practice. Consequently, the empowerment discourse can be qualified as misleading and, in the end, not helping to restore confidence in the Single Market.

With respect to designing law and policy as well as with regard to law enforcement, we come to the same conclusion: they empower the Commission instead of the citizens and consumers.

With respect to designing law and policy, the decision-making authority is put in a responsive position as opposed to the more steering position it has in traditional public decision-making. That alone does not have to be problematic. However, it becomes problematic when we consider principles of equality and accountability as they function in representative democracy. As long as it is not clear whose voices are actually heard and which mechanisms safeguard an equal and efficient opportunity to have a say in policy-making or what principles determine a response from decision-making authorities, the empowerment instruments merely provide an opportunity for arbitrary responsiveness. Furthermore, the empowerment discourse tends to put the focus on the individual, at the expense of cohesion, collective action and community building.

Recent empowerment tools of law enforcement demonstrate a noticeable governance shift from judicial enforcement to alternative dispute resolution, small claims and to more administrative enforcement. While the EU does not have a competence in regulating either procedural or institutional issues in national laws of the Member States, the EU legislator has been actively introducing EU standards to guide and at times constrain the Member States' enforcement models. These EU standards mostly impose goal-driven (effective enforcement-effective judicial protection) obligations on the Member States and they have a highly general character without providing practical or financial guidance on designing procedures.

With regard to the institutional design of consumer law enforcement, the EU went further. The prioritization of public authorities cannot be reconciled with the Commission's consumer empowerment strategies. While public authorities play an undeniable role in the enforcement of consumer law, this role is more nuanced. Public authorities' role in judicial enforcement through lodging collective or public interest actions with regard to ADR schemes, either as operators or merely as advocating such schemes, can grow into an important contribution to consumer empowerment. But consumer empowerment needs civil society and strong private organizations as well. They cannot be excluded from the operation of an effective institutional system.

References

Bakardjieva-Engelbrekt, A. 2006. Grey zones, legitimacy concerns and boomerang effects: On the implications of extending the acquis to the countries of Central and Eastern Europe, in Wahl, Nils and Per Kramér (eds.), *Swedish Yearbook of European Law*, Oxford: Hart Publishing, 1–36.

Bakardjieva-Engelbrekt, A. 2009. Public and private enforcement of Consumer Law in Central and Eastern Europe: Institutional choice in the shadow of EU enlargement, in F. Cafaggi and H.W. Micklitz (eds.), *New Frontiers of Consumer Protection. The Interplay Between Private and Public Enforcement*. Antwerp: Intersentia, 47–92.

Bouza García, L. and Del Río Villar, S. 2012. The ECI as a Democratic Innovation: Analysing its Ability to Promote Inclusion, Empowerment and Responsiveness. *European Civil Society. Perspectives on European Politics and Society*, 13, 312–24.

Coase, R.H. 1960. The Problem of Social Cost. *Journal of Law and Economics*, 3, 1–44.

Coase, R.H. 1937. The Nature of the firm. *Economica*, 4(16), 386–405.

Davies, J. 2011. *The European Consumer Citizen in Law and Policy*. Basingstoke, Hampshire: Palgrave.

Davies, J. and Szyszczak, E. 2010. ADR: Effective Protection of Consumer Rights?. *European Law Review*, 35, 695–706.

Dawson, M. 2011. *New governance and the Transformation of European Law. Coordinating EU Social Law and Policy*. Cambridge: Cambridge University Press.

De Geest, G. 2002. The Signing-Without-Reading Problem: An analysis of the European Directive on Unfair Contract Terms', *Festschrift für Claus Ott*, Wiesbaden: Deutscher Universitätsverlag, 230–31.

De Moor-van Vugt, A. 2011. Handhaving en toezicht in een Europese context, in *De consument en de andere kant van de elektriciteitsmarkt: inleidingen op het openingscongres van het Centrum voor Energievraagstukken Universiteit van Amsterdam op 27 januari 2010*, edited by S. Pront-van Bommel, Amsterdam: Universiteit van Amsterdam, Centrum voor Energievraagstukken, 62–95.

De Witte, B. *et al.* 2010. Legislating after Lisbon. New Opportunities for the European Parliament. *EUDO report* 2010/1.

DG SANCO. 2007. Healthy Democracy: Consultation and Action Following the DG SANCO Peer Review Group on Stakeholder Involvement. February 2007.

Dougan, M. 2011. What are we to make of the Citizens' Initiative?. *Common Market Law Review*, 48, 1807–48.

Emmanouilidis, J.A. and Stratulat, C. 2010. Implementing Lisbon: a critical appraisal of the Citizens' Initiative, *EPC Policy Brief*, June 2010.

Eurobarometer. 2004. Special Eurobarometer 2004 no. 195 European Union citizens and access to justice, Fieldwork: September 2003, Publication: October 2004.

Eurobarometer. 2011. Special Eurobarometer 2011 no. 342. Consumer Empowerment Report. Fieldwork: February – April 2010, Publication: April 2011.

European Commission. 2002. Report from the Commission to the Council and the European Parliament on the State of the Internal Market for Services, presented under the first stage of the Internal Market Strategy for Services, COM (2002) 441 final.

European Commission. 2007a. Communication from the Commission to the European Parliament, the Council, the European Economic and Social Committee and the Committee of the Regions, A Single Market for 21st century Europe, COM (2007) 724 final.

European Commission. 2007b. Communication from the Commission to the European Parliament, the Council, the European Economic and Social Committee and the Committee of the Regions accompanying the Communication on 'A single market for 21st century Europe' – Services of general interest, including social services of general interest: a new European commitment, COM(2007) 725 final.

European Commission. 2007c. Communication from the Commission to the European Parliament, the Council, the European Economic and Social Committee and the Committee of the Regions. Opportunities, access and solidarity: towards a new social vision for 21st century Europe, COM(2007) 726 final.

European Commission. 2007d. Communication from the Commission to the Council, the European Parliament and the European Economic and Social Committee and the Committee of the Regions. EU Consumer Policy Strategy 2007–2013 – Empowering Consumers, Enhancing Welfare, Effectively Protecting Them, COM(2007) 99 final.

European Commission. 2007e. Commission Staff Working Document. Outcome of the public consultation on the Green Paper on a European Citizens' Initiative. Accompanying document to the Proposal for a regulation of the European Parliament and of the Council on the citizens' initiative, SEC(2010) 370.

European Commission. 2008a. Green Paper on consumer collective redress, COM(2008) 794 final.

European Commission. 2008b. Commission Staff Working Paper accompanying the white paper on Damages actions for breach of the EC antitrust rules, SEC(2008) 404.

European Commission. 2009. Communication from the Commission to the European Parliament, the Council, the European Economic and Social Committee and the Committee of the Regions on the enforcement of consumer acquis, COM(2009) 330 final.

European Commission. 2010a. Communication from the Commission. Europe 2020. A Strategy for smart, sustainable and inclusive growth, COM(2010) 2020 final.

European Commission. 2010b. Proposal for a Regulation of the European Parliament and of the Council on the citizens' initiative, COM(2010) 119 final.

European Commission. 2011a. Communication from the Commission to the European Parliament, the Council, the Economic and Social Committee and the Committee of the Regions, Single Market Act. Twelve levers to boost growth and strengthen confidence. 'Working together to create new growth', COM (2011) 206 final.

European Commission. 2011b. Proposal for a Regulation of the European Parliament and of the Council on a consumer programme 2014–2020, COM (2011) 707 final.

European Commission. 2011c. Commission Staff Working Paper. Consumer empowerment in the EU, SEC(2011) 469 final.

European Commission. 2011d. Commission staff working document. Public consultation. Towards a coherent European approach to Collective Redress, SEC(2011)173 final.

European Commission. 2011e. Communication from the Commission to the European Parliament, the Council, the European Economic and Social Committee and the Committee of the Regions. Communication on Alternative dispute resolution for consumer disputes in the Single Market, – COM (2011) 791 final.

European Commission. 2012. Commission Staff Working Document. Delivering the Single Market Act: State of Play, SWD (2012) 21 final.

Everson, M. 1995. The Legacy of the Market Citizen in *New Legal Dynamics of European Union*, edited by J. Shaw and G. More. Oxford: Oxford Clarendon Press, 73–90.

Gerber, David J. 2009. Competition Law and the Institutional Embeddedness of Economics. in *Economic Theory and Competition Law*. Edited by J. Drexl, L. Idot, J. Monéger. Cheltenham: Edward Elgar, 20–44.

Gormley, L.W. 2006. The internal market: history and evolution. In *Regulating the Internal Market*, edited by N.N. Shuibhne. Cheltenham: Edward Elgar, 14–28.

Hoskins, B. 2009. Monitoring Active Citizenship in the European Union: The Process, the Results and initial Explanations, *CADMO, Giornale Italiano di Pedogagia Sperimentale*, XVII.I.

Hoskins, B. and D'Hombres, B. 2008. Does Formal Education Have an Impact on Active Citizenship Behaviour?. *European Educational Research Journal*, 386–402.

ICN 2012 International Competition network, Competition Policy implementation Working Group: sub group 1, Agency effectiveness project, http://www.internationalcompetitionnetwork.org/working-groups/current/agency-effectiveness.aspx [accessed 7 September 2012].

Kelemen, R.D. 2012. Eurolegalism and Democracy, *Journal of Common Market Studies*, 50, 55–71.

Kohler-Koch, B. 2010. Civil Society and EU democracy: 'astroturf' representation?, *Journal of European Public Policy*, 17(1), 100–16.

Klein, P.G. 2000. New Institutional Economics, in *Encyclopaedia of Law and Economics*, edited by B. Bouckaert and G. de Geest. Cheltenham: Edward Elgar, 456–89.

Micklitz, H.-W. 2009. Universal Services: Nucleus for a Social European Private Law, *EUI Working Paper Law* No. 2009/12.

Micklitz, H.-W. 2012. Do Consumers and Businesses need a new Architecture of Consumer Law? A Thought-Provoking Impulse. *EUI Working Papers Law* 2012/23.

Monaghan, E. 2012. Assessing Participation and Democracy in the EU: the Case of the European Citizens' Initiative. *Perspectives on European Politics and Society*, 13, 285–98.

OECD. 2008. Global Forum on Competition. The interface between competition and consumer policies, Background Note, DAF/COMP/GF(2008)4.

Ottow, A. 2012. Europeanization of the Supervision of Competitive Markets. European Public Law. 18(1), 191–221.

Polinsky, M. and Shavell, S. 2000. The economic theory of public enforcement of law, *Journal of Economic Literature*, 38(1) 45–77.

Ramsay, I. 1985. 'Framework for regulation of the consumer marketplace', *Journal of Consumer Policy*, 8, 353–72.

Sauron, J-L. 2011. The European Citizens' Initiative; not such a good idea? *Foundation Robert Schuman Policy Paper*, European Issue no. 192.

Scott, C. and Black, J. 2000. *Cranstons' Consumers and the Law*, London: Butterworths, 3rd Edition.

Stiglitz, J. 2002. Participation and Development: Perspectives from the Comprehensive Development Paradigm. *Review of Development Economics, Special Issue on Democracy, Participation and Development*, 6 (2), 163–82.

Stuyck, J., Terryn, E., Colaert, V., van Dyck, T., Peretz, N., Hoekx, N. and Tereszkiewicz, P. 2007. *An analysis and evaluation of alternative means of consumer redress other than redress through ordinary judicial proceedings*, Final report, Leuven. Available at http://ec.europa.eu/consumers/redress/reports_studies/comparative_report_en.pdf.

Szeligowska, D. and Mincheva, E. 2012. The European Citizens' Initiative – Empowering European Citizens within the Institutional Triangle: A Political and Legal Analysis. *Perspectives on European Politics and Society*, 13, 270–84.

Thoresen. 2002. W. Thoresen (ed), Developing Consumer Citizenship, *Conference report Hamar 20–23 April 2002*. Available at http://fulltekst.bibsys.no/hihm/oppdragsrapport/2002/04/opprapp04_2002.pdf.

Trzaskowski, R. 2010. The European Citizens' Initiative: a victory for democracy of a marketing trick? *European View*, 9, 263–6.

Van den Bergh, R. 2007. Should consumer protection law be publicly enforced? in *Collective Consumer Interests and How They are Served Best in Europe; Legal aspects and policy issues on the border between private law and public policy*, edited by M. Loos and W. Van Boom. Amsterdam: Europa Law Publishing, pp. 179–203.

Van den Bergh, R.J. and Visscher, L. 2008. 'The preventive function of collective actions for damages in consumer law', *Erasmus Law Review*, 1(2), 5–30.

Verhoeven, M. 2010. The 'Constanzo Obligation' and the Principle of National Institutional Autonomy: Supervision as a Bridge to Close the Gap? *Review of European Administrative law*, 3(1), 23–64.

Chapter 7

The Politics of Inclusion: Comparing the Contribution of Civil Society Actors to EU Legitimacy

Petra Guasti*

Introduction

Political and scholarly debates abound as regards the nature and conditions of legitimacy of European governance.[1] Assuming that civil society 'is a space in which the citizens can be empowered and take on the role of political subjects, as well as a forum testing the legitimacy of political power as regards "the will of the people"' (Eriksen and Fossum 2012: xiii), the 'new politics of European civil society' have been explored from conceptual, normative and empirical perspectives.[2] This chapter contributes to unravelling the puzzle of how civil society relates to the legitimacy and contributes to the legitimation of the European Union (EU). To this end, it explores two questions:

1. What role does civil society assume regarding the impacts of European constitutionalization at the domestic level; is it an active or a passive player and are we witnessing the transnationalization of European civil society?
2. What are the conditions under which civil society can be expected to enhance the legitimacy of the emerging EU polity?

---

* The author would like to express thanks to Professor Ulrike Liebert for her long-term support, intellectually stimulating collaboration and encouragement to strive for academic excellence, to her ConstEPS colleagues Dr. Tatjana Evas, Dr. Alexander Gattig, Dr. Aleksandra Maatsch, Dr. Kathrin Packham and Ewelina Pawlak, M.A. for their collaboration and support, to Professor Beate Kohler-Koch and Professor Dagmar Schiek for their generous encouragement and help to see the light at the end of the tunnel and last but not least to Dr. Zdenka Mansfeldova for the numerous years of her kind support and wise advice.

1 E.g. Lord and Beetham 2001, Craig 2003, Erne 2008, Føllesdal 2004, Héritier 1999, Magnette 2003, Kohler-Koch, De Biévre and Maloney 2008, Kohler-Koch and Larat 2008, Kohler-Koch and Rittberger 2007, Kohler-Koch and Quittkat 2013, Paolini 2007, Smith 2002, Liebert 2011.

2 See the conceptual, normative theoretical and empirical contributions in Liebert and Trenz 2010.

In line with the focus of this book, this chapter concentrates on employer associations', trade unions and lobby organizations which form an important part of civil society most likely to be involved in legitimizing the EU economic and social model. The theoretical framework consists of a model of viable civic participation in the European political arena. It is utilized here in order to assess the participatory element of legitimizing EU economic and social policies. The chapter's objective is to gauge the role of trade unions and employer associations both at EU and national levels and the emerging transnationalization of civil society through increasing communication and cooperation amongst EU and national-level organizations.

The chapter is organized in three parts – theory, methodology and empirical analysis. The first part reviews the state of the art of the literature on EU legitimacy and civil society, and develops the theoretical model – a three-dimensional conception of legitimacy – and the analytical framework. The second part describes the operationalization of this framework and the research methodology. The third part presents findings from qualitative and quantitative empirical research. This is structured in five sections: sections one, two, three and four assess civil society practices of engaging with the TCE (Treaty establishing a Constitution for Europe)[3] in the light of four criteria on which the procedural legitimation of the EU rests (for more on procedural legitimation of the EU, see Lord 1998). These criteria are transparency, inclusion, balance of interests and representation; their requisite conditions include visibility in public spheres, vertical and horizontal cooperation networks as well as channels and resources for European political communication with citizens. The fifth section summarizes the empirical findings and the concluding part reviews the posed questions regarding the preconditions for civil society to overcome the current deficits and contribute to providing the emerging EU polity with a democratic legitimation process.[4]

EU Legitimacy and Civil Society: Theoretical Model and Analytical Framework

In EU research literature, the understanding of democratic legitimacy is rooted in different assumptions about the EU as an international organization vs. an emerging political entity.[5] On the one hand, intergovernmental approaches and

---

3   Treaty establishing a Constitution for Europe, signed by 25 EU member governments in December 2004 and after a long process adopted in an altered form as the Lisbon Treaty in December 2009.

4   In this chapter, distinction is drawn between legitimacy as a theoretical concept and one of the key preconditions for democratic order and legitimation, which refer to the process of gaining legitimacy. Legitimation takes place in the public sphere by participation of citizens.

5   In recent years, the literature on legitimacy, and on EU legitimacy in particular, has flourished (Beetham and Lord 1998, Bellamy 2001, Bellamy and Castiglione 1998,

conceptions of the EU as an international organization or regulatory regime hold that its authority derives from indirect sources of democratic legitimacy or that national governments are held accountable for EU-level decision-making. These approaches identify the European Council and the Council of Ministers as the pillars on which the EU's legitimation ultimately rests.[6] On the other hand, federalists conceptualize the EU as a polity evolving into the direction of a multinational supranational state where ever more political and administrative competencies once held by the nation states are being transferred to EU level. Thus, EU institutions need their own direct sources of democratic legitimacy.

According to the federalists, the fact that these standards are currently not met by EU decision-making has led to legitimacy deficits (Lord and Beetham 2001). As a result, federalist theorists are critical of the current construction of the EU polity and propose possible solutions such as increasing the competences of the European parliament, to directly elect the Commission President or participatory policy-networks. The latter, in particular, facilitate the incorporation of organized interests and of stake-holders (Héritier 1999). According to Banchoff and Smith, these 'new modes of governance' of the EU add to the traditional channels of vertical democratic accountability, but they do not replace them. Rather, they can strengthen output legitimacy in addition to indirect legitimacy 'borrowed' from the national level (1999: 15).

The Concept of EU Legitimacy

Legitimacy is a central category for analyzing why citizens have trust in the authority of institutions they believe to normatively deserve their obedience and, thus, also trust the future compliance of their fellow citizens.[7] Four basic meanings of the concept of legitimacy have been distinguished: legitimacy as legality, legitimacy as justifiability, legitimacy as compliance and legitimacy as

---

Duff 2003, Føllesdal 2004, Kohler-Koch and Rittberger 2007, Lord and Harris 2006, Meny 2003, Schmitter 2001a, 2001b, 2002, 2003 and 2007, Walker 2003).

6   Early functionalists, such as Haas, have conceptualized the European Community as an international organization, whose legitimacy was linked to two pillars: 1. open and prolific participation of voluntary interest groups in decision-making and 2. effective performance of functions perceived crucial by its units (Haas 1964: 195–6). This focus on participation has been revitalized by Schmitter's proposal to view the EU as a system of inclusion of aggregated interests and European governance arrangements as policy 'sites' where stake-holders and knowledge-holders would negotiate the definition of policies under the supervision of the EU institutions (Schmitter 2001b).

7   The current debates on trust and the relationship between trust and viability of democratic regimes is very vivid; for the sake of space we refer here to seminal pieces such as Rothstein and Uslaner 2005, Della Porta 2000, Fukuyama 1995, Sztompka 1999 and Gambetta 1998, and see trust as a necessary component for the legitimacy of the emerging European polity. As such, trust can only be achieved through transparency, inclusion, balance of interests and representation.

problem solving. Each of these depends on different mechanisms or institutional arrangements, for instance rule of law or democratic rule, participation or actual consent, policy-output and accountability procedures. These correspond to three basic types of legitimacy: 1. regime legitimacy or the extent to which justice is achieved within the polity's institutions vis-à-vis representation, the protection of individual and minority interests and so on, 2. polity legitimacy or the overall support for and the stability of the polity as a 'self-standing political community' and 3. performance (output) legitimacy or the capacity of a given polity to deliver public goods effectively and efficiently (Beetham and Lord 1998). In the political process, all three types may be interlinked; here, they are differentiated for analytical purposes only.

Moreover, Christopher Lord and Paul Magnette have identified four vectors of EU legitimation, understood as ideal and not real type processes: 1. *indirect* or derivative legitimation of the Union and its institutions depending on the legitimacy of the Union's component states, the Union's respect for sovereignty and on its ability to serve its purpose, 2. *parliamentary* legitimation where EU policies and institutions are legitimated by a combination of elected parliamentary bodies and the Member States, thus serving the purpose of a series of people and of a citizenry divided along the lines of cultural identity, 3. *technocratic* legitimation where EU institutions are legitimated by their ability to offer solutions to problems and 4. *procedural* legitimation which requires the observance of certain procedures, namely transparency, balance of interests, proportionality, legal certainty, consultation or inclusion of stake-holders (2004: 184–9). The present analysis focuses on the fourth type defined by procedural criteria, making legitimation dependent on four key criteria: transparency, inclusion, balance of interests and representation.

European Civil Society

Following the theoretical literature, the term civil society has evolved over many centuries, if not millennia,[8] going through multiple conceptual and connotative changes, which have been widely discussed[9] and which have eventually led to political dispute (Green 1997).[10] According to Cohen, modern civil society

---

8   Theoretical literature places the origins of the term 'civil society' – *societas civilis* – in antiquity (Arato and Cohen 1990: 84–6).

9   The concept is subject to avid academic discussions, e.g. between Christoph Bryant and Krishan Kumar in *The British Journal of Sociology* (Bryant 1993, Kumar 1993 and 1994, Neocleous 1995, also Alexander 1997, Habermas 2003, 2011, Keane 1988, Seligman 1992, Waltzer 1998).

10   The substance of the dispute is about the definition of the relationship between the state and civil society, which especially in post-communist countries is considered to be essentially inconsistent. Based on historical experience, civil society is regarded as the opposition to state power (Arato and Cohen 1990, Kumar 1993).

is formed and reproduced through varying forms of collective activities and institutionalized on the basis of law and subjective rules, which play an important role in stabilizing social differentiation (Cohen, in Arato and Cohen 1990: 37).

In this chapter, the term civil society delineates the area between the sphere of private interests and the state. It is an area of voluntary association outside the spheres of market, state and private lives in which people realize how interrelated their world is. From the theoretical and historical literature on civil society it can be concluded that the emergence of civil society is the result of democratic politics based on the direct participation of citizens aiming to influence public affairs. In order to be able to include trade unions and employer associations into our analysis, market is here understood as profit-generating arena with which both organized civil society and economic civil society (i.e. trade unions and employer associations) engage in multiple, often conflicting ways.

In current citizenship research, authors such as Waltzer (1998) and Meehan (2000) have acknowledged civil society as a useful frame for active (European or global) citizenship. Delanty and Rumford conceive of European civil society as predominantly rooted in national civil societies. In their view, national civil society serves as protection against economic globalization by establishing a basis for maintaining the integrity of the nation state (Delanty and Rumford 2005). Critical authors, such as Meehan, state that it is the supranational, rather than the domestic, arena that provides for a European citizenship. However, in her view European citizenship is currently struggling between market citizenship, which defines citizens predominantly as producers and consumers, and a liberal (or libertarian) notion of privatized citizenship (Meehan 2000).

According to Obradovic, the aim of European governance is to establish institutional opportunities for the participation of stake-holders in the decision-making process via civil dialogue. From her examination of the civil and social dialogue in European Governance, she concludes that economic dialogue prevails over civil and social dialogue.[11] Moreover, even though the Commission supports the involvement of civic groups in European governance[12] for increasing its efficiency, the boundaries between social and civil dialogue in Europe are blurred. As CSOs, unlike the social partners, are perceived as diffuse, unstable partners, their contribution is limited (Obradovic 2005, Obradovic and Vizcaino 2006).

Hence, in the context of European Governance the involvement of civil society is seen less as a reality and more as a normative project aimed at improving both governance (efficiency) and democracy (legitimacy), whereas the social

---

11 Although, as Obradovic points out, the idea of civic dialogue was launched to counterbalance the involvement of the sphere of production in European governance, the currently prevailing notion of civil dialogue is that it is complementary rather than contradictory to social dialogue (Obradovic 2005: 322).

12 There are numerous organizations (over 160) and around 1500 interest groups, involved in regular consultations with the Commission, but this is mainly in the phase of pre-drafting legislation (Obradovic 2005, see also Greenwood 2003).

partners (i.e. trade unions and employer associations) engaged in social dialogue are an important part of European governance. Here we intend to compare the participants of civic and social dialogues to assess both their existing and potential contribution to the democratic legitimacy in Europe.

Analytical Model

As a framework for analyzing the role of civil society for the democratic legitimation (i.e. the process of achieving democratic legitimacy) of the EU, an analytical model of viable civic participation in the EU's multilevel polity is proposed (Figure 1). Although national and European levels are differentiated, the figure suggests that processes as well as actors interact across both levels, as their operations often have implications for both national and European arenas. Here, processes are understood to include (a) relations of representation, (b) networks of communication, interaction and cooperation among CSOs and (c) access to public opinion and political will formation, through mass-mediated public spheres or through inclusion in institutional decision-making. As for the actors, Figure 7.1 distinguishes between citizens on the one hand and EU-level institutions on the other hand, with civil society as intermediary organizations that encompass both economic actors such as employer associations and trade unions, as well as civil society actors at the national level and EU-level CSOs, the so-called 'umbrella organizations' (e.g. European Trade Union Confederation, ETUC).

Data and Methodology

The analytical framework developed above rests on two key concepts; democratic legitimacy and civil society. For the purpose of the present empirical analysis, civil society is operationalized in terms of organized as well as individual forms of civic and political participation; that is, it comprises CSOs and civic forms of individual political participation.[13] Legitimacy is operationalized as a process of legitimation in which civil society and citizens have the theoretical potential to play an integral role. The degree to which civil society engages with the governance structure, the degree of its inclusion, is thus related to the degree of legitimacy. A combination of two different data sets from the ConstEPS research project[14] will be used for

---

13   The basic definition of civil society organization is that of an institutionalized form of civil society. The type of organizations included in this definition varies between countries, but in this research it includes various interest and advocacy groups with an institutionalized structure.

14   The ConstEPS research project 'Citizenship and Constitutionalization: Transforming the Public Sphere in East-West European Integration' was based at the Jean Monnet Centre for European Studies of the University of Bremen, directed by Professor Ulrike Liebert and funded by the Volkswagen Foundation (2005–2008).

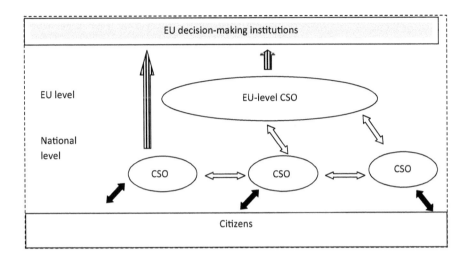

Figure 7.1   Model of viable civic participation in the EU's multilevel polity

Note: CSO = civil society organizations, (a) black arrows between citizens and CSOs = representation, (b) white arrows between CSOs on national level and between CSOs on national and EU level = cooperation networks and access to national public spheres, (c) black and white arrows between CSOs on national and EU level and EU decision-making institutions = inclusion in EU decision-making.

Source: author.

developing theoretically structured and empirically grounded arguments regarding the potentials of civil society for enhancing the democratic legitimation of the European polity. These data sets include (1) the ConstEPS media data set (2004–2005) and (2) the ConstEPS civil society data set (2007).

1. The ConstEPS media data set covers the TCE ratification period during October 2004 to October 2005 across six EU Member States. The data set has been constructed from 8540 articles selected from 36 printed media. From these, a sample of 185 articles was drawn for a qualitative analysis of European political discourses in the Czech Republic, Estonia and Poland (as new Member States) and France, Germany and the UK (as old Member States). The selection of a representative sample of print media articles for qualitative political discourse analysis was based on the following criteria: (1) the overall coverage by month, (2) the share of the periodicals over time and (3) the coverage of key events in the ratification debate.
2. The ConstEPS CSO data set was constructed from interviews that ConstEPS team members and collaborators conducted with national CSOs in the six ConstEPS countries between February and June 2007. In each

country, approximately 24 semi-structured interviews were held with non-governmental organizations (NGOs), political parties and economic organizations. In addition to comprising CSOs present in the ConstEPS media sample, the sampling included national-level organizations with links to EU-level umbrella organizations and/or represented in the European Social and Economic Council (top-down principle), as well as organizations influential in TCE politics at the national level (bottom-up principle). The data set used in the present analysis includes 95 interviews with both European and national-level CSOs (NGOs and economic CSOs such as trade unions and employer associations) from both new and old Member States (Czech Republic, Estonia, France, Germany, Poland and the UK). The analysis was based on both qualitative and quantitative methods, including statistical and network analysis.

Empirical Findings

The presentation of empirical findings is structured in five parts: First, the ConstEPS media data set is analyzed for establishing whether and to what extent, in the TCE ratification process, CSOs have gained access to the print media for providing information on CSOs' positions to the general public. Second, based on the ConstEPS CSO interview data set, the linkages among actors and institutions are scrutinized. Here, a network analysis is conducted for identifying the patterns of CSOs' linkages to EU institutions and political parties on the one hand and to citizens and other CSOs on the other. During the course of the analysis, particular attention will be paid to economic CSOs. Based on the existing literature as well as legal differentiation in the civil and social dialogues, we expect economic CSOs such as trade unions and employer associations to be more visible as well as more active.

CSO Visibility in the Mass Media

By shedding light on the EU's politics of treaty reform, public debates are a mechanism and precondition for engendering EU transparency vis-à-vis the general public. Empirically, the visibility of CSOs in the public sphere has been measured by an analysis of print media coverage of TCE ratification, based on comparative political discourse analysis, assessing the relative visibility of CSOs' positions (vis-à-vis those of state and EU actors) on key issues of EU polity building (established by the TCE).

The comparative print media-based European political discourse analysis helps identify similarities and differences in the patterns of how organized civil society has gained access to national public spheres and, thus, has rendered visible EU treaty reform in general and its own position in particular.

From the comparative analysis of CSO visibility in the British, Czech, Estonian, French, German, Latvian, and Polish TCE debates, three clusters of cases emerge, each defined by a differing level of active involvement on the part of organized civil society:

The first cluster includes countries with highly involved CSOs – in our case, only France falls into this category so far. In France, the dominant organized CSOs were lobby groups, when measuring primarily the extent of their visibility. However, if both the visibility and number of articles in which CSOs were mentioned are taken into the consideration, then trade unions appear to be important as well.[15] Present in French debates were also advocacy groups and social movements, such as ATTAC, and critics of globalization, as well as various NGOs.

The second cluster – the most highly populated one – includes countries with medium visibility of organized civil society. Here, in terms of numbers of occurrences, Polish and UK-based CSOs lead this second group, followed by Germans and Estonians. However, if we also take into account the number of articles referring to CSOs, German and Czech ones appear to dominate the group (see Table 7.2 below). In Germany, the most visible types of organized civil society were think-tanks, followed by 'general CSO' and social movements. In Germany and the UK, the visibility of organized civil society can be mainly attributed to think-tanks, followed by employer associations and social movements. While the think-tanks were also the most visible category in Estonia, the second largest category here were transnational NGOs such as the Estonia Open Foundation. Trade unions only appeared once in our data for Estonia. The lack of visibility of trade unions is also an interesting finding from the Polish case. Here, the church clearly dominated other civil society organizations in the ratification debate (Table 7.1).

The third cluster of CSOs who gained access to and became visible in national ratification debates is constituted by those from the Czech Republic, with a rather limited involvement of organized civil society actors in the debate, with the exception of think-tanks. The analysis of the Czech media sample helped identify domestic think-tanks, such as the Institute for International Relations (UMV), the Association for International Issues (AMO) and the Centre for Economy and Politics (CEP). Their members contributed to the media both actively (writing articles) and passively (being cited by the media). In terms of foreign think-tanks, the Heritage Foundation – a conservative US think-tank – was also visible (Rakušanová 2006).

---

15   In the course of the analysis, the number of times the particular type of organized civil society appeared in the media, as well as the number of articles in which the organized civil society was mentioned, was measured. The number of articles was used to provide a certain corrective of the differences in terms of style.

Table 7.1   CSO visibility in national media debates on EU treaty ratification, by Member States

Category of Organization	Czech Republic	Estonia	France	Germany	Poland	United Kingdom
Trade unions		1 (1)	7 (5)			
Lobby			14 (2)			
Employer associations	2 (2)		1 (1)	1 (1)		1 (1)
Civil society (general)		5 (1)	1 (1)	4 (1)		
Foundations					1 (1)	
Churches					13 (2)	
Charities						
Advocacy groups			3 (3)			
Social movements			2 (2)	2 (1)		1 (1)
Think-tanks	5 (4)	7 (2)		6 (6)		11 (2)
Professional associations						
Other NGOs			1 (1)			
Total	**7 (6)**	**13 (4)**	**29 (15)**	**13 (9)**	**14 (3)**	**14 (4)**

Note: Numbers refer to total amount of occurrences of CSO category, numbers in parentheses to number of print articles with at least one occurrence of CSO category. The CSOs highlighted in grey are part of economic civil society.

Source: ConstEPS media data set (Oct 2004–Oct 2005).

Comparing East and West, the overall visibility of organized civil society in national ratification debate was lower in the new Member States (NMS) than in the old ones (OMS), both in terms of the number of times CSOs were mentioned in the media and the number of articles that made references to organized civil society (Table 7.2). The dominant type of CSO in one of the new Member States – Poland – was the (Catholic) Church while think-tanks were more visible than other types of CSOs in both Estonia and the Czech Republic. To a much lesser degree, trade unions and employer associations gained visibility in the media as participants in the ratification debates in the NMS.

National think-tanks were the most visible type of organized civil society in the ratification debate, not only in NMS but also EU-wide, both in terms of the number of times they appeared in the media and the number of articles that included a reference to them. The second most visible category was lobby groups. In the OMS, the social partners – both trade unions and employers associations – were also more present in the ratification debates than their counterparts in the NMS (see Table 7.2).

Table 7.2   CSO visibility in media ratification debates, by old and new Member States

Category of CSO	NMS (No. of articles)	OMS (No. of articles)
Interest organizations	0	0
Trade unions	1 (1)	7 (5)
Lobby		14 (2)
Employer associations	2 (2)	3 (3)
Civil society (general)	5 (1)	5 (2)
Foundations	1 (1)	0
Churches	13 (2)	0
Charities	0	0
Community groups	0	0
Advocacy groups	0	3 (3)
Social movements	0	5 (4)
Watchdog organizations	0	0
Think-tanks	12 (6)	17 (8)
Umbrella organizations	0	0
Professional associations	0	0
Other NGOs	0	1 (1)
Total (articles mentioned)	**34 (13)**	**56 (28)**
Total (articles analyzed)	**88**	**97**

Note: Numbers refer to total amount of occurrences of CSO category, numbers in parentheses to number of print articles with at least one occurrence of CSO category. The CSOs highlighted in grey are part of economic civil society.

Source: ConstEPS data set (Oct 2004–Oct 2005).

There are different ways of interpreting the low level of visibility of CSO in the mass media. The above findings might support Delanty and Rumford's (2005) argument that European civil society remains predominantly rooted in national civil societies which serves as a protection against economic globalization rather than a catalyst of Europeanization. Furthermore, the observed difference between the visibility of economic civil society in OMS and NMS (which accounts for most of the difference between the two groups) can be explained by the inability of economic civil society, in particular of the trade unions in the NMS, to gain ground they lost in the process of societal transformation. In line with Delanty and Rumford's argument and findings of authors such as Pleines (2006), trade unions in NMS have not yet seen or realized the full potential offered to them by an active involvement in European governance (although they take part in ETUC and so on).

However, the limited access of civil society as a whole to European political discourses in national public spheres might also be a result of other factors. On the one hand, the prevalence of top-down Europeanization processes might reduce national civil society to a rather limited role (Della Porta and Caiani 2006). In line with this argument, Maurer *et al.* (2005: 4–22) have implied that the role of civil society organizations in the European constitutional process was not to inform citizens about their positions vis-à-vis the TCE, but rather to mobilize them for participating in referenda, as well as to establish supportive channels of communication, participation and influence for state and EU institutions. If this was the case, our data shows that printed media was not the channel that civil society used for mobilization.

On the other hand, assuming that the establishment of European civil society proceeds along functional lines, ad-hoc coalitions for key issues of shared concern would emerge from transnational networks and umbrella organizations aimed at bridging pre-existing national civil societies. Such expectations would be consonant with research findings from the project 'Organized Civil Society and the European Governance' (CIVGOV), as building advocacy coalitions for environmental or antiracist concerns appears a valuable and effective civil society strategy vis-à-vis the EU (Ruzza 2005, 2006). This strategic orientation would explain the relatively limited attempts of national NGOs to get access to general public spheres or to become visible in national print media: national CSOs might simply use the more effective, informal channels of communication about EU issues of shared concern, via face-to-face communication, telephone or internet.

After having explored CSO public visibility as a mechanism for enhancing transparency – defined above as the first criterion for procedural legitimation – the next section turns to the second defining precondition for EU procedural legitimation: CSO inclusion through cooperation networks that engage with EU treaty reform politics.

CSO Inclusion in Vertical and Horizontal Cooperation Networks[16]

Having selected *inclusion* and *balance of interests* as two additional defining criteria on which legitimation through democratic procedures rests (see above), this section presents findings from vertical and horizontal network analysis. CSOs may develop vertical networks with EU institutions and actors and horizontal networks among themselves. The question is whether and how these networks

---

16   I would like to thank Ewelina Pawlak for her help with creating the network analysis matrixes and graphs. On NGO networks in multi-level governance, compare Pleines 2008.

balance a) the interests of economic organizations (trade unions and employer organizations) and b) the interests of CSO from OMS and NMS.

The empirical network analysis shows that the vertical and horizontal networks vary considerably in NMS. In the Czech Republic, trade unions tend to maintain relationships with their EU-level counterparts and other organizations, while employer organizations are equipped with numerous linkages connecting them to both their European counterparts and to EU-level political actors. Czech employers tend to have stronger political links than Czech NGOs and think-tanks. Polish economic organizations are less well connected than Czech trade unions and employer organizations and exhibit fewer links to EU-level political actors. In Estonia, as in the Czech Republic, economic CSOs have stronger links at the EU level than other organization types. Comparing the density of vertical networks of the Czech Republic, Estonia and Poland, respectively, stronger links between national and EU-level organizations can be found in Poland and in the Czech Republic than in Estonia. Also, Estonian organizations show a stronger tendency toward bilateral, rather than multilateral, networks.

Turning the focus now on the OMS, the findings are also diverse. Germany exhibits a similar pattern to that observed in the Czech Republic; nevertheless, the German economic CSOs do not seem to entertain stronger networks than their NGO counterparts. In the UK, in contrast with the other OMS under study, economic CSOs, trade unions and employers have established comparatively rather strong multilateral networks of cooperation. Significantly, British economic CSOs seem to be less in touch with political party groupings in the European Parliament than their counterparts in other Member States.

Similarly to the case of the UK, the network analysis of French and German economic CSOs shows that both have developed multilateral domestic as well as transnational networks. In general, in OMS, we find a larger differentiation of such networks. In France, for instance, economic CSOs concentrate on the relationship with European political parties and transnational civil society and economic actors. In Germany, economic civil society actors tend to prefer institutional partners. German economic CSOs developed the strongest links to EU-level institutions – both the European Commission and the European Parliament. While German civil society actors prefer domestic institutions, such as the German Government and the Parliament, British economic CSOs have strong transnational civil society links and links to transnational economic actors.

Empirically, CSOs' inclusion has been measured by vertical interactions with EU institutions relative to national institutions and organizations. The findings from the network analysis of CSO can be summarized as follows: (1) economic organizations are generally better connected to the EU than NGOs, (2) both employer organizations and trade unions are often also part of multilateral transnational networks and (3) moreover, economic organizations often have horizontal links to European political parties.

Given the rich evidence, it seems reasonable to conclude that CSOs are by no means excluded from EU decision-making institutions and organizations.

Inclusion as the second condition for EU legitimacy is present, at least partially. Across all Member States, organized civil society actors did develop bilateral as well as multilateral links to EU-level organizations and party groupings in the European Parliament. Yet network analysis exhibits a complex and highly asymmetric pattern of inclusion, to the advantage of economic organizations. Furthermore, CSOs from the NMS seem to lag behind in establishing multilateral networks.

The question is whether and how CSOs – whether more or less included in vertical or horizontal networks of cooperation – make selective use of the channels of European political communication – conceived here as a condition for reaching out to and mobilizing mass publics for engaging in EU constitutional politics.

CSO in European Political Communication

Turning to the third step of the empirical analysis, evidence is presented regarding the multiple channels of European political communication that CSOs have used for engaging with the drafting and ratification of the TCE. The analysis is based on respondents' evaluation of the effectiveness of alternative modes of communication in EU constitutional politics. Generally speaking, it can be said that the ConstEPS data shows that CSOs have not only gained access to the mass media but have used a variety of other channels of European political communication, as well; from the internet over informal campaigns to social partnership dialogue and EU political consultations, both at the national and European levels.

Economic CSOs favoured social dialogue, political consultations at the national and European levels and activities directed against (Euro-sceptical) political parties. In Estonia, civil society actors utilized institutional debates (Convention), political consultations and transnational communication, including participation in the European Economic and Social Committee. In Poland, more pro-active forms of communication were used by civil society, such as internet-based communication, petitions, conferences at the European level and the media. As for the OMS, UK-based organizations also ranked the mass media and media-related campaigns highest in their domestic engagement with EU treaty ratification. German actors were more oriented towards political communication within EU institutions, such as the Convention or the European Economic and Social Committee on the one hand and towards developing transnational links on the other.

The empirical findings show that due to the high level of politicization of mass media debates dominated by political parties (e.g. in France and the Czech Republic), civil society organizations engage with channels of access and communication other than the printed mass media, including internet campaigns, informal campaigns, social partnership dialogue or political consultations at the national and European levels. Thus, rather than limiting themselves to the intermediary communicative role of the print media, CSOs also used more informal but direct communication channels towards both decision makers and citizens. Furthermore, the data confirms the fact that CSOs preferred activities aimed directly at national and European institutions, rather than communicating to the public via media.

To sum up, for engaging with EU constitutional reforms, CSOs use multiple channels of European political communication that combine intermediaries such as the print media with forms of direct communication with both decision makers and citizens.

CSOs as Agents of Citizen Representation vis-à-vis EU Institutions

The fourth condition for EU procedural legitimation examined here is *representation*. As the data demonstrates, civil society organizations utilize various channels of communication with citizens and the public at large. They engage in a range of activities directed at citizens, not only through national and EU institutions. The aim is to comparatively explore whether CSOs prefer to communicate with the public via the mass media or through alternative communication channels, and how CSOs from the OMS and NMS compare to each other.

As Figure 7.2 shows, two different patterns can be detected: In countries like Estonia, Germany, Poland, the UK and at the EU level, economic organizations were more often involved in citizen-related communication than NGOs. By comparison, in the Czech Republic and in France, NGOs were more engaged in this respect. CSO engagement with citizens also varies as regards its intensity: While in Estonia and at the EU level on average over 80 per cent of CSOs claim to be involved in citizen-related activities, in the UK and the Czech Republic the number is just over 40 per cent and in Germany and Poland little more than 30 per cent.

CSO engagement with citizens took two main forms, direct and indirect ones (through umbrella organizations and transnational structures). When passive CSOs were asked for the reasons for their non-involvement in this field, answers can be classified in the following four categories: (1) lack of interest or it was not part of the organization's priorities, for instance producer organizations, employer organizations and some advocacy groups, (2) opposition to such activities, for instance by some Euro-sceptical groups, (3) lack of invitation to participate, for instance on the part of some Euro-critical and Euro-sceptical[17] groups and trade unions and 4) missing domestic debate or discontinuation of domestic debate after the ratification failure (some economic organizations).

As for the national vs. European institutions being addressed, there is no clear pattern accruing among the countries under study. Economic CSOs were very active at the EU level, in the UK, in Poland and in Germany, less active in France and in the Czech Republic, and passive in Estonia. Similarly, as regards activities of

---

17   The difference is made between Euro-critical organizations, which are vocal critics of specific aspects of the emerging European polity, and Euro-sceptical groups, which are critics of the enlargement process as such.

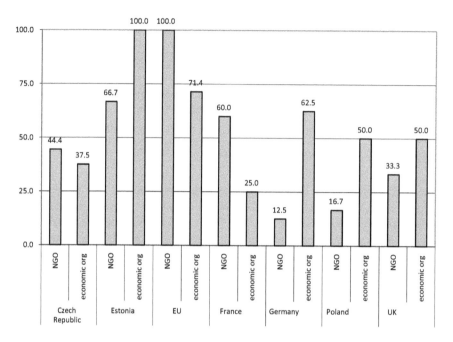

Figure 7.2   Involvement in activities engaging the public, civil society and citizens

Source: ConstEPS Interviews (N=76).

NGOs in this area, no clear pattern has emerged. The EU-level CSOs addressed all institutions, with the exception of political parties. Polish, as well as British, and to a lesser extent also German CSOs talked to national governments and parliaments. French and Czech CSOs were much less active, but they communicated with the Constitutional Convention, national governments, the national and the European Parliaments and the Commission. Moreover, economic interest organizations stated that they addressed the Constitutional Convention to a much smaller degree than NGOs.

The data presented here supports the claim that civil society organizations combine media communication with direct channels of communication to both citizens and to national and European-level institutions. Yet the communication towards institutions seems to be relatively stronger than that towards citizens.

Summary of Findings

The empirical results presented here confirm the relatively low visibility of organized civil society during the constitutional reform process as it was reflected by the mass media. This supports the findings of Della Porta and Caiani (2006) regarding the

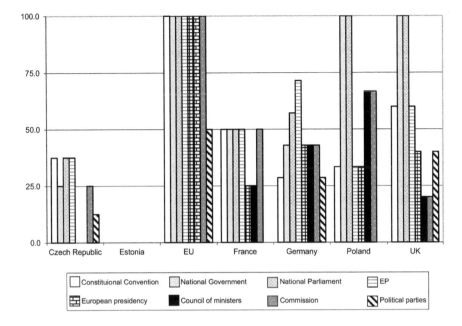

Figure 7.3   Institutions addressed by economic organizations regarding TCE

Source: ConstEPS Interview (N=68).

marginalization of civil society in processes of top-down Europeanization. Albeit to a lesser degree, they also support the argument developed by Maurer *et al.* (2005) introduced above.

The cross-national comparative analysis of organized civil society shows that national CSOs tend to have both bilateral and multilateral links to EU-level organizations and party groupings in the European Parliament. Here, economic CSOs are generally better connected than other types of CSO such as NGOs. Both employer organizations and trade unions are often part of multilateral transnational networks; economic CSOs also more actively developed horizontal links to European political parties.

The analysis has also shown that civil society organizations use multiple channels of communication, combining the intermediary role of printed media with more direct channels of communication, directed towards both decision makers and citizens. In this respect, lobby groups are the most effective economic CSOs in both communications with media and with decision makers.

Looking at the fourth vector of legitimation outlined in the theoretical part above, large differences could be detected between the civil society and economic actors with respect to the four procedural conditions (or criteria), 'transparency', 'inclusion', 'balance of interests' and 'representation'. Out of the 94 CSOs under study, no less than 27 are represented in the European Economic and Social Committee, among which the overwhelming majority are economic actors. Those CSOs that were included tended to exhibit positive positions on European integration and the TCE. On the other hand, Euro-sceptical groups tended to be excluded from the same vertical networks.

The correlation analysis of the four conditions for EU procedural legitimation (transparency, inclusion, balanced interests and representation) and CSO attitudes on the EU and the TCE shows that both are correlated among economic CSO actors (Guasti 2009). Furthermore, a negative correlation exists between the networks of economic CSO and their position on the Constitution. This means then that pro-European and Euro-sceptical groups tend to avoid interaction with each other.

Conclusions

The aim of this chapter was to explore the potential of civil society to contribute to the legitimation of the emerging European polity, and to compare between actors engaged in civic and social dialogue (i.e. between civil society such as NGOs and advocacy groups on the one hand, and social partners such as trade unions and employer associations, including lobby organizations on the other). Developing a four-step empirical analysis, the chapter has adopted four criteria on which procedural legitimation through civil society depends – transparency, inclusion, balance of interests and representation.

The findings from our research further confirmed the arguments reported by the Civil Society Contact Group (Fazi and Smith 2006), namely that the main aim of CSOs at the EU level appeared to be networking and lobbying. The academic as well as the official discourse on civil society's role in the establishment of the new European democratic order is incoherent and fluid both in institutional and temporal terms; i.e. there is no unitary discourse on civil society, but rather multiple discourses by different institutions and at different time periods. By contrast, the self-description by civil society on the European level is clearly utilitarian; pointing to its goal to reach the level of impact and efficiency that the partners of the social dialogue already have. Therefore, we find an inconsistency between the official roles attributed to organized civil society by EU institutions and EU elites and their practical expectations.

Concerning the conditions for civil society to contribute to the legitimation of European constitutionalization, empirical evidence is mixed, pointing to half-filled as well as partially empty glasses. Regarding the deficits, the main findings about civil society engagement with EU constitutional politics can be summarized in three arguments concerning key impediments to EU legitimation:

Firstly, the condition of *transparency* is weakened, on the one hand, by top-down processes of Europeanization that constrain the access of bottom-up civil society to national public spheres. On the other hand, it is also undermined by a lack of norms or procedures for checking the democratic credentials of actors who do have access to or even control means of mass communication with biased discourses about the EU.

Secondly, the condition of *balanced inclusion* is undermined by differential access to EU decision-making processes, where economic CSOs tend to have more advantages as compared to other types of CSO (such as think-tanks etc.). It is also undermined due to qualitative differentiation in the status and nature of civil and social dialogue regarding the formal inclusion of civil society in the TCE and in EU governance (Erne 2008, Fazi and Smith 2006, Kohler-Koch, De Biévre and Maloney 2008, Kohler-Koch and Larat 2008, Kohler-Koch and Quittkat 2013, Obradovic 2005).

Thirdly, the condition of *representation* through CSOs is weakened by the relative marginalization of citizens in civil society's vertical communication and cooperation networks, compared to the centrality of EU decision-making institutions in vertical interactions.

These impediments arguably originate in the process of top-down Europeanization. This faces CSOs with a dilemma: Given their limited resources, the organizations under study choose to concentrate predominantly on EU or national-level institutions and parliamentary party groups, rather than citizens. For maximizing their influence on European constitutionalization, they unwillingly contribute to widening the gap between civil society and citizens. While close contact to the citizens is one of the goals the emerging European civil society sets for itself, it is in contradiction to the role expectations European institutions attribute to civil society. It is paradoxical that by contrast, the so-called 'Euro-sceptic' organizations remain closer in touch with the citizens, while their access to European-level institutions remains limited. However, the impact of these groups on public opinion does not remain limited. As Liebert points out, the European civil society is caught in its dual nature as loyal (and dependent) partner of the EU institutions and its original role of challenging and contentious agent in the process of EU polity formation (2011: 119).

To summarize, civil society is found to be an active player in the politics of EU constitutional treaty reform; however, an actor with generally speaking limited access and impact. Another effect of the constitutionalization process is the emerging transnationalization of civil society – growing communication and cooperation among CSOs across national boundaries. Horizontal interaction takes place along ideological lines and the interaction among pro-European and Euro-critical organizations remains virtually non-existent. Key factors in the emerging transnationalization is the access to decision-making processes as well as the intention to maximize policy impact by joining efforts. Nonetheless, in terms of transnationalization, we still witness struggles to overcome the East-West divide. CSOs from the old and the new Member States are still in the process of learning to communicate with each other, to define a shared ground as well as a common agenda. This has been highlighted by the contentions about the TCE, especially the failure of the French referendum that put the spotlight on the political conflict about European integration and the politicization of national public spheres.

The chapter thus concludes that trade unions and employer associations both at EU and national levels are active players in EU policy development, although their impact and access are overall limited. A side effect of this is the emerging transnationalization of socio-economic civil society through increasing communication and cooperation among EU and national-level organizations.

In this current constellation, civil society does not offer a panacea for resolving the democratic legitimation deficit of the European Union. Democracy in the enlarged EU remains severely handicapped by a lack of strong commitment to change the current practices of citizens' and civil society's involvement in European governance. It is constrained by a lack of political will to implement deep changes of the existing structures, namely channels of communications and patterns of conduct. To answer the second question posed in the introduction – these are some of the conditions required by the emerging transnational European civil society to contribute to enhancing the democratic order of the European polity.

Bibliography

Alexander, J. 1997. The paradoxes of civil society. *International Sociology*, 12(2), 115–33.
Arato, A. and Cohen, J.L. 1990. *Civil Society and Political Theory*. Cambridge and London: MIT.
Banchoff, T. and Smith, P.M. (eds) 1999. *Legitimacy and the European Union: The Contested Polity*. London: Routledge.
Beetham, D. and Lord, C. 1998. *Legitimacy and the European Union*. London/ New York: Longman.
Bellamy, R. 2001. The 'Right to Have Rights': Citizenship Practice and the Political Constitution of the EU, in *Citizenship and Governance in the European Union*, edited by R. Bellamy and A. Warleigh. London: Continuum, pp. 41–70.
Bellamy, R. and Castiglione, D. 1998. Between Cosmopolis and Community: Three Models of Rights and Democracy within the European Union in *Reimagining Political Community*, edited by D. Archibugi, D. Held and M. Kolher, Oxford: Polity Press, pp. 152–78.
Bellamy, R. and Warleigh, A. (eds) 2001. *Citizenship and Governance in the European Union*. London: Continuum.
Bryant, C.G.A. 1993. Social self-organisation, civility and sociology: a comment on Kumar's 'Civil Society'. *The British Journal of Sociology*, 44(3), 397–401.
Craig, P. 2003. *What Constitution Does Europe need: the House that Giscard Built: Constitutional Room with a View*. London: The Federal Trust.
Delanty, G. and Rumford, C. 2005. Rethinking European Society. The Global Civil Society Context, in *Rethinking Europe. Social Theory and the Implications of Europeanization*, edited by G. Delanty and C. Rumford. London and New York: Routledge, 168–83.

Della Porta, D. 2000. Social Capital, Belief in Government and Political Corruption in *Disaffected Democracies: What's Troubling the Trilateral Countries?* edited by S.J. Pharr and R.D. Putnam. Princeton: Princeton University Press, 202–29.

Della Porta, D. and Caiani, M. 2006. The Europeanization of public discourse in Italy: a top-down process. *European Union Politics*, 7(1), 77–112.

Duff, A. 2003. *A Liberal Reaction to the European Convention and the Intergovernmental Conference*, London: Federal Trust.

Eriksen, E.O. 2005. An Emerging European Public Sphere. *European Journal of Social Theory*, 8(3), 341–63.

Eriksen, E.O. and Fossum, J.E. 2004. Europe in search of its legitimacy: the strategies of legitimation assessed. *International Political Science Review*, 25(4), 435–59.

Eriksen, E.O. and Fossum, J.E. 2012. *Rethinking Democracy and the European Union*. London: Routledge.

Erne, R. 2008. *European Unions: Labors' Quest for Transnational Democracy.* Ithaca: Cornell University Press.

Fazi, E. and Smith, J. 2006. *Civil Dialogue: Making it work better.* Brussels: CSCG.

Føllesdal, A. 2004. The seven Habits of highly legitimate new Models of Governance. *NEWGOV Paper.* Available at: http://www.follesdal.net/ms/Follesdal-2005-Leg-nmg-NEWGOV.pdf [accessed: 18.10.2010].

Fukuyama, F. 1995. *Trust. The Social Virtues and the Creation of Prosperity.* New York: Free Press.

Gambetta, D. (ed) 1998. *Trust: Making and Breaking Cooperative Relations.* Oxford: Basil Blackwell.

Green, A.T. 1997. Občanská společnost, ideje a utváření politiky. *Sociologický časopis,* 33(3), 309–20.

Greenwood, J. 2003. *Interest Representation in the European Union.* Houndmills: Palgrave Macmillan.

Guasti, P. 2009. *European Civil Society and the Legitimacy of the European Polity.* Paper in the 21. IPSA World Congress: Panel 'Civil Society and the Public Sphere in the Reconstruction of Democracy in Europe', (Santiago de Chile, Chile).

Haas, E.B. 1964. *Beyond the Nation State. Functionalism and International Organizations.* Stanford: Stanford University Press.

Habermas, J. 2003. *The Future of Human Nature.* Oxford: Polity Press.

Habermas, J. 2011. *Zur Verfassung Europas. Ein Essay.* Frankfurt: Suhrkamp.

Héretier, A. 1999. Elements of democratic legitimation in Europe: an alternative perspective. *Journal of European Public Policy*, 6(2), 269–82.

Howard, M.M. 2003. *The Weakness of Civil Society in Post-Communist Europe.* Cambridge: Cambridge University Press.

Keane, J. 1988. *Democracy and Civil Society.* London: Verso.

Kohler-Koch, B. and Buth, V. 2013. The balancing act of European civil society.

Between professionalism and grass roots, in *De-Mystification of Participatory Democracy. EU –Governance and Civil Society* edited by B. Kohler-Koch and C. Quittkat. Oxford: Oxford University Press, 195–224.

Kohler-Koch, B., De Biévre, D. and Maloney, W. 2008. *Opening EU Governance to Civil Society – Gains and Challenges*, CONNEX Report Series, Vol. 5. Mannheim: MZES.

Kohler-Koch, B. and Larat, F. 2008. *Efficient and Democratic Governance in the European Union*. CONNEX Report Series Vol. 9. Mannheim: MZES.

Kohler-Koch, B. and Quittkat, C. 2013. *De-Mystification of Participatory Democracy. EU – Governance and Civil Society*. Oxford: Oxford University Press.

Kohler-Koch, B. and Rittberger, B. 2007. *Debating the Democratic Legitimacy of the European Union*. Lanham: Rowman & Littlefield Publishers.

Kopecky, P. and Mudde, C. 2002. Two sides of Euroscepticism: party positions on European integration in East Central Europe. *European Union Politics*, 3(3), 297–326.

Kumar, K. 1993. Civil society: an inquiry into the usefulness of an historical term. *The British Journal of Sociology*, 44(3), 375–95.

Kumar, K. 1994. Civil society again: a reply to Christopher Bryant's 'Social self-organisation, civility and sociology'. *The British Journal of Sociology*, 45(1), 127–31.

Liebert, U. 2006. Structuring political Conflict about Europe: Media, Parliaments and constitutional Treaty Ratification. *ConstEPS internal Material No. IV. Outline for country case studies*. Bremen: CEuS.

Liebert, U. 2011. Exit, voice or loyalty: The new politics of European civil society. in *The new politics of European Civil Society*, edited by U. Liebert and H.J. Trenz. London: Routledge.

Liebert, U. and Trenz, H.-J. 2010. *The New Politics of European Civil Society*. London and New York: Routledge.

Lord, C. 1998. *Democracy in the European Union*. Sheffield: Sheffield Academic Press.

Lord, C. and Beetham, D. 2001. Legitimizing the EU: Is there a 'Post-parliamentary Basis' for its Legitimation?. *Journal of Common Market Studies*, 39(3), 443–62.

Lord, C. and Harris, E. 2006. *Democracy in the New Europe*. London: Palgrave Macmillan.

Lord, C. and Magnette, P. 2004. E Pluribus Unum? Creative Disagreement about Legitimacy in the EU. *Journal of Common Market Studies*, 42(1), 183–202.

Maatsch, S. and Gattig A. 2008. Technical coding guidelines for comparative print media/text analysis using ATLAS.ti computer software. *RECON Working Paper*, Jean Monnet Centre for European Studies, University of Bremen; available at http://www.monnet-centre.uni- bremen.de/pdf/wp/MaatschGattig_RECONWP5_ManualATLAS.ti_2008.pdf.

Magnette, P. 2003. Will the EU be More Legitimate after the Convention? in *The Convention on the Future of Europe Working Towards and EU Constitution*, edited by J. Shaw, P. Magnette, L. Hoffman and A. Verges Bausili. London: The Federal Trust.

Maurer, A. *et al.* 2005. Ratifikationsverfahren zum EU-Verfassungsvertrag. *Diskussionspapier der FG 1*, 2005/5 Berlin.

Meehan, E. 2000. Europeanization and citizenship of European Union. *Yearbook of European Studies*, 14(1), 157–77.

Meny, Y. 2003. 'Della Demokratie en Europe: Old Concepts and New Challenges'. *Journal of Common Market Studies*, 41(1), 1–13.

Neocleous, M. 1995. From civil society to the social. *The British Journal of Sociology*, 46(3), 395–408.

Obradovic, D. 2005. Civil society and the social dialogue in European governance. *Yearbook on European Law*, 24(1), 261–328.

Obradovic, D. and Alonso Vizcaino, J.M. 2006. Good governance requirements for the participation of interest groups in EU consultation, in *Participation of Civil Society in New Modes of Governance. The Case of the New EU Member States. Part 3: Involvement at the EU Level, Arbeitspapiere und Materialien, No. 76 – 9/2006*, edited by H. Pleines. Universität Bremen: Forschungsstelle Osteuropa, 19–44.

Paolini, G. 2007. *The Legitimacy Deficit of the European Union and the Role of National Parliaments*. Fiesole: EUI Dissertation.

Pleines H. (ed) 2006. *Participation of Civil Society in New Modes of Governance. The Case of the New EU Member States. Part 3: Involvement at the EU Level, Arbeitspapiere und Materialien. No. 76 – 9/2006*. Universität Bremen: Forschungsstelle Osteuropa, 19–44.

Pleines, H. 2008. 'Czech Environmental NGOs: Actors or agents in EU multilevel governance?'. *NewGov Policy Brief* No. 20, 2008.

Rakušanová, P. 2006. The Constitutional Debate – a One Man Show? Václav Klaus and the Constitutional Discourse in the Czech Media. *ConstEPS Working Paper* No. 2006/6. Bremen: Bremen University.

Rothstein, B., Uslaner, E.M. 2005. 'All for All: Equality, Corruption, and Social Trust'. *World Politics* 58 (October), 41–72.

Ruzza, C. 2005. *Organized Civil Society and the EU*. Paper presented at the 3rd ECPR general Conference. Budapest.

Ruzza, C. 2006. European institutions and the policy discourse of organised civil society, in *Civil society and legitimate European governance*, edited by S. Smismans. London: Elgar, 169–95.

Schmitter, P. 2001a. *What is there to Legitimize in the European Union and how this might be accomplished?* Mimeo: EUI.

Schmitter, P. 2001b. *How to Democratize the EU ... and why bother?* Oxford: Rowman & Littlefield Publishers.

Schmitter, P. 2002. Organized labor between the practice of democracy and the prospect of democratization of Europe, in *Europe – One Labour Market?* edited by L. Magnusson and J. Ottosson. Bruxelles: Peter Lang.

Schmitter, P. 2003. Democracy in Europe and Europe's democratization. *Journal of Democracy*, 14(4), 71–85.

Schmitter, P. 2007. *Political Accountability in 'Real-Existing'Democracies: Meaning and Mechanisms.* Firenze: Instituto Universario Europeo.

Seligman, A.B. 1992. *The Idea of Civil Society.* New York: Free Press.

Smith, M. 2002. Civil Society: Interest Groups and Social Movements in *Studying Politics: An Introduction to Political Science*, edited by R. Dyck Scarborough: Nelson, 290–310.

Sztompka, P. 1999. *Trust: A Sociological Theory.* Cambridge: Cambridge University Press.

Walker, N. 2003. Constitutionalising enlargement, enlarging constitutionalism. *European Law Journal*, 9(3), 365–85.

Waltzer, M. 1998. *Towards a Global Civil Society.* Providence: Berghahn Books.

Chapter 8

EU Internal and External Social Policy in Times of Global Crisis

Rebecca Zahn

Introduction

The European Union (EU) and its predecessors have considerably expanded their competences for developing social policy since the adoption of the Single European Act in 1986. The underlying rationale for such a European internal social policy, which also impacts on Member States, has hitherto been the demand for broad equivalence in labour standards. However, the competence regime does not cover the full breadth of social policy at national levels and at times the need for political compromise halts social policy legislation. Accordingly, in order to achieve its social policy goals, the EU has increasingly relied upon soft law mechanisms and dialogue instead of hard law mechanisms to adopt minimum standards.

Since the early 1990s, the EU has also been active in promoting social policy beyond its Member States by incorporating social values into EU external relations. This has been in response to calls for a 'social side' to globalization in order to counter-balance the economic facets of world trade. Thus, the European Commission has repeatedly committed itself to supporting a social side to globalization. Moreover, the EU has 'shifted from a rather narrow approach of promoting core labour standards through trade policies to a broader and more ambitious social agenda' (Orbie and Tortell 2009: 1). In promoting this external social policy and after initial failed attempts at fostering agreement on a hard law approach, the EU has focused on a soft law and dialogue-oriented approach, thus mirroring the mechanisms used in recent years in the development of an internal EU social policy. At first glance, one might thus assume that there exists a level of interdependence between the EU's internal and external social policies. If parallels can be drawn then recent events, in particular the entry into force of the Treaty of Lisbon and the ongoing global economic crisis, call for a reassessment of such an argument in order to determine the effects of both events on the EU's internal and external social policies.

This chapter thus proposes to examine whether parallels exist between the EU's internal and external social policy approaches. In order to do so, the chapter first outlines the development of the EU's internal and external social policies. It then describes the effects of the entry into force of the Lisbon Treaty and of the ongoing global economic crisis on the EU's internal and external social policies.

Finally, the chapter discusses the impact of the Lisbon Treaty and the global economic crisis in order to assess whether parallels between internal and external social policy approaches can be drawn or whether both are developing in distinct and different ways.

EU Internal Social Policy

The concept of an EU internal social policy has its origins in a report written by a group of independent experts appointed by the Governing Body of the International Labour Organization (ILO). The report (1956: 40–41) noted that:

> So long as we confine our attention to international differences in the general level of costs per unit of labour time, we do not consider it necessary or practicable that special measures to 'harmonise' social policies or social conditions should precede or accompany measures to promote greater freedom of international trade.

As a result, European social policy in the founding Treaty of the European Economic Community (EEC) was limited to the free movement of workers, equal pay and cooperation in the area of social security. The Treaty also made provisions for cooperation between the EEC and the ILO and it was hoped that ILO Conventions could be used to 'solve certain of the social problems connected with closer European economic co-operation' (ILO 1956: 116). However, effective cooperation between the two organizations has proved to be sporadic. Within the EU, any attempts that have been made to introduce a comprehensive policy – largely under the banner of a so-called European Social Model – have been dependent on the effective accommodation of political interests (Weinstock 1989). As a result, the European Social Model is patchy in its coverage of rights.

The European institutions have from time to time adopted key roles in trying to advance a catalogue of rights.[1] This was facilitated by the introduction of a limited amount of legislative competence in the field of labour law beginning with the Single European Act in 1986. Current legislative competences in the area of social policy include not only the provisions contained in the EU Treaties which enable the EU institutions to act in order to facilitate the free movement of workers, but also Article 153 of the Treaty on the Functioning of the European Union (TFEU) which allows for the introduction of directives on working conditions, information and consultation of workers and equality at work between men and women. There is also the option to make rules on matters related to employment law through the 'social dialogue'. Introduced by the Treaty of Maastricht in 1993, the social dialogue involves discussions, consultations, negotiations and joint actions by

---

1   Däubler (1989) describes repeated attempts to introduce a European charter of social rights from 1965 to 1984.

representatives of the two sides of industry – management and labour – within an EU law framework. The agreements concluded between the two sides may be given force of law through a Council decision (Article 155 TFEU), thereby turning the agreements into a Directive.

Particularly following the entry into force of the Maastricht Treaty, the European Commission together with the social partners took advantage of the Treaty provisions through social dialogue in actively pursuing a social policy. However, a period of legislative stagnation which characterized the end of the 20th century resulted in a change of approach by the Commission which, keen to avoid a return to the political stalemate that had occurred during the recession of the 1980s, turned to a new *modus operandi* for social integration: since the turn of the century, the emphasis has been on soft law mechanisms – 'framework agreements, joint declarations and guidelines and codes of conduct' (Marginson 2006: 103) – in order to achieve some sort of harmonization in the sphere of social policy. This shift to new forms of governance[2] was accompanied by the launch of the EU's Lisbon Strategy in 2000 which aimed to turn the EU into 'the most dynamic and competitive knowledge-based economy in the world, capable of sustainable economic growth with more and better jobs and greater social cohesion' (European Council 2000) by 2010. The social goals of the Lisbon Strategy sought to 'modernise the European Social Model and to build an active welfare state'. The main policy instrument, introduced to achieve this, was the Open Method of Coordination (OMC) – 'a coordinated and Commission-facilitated inter-governmental process' (European Council 2000) – which has been described as a 'means of spreading best practice and achieving greater convergence towards the main EU goals' (Commission 2002). It 'combines processes of common target setting by member states, cross-country benchmarking and periodic review' (Marginson 2006: 103). Scott and Trubek (2002: 4–5) explain that:

> The OMC aims to coordinate the actions of several Member States in a given policy domain and to create conditions for mutual learning that hopefully will induce some degree of voluntary policy convergence. Under the OMC, the Member States agree on a set of policy objectives but remain free to pursue these objectives in ways that make sense within their national contexts and at differing tempos.

The OMC can therefore be seen as 'a response to regulatory failure, as well as a response to the "joint decision trap" or the "competency gap" in social policy

---

2   There is a vast amount of literature on this topic. For a good overview of the shift to new forms of governance including references to other literature, see Armstrong and Kilpatrick 2007; Armstrong 2010; Sabel and Zeitlin 2010; Dawson 2011; Dawson and de Witte 2012.

and in other policy areas'.[3] Advocates of the method (Ashiagbor 2004: 308) argue that, as a form of governance, the OMC 'has the potential to achieve policy coordination without threatening jealously-guarded national sovereignty, *and* to allow Member States to implement policy in accordance with their socio-economic development'. Moreover, 'with an increasingly differentiated European Union, and in light of [...] enlargement, the coordination approach is appealing, as it does not seek to establish a single common framework, but instead, to put the EU Member States on a path towards achieving common objectives' (De la Porte 2002: 39). In this respect, the OMC's strength lies in its potential as a normative tool which can be used to enshrine a series of common values within the national policies of Member States so that the ultimate goals are the same, yet the methods for achievement can be adapted to better suit domestic frameworks. Empirical evidence seems to suggest that the OMC has indeed contributed to planning and evaluation in policy development in certain countries (Zeitlin and Pochet 2005; Heidenreich and Zeitlin 2009). It can be asserted that the process embraces the principle of subsidiarity which is increasingly promoted alongside the aspiration for a democratically accountable Union (Ashiagbor 2004).

Opponents of the OMC (De la Porte 2002: 50) challenge its effectiveness and argue that it only 'impacts on domestic policy-making, when the European objectives coincide with the national policy objectives'. In a recent article, De la Porte and Pochet (2012: 342) confirm this suspicion by looking at the OMC in social exclusion which was 'used for conceptualising and debating child poverty [when] this was in line with national priorities' but which 'was largely ignored by governments' when 'issues were not framed according to the domestic agenda'. Streeck (1995: 424) criticizes that a shift from hard to soft law in social policy (which he describes as 'neo-voluntarism') could lead to 'a type of social policy that tries to do with a minimum of compulsory modification of both market outcomes and national policy choices, presenting itself as an alternative to hard regulation as well as to no regulation at all'. Moreover, according to Hatzopoulos (2007: 318–19), the OMC may:

> Damage the future legitimacy of the EU and its institutions [...] as it does not confer any new competencies on them but specifically limits their reach on national policies in the fields concerned. More importantly still, there is a risk that the OMC replaces the classic Community method in fields where the latter currently prevails.

Although the Lisbon Strategy and the OMC can be criticized for a lack of effective time constraints on implementation or enforcement mechanisms to ensure

---

3   Ashiagbor (2004: 318). The 'joint decision trap' or the 'competency gap' describes a situation where 'the national capacity to regulate markets is severely reduced as a result of economic integration, whilst the problem-solving capacity at European level is constrained by conflicts of interest among governments'.

compliance, there seems to be a general consensus (Goetschy 2009: 222) that the Lisbon Strategy 'enlarged the EU employment and social agenda on matters of national priority'.

The introduction of the Charter of Fundamental Rights by the Treaty of Nice in 2000 – albeit as a non-legally binding document – contributed to this feeling of consensus. The Charter sets out the full range of civil, political, economic and social rights of European citizens and all persons resident in the EU. The Council acknowledged its primary objective as being to make citizens' rights 'more visible' through consolidation and restatement of pre-existing texts rather than to establish any new rights. The Charter stresses the importance of fundamental social rights by placing them alongside more easily recognizable fundamental rights such as the right to life (Article 2) or the prohibition of torture (Article 4). In this it is exceptional as it is the first international document to recognize the indivisibility of human rights by placing civil, political, social, cultural and economic rights on the same level. On the one hand, the introduction of the Charter functioned 'as a limit to the exercise of the powers of the EU institutions and the Member States acting as decentralized European administration' (De Schutter 2005). On the other hand, the placement of the full range of rights within a single document arguably signifies a process of deconstruction of the traditional hierarchy of rights within EU law which prioritizes economic over social rights. Placing the OMC against this backdrop of fundamental rights protection 'suggests possibilities for stimulating governmental actors to reflect upon and to develop the protection of fundamental rights in policy-making while also holding states to account for their performance through systematic and periodic analysis and review' (Armstrong 2005: 2). The viability of using the OMC to stem the rights agenda has been questioned. As the OMC is more of a political exercise than an expert evaluation, its independence and effectiveness is far from assured (Armstrong 2005). Moreover, the ability of the OMC to encourage the EU institutions to act to promote fundamental rights is somewhat limited. As Armstrong (2005: 4) points out, the 'OMC, while it may provide EU institutions with information, is not primarily intended as a tool to stimulate those institutions to act: rather it is intended to promote policy reflection by the Member States'. Both of these negative arguments can, however, also be turned into positive suggestions for the use of the OMC in strengthening the social rights agenda: 'the virtue of the OMC is that it is a political process intended to shift political expectations and institutional cultures and, therefore, to open the way to mainstream fundamental rights into domestic policies' (Armstrong 2005: 5). Thus, despite its uncertain status prior to the entry into force of the Lisbon Treaty, the Charter's symbolic value as an aspirational statement or bill of rights should not be underestimated.

The Lisbon Strategy came to an end in 2010 when, following a broad consultation, the European Commission launched the Europe 2020 Strategy whose aim is to 'turn the EU into a smart, sustainable and inclusive economy delivering high levels of employment, productivity and social cohesion […], taking into account different needs, different starting points and national specificities so as to promote growth for all' (European Commission 2010a). The Strategy combines five EU headline targets, which are to be translated into national targets, a number of flagship initiatives and integrated guidelines for employment and economic policies (European Commission 2012). Although the 'OMC label is no longer used [...], policy coordination remains a central component for policy-making in economic, employment, social and other policy areas' (De la Porte and Pochet 2012: 339), there have been suggestions (Vanhercke 2011) that the EU 2020 Strategy, rather than providing for innovative new forms of governance, instead tries to strengthen the existing framework. Thus, similar to Lisbon 2010, it could be argued that the coexistence of soft law mechanisms alongside hard policy goals under the Europe 2020 Strategy leaves little room for the development of new legislative initiatives. On the other hand (Vanhercke 2011: 8), 'one of the most striking features of the Europe 2020 Strategy is its insistence on targets, and the monitoring of progress towards these'. In this respect (Vandenbroucke 2012: 33), 'Europe 2020 offers something to hold on to' and it may be that the use of soft law mechanisms combined with specific targets will result in a process 'whereby the European social model can gradually be better defined'. This then may eventually lead to a European Social Model with a wider and more effective coverage of rights.

As it stands, the European Social Model has a curious character. Initially conceived of as a 'market-correcting' tool (Schiek 2012: 50) and then gradually widened through increased legislative competence so as to foster 'socio-economic integration' (Schiek 2012: 50), it never developed as an all-encompassing and comprehensive European social policy. The switch from hard to soft law mechanisms as the preferred instruments for the development of European internal social policy makes it difficult to predict the future of the European Social Model. While the OMC keeps social issues on the EU's agenda, it is 'not primarily aimed at social policy, but rather at structural change of the Member States' economies which should enhance competitiveness of the EU economy as a whole' (Schiek 2012: 50–51). The Charter of Fundamental Rights has the potential to legitimize European internal social policy as a policy in its own right rather than one linked to economic integration. Whether the Charter will have such an effect is, however, open to speculation. This is discussed in more detail below in relation to the entry into force of the Lisbon Treaty.

EU External Social Policy

The EU's 'external social policy' is not a clearly defined area of competence set out in the Treaties. Any competence that the EU lays claim to is derived from its internal social policy and is pursued through external policy instruments in the areas of trade, development or foreign and security policy where the EU has defined competences. As illustrated above, the EU's competence in internal social policy is rather limited and, as a result, external competence is far from wide-reaching. The 'social' aspect of 'external social policy' is also a vague concept. The ILO's World Commission on the Social Dimension of Globalisation (2004) defines 'social' in the broadest sense as everything that is development-related, ranging from poverty reduction and economic growth, to health and education, democratic development and human rights. A study commissioned by the European Parliament (Eichhorst *et al.*: 20) in 2010 defines 'social' more narrowly in terms of 'working conditions, labour rights and associated policy-making', thereby mirroring the EU's internal ambit on social policy. This chapter copies this narrow approach and borrows the European Parliament's definition in order to look at whether parallels exist between the EU's role in promoting working conditions and labour rights internally and externally.

The main point of reference to determine the EU's competence in the sphere of external social policy is the Court of Justice of the European Union's (CJEU) Opinion 2/91 on the division of competences between the European Community and the Member States to conclude an ILO Convention on Chemicals at Work.[4] In its Opinion the CJEU first reiterated a previous Opinion (1/76)[5] where it stated that:

> Whenever Community law has created for the institutions of the Community powers within its internal system for the purpose of attaining a specific objective, the Community has authority to enter into the international commitments necessary for the attainment of that objective even in the absence of an express provision in that connexion (para 3).

Based on this reasoning, the Court ruled that external Community competence is exclusive in areas where the Community has already adopted harmonizing legislation. However, the Court went on to clarify that the nature of Community competence also depends on the scope of the measures in question. Thus, whenever the EU sets minimum labour standards, as is the case most of the time, external competence is shared by the Union and the Member States. This effectively limits the competence of the EU to those areas in which it can act internally, thereby excluding most collective labour rights and competence in respect of setting wage standards, both of which could be of particular importance when working towards a social side to globalization. Cooperation with Member States in external social policy also deprives the EU of the ability to act with one voice and diverging interests between Member States and EU institutions have the potential to hamper the development of an effective and coherent external social policy.

EU initiatives in external social policy can be traced back to the early 1990s when the European Commission began to push for a social dimension to its external relations. In particular, the EU and its Member States focused their attention on the promotion of 'the most fundamental standards linked with respect for human rights: abolition of slavery, forced labour and child labour, freedom to

---

4   [1993] ECR I-01061.
5   [1977] ECR 741.

organise, and, the right to collective bargaining' (Orbie and Tortell 2009: 6). This initial rationale for an external social policy – based on human rights principles – stands in stark contrast to the considerations given to the introduction of an internal social policy; namely, whether social harmonization was necessary to promote economic integration. Even though there have been moves away from the economic argument as justification for the existence of an internal social policy – the introduction of the Charter of Fundamental Rights is a recent example[6] – the fundamental underlying difference between the EU's internal and external social policies remains; one is based on principles of fundamental human rights, the other traces its roots to economic harmonization. However, the means by which the EU has given effect to its two policies throws up interesting parallels.

Initial attempts by the EU in its external social policy to ensure the observance of core labour standards concentrated on a hard law approach by advocating the introduction of social clauses into trade policy in order to encourage respect for core labour standards by rewarding those countries that adhered to them.[7] Driven by the establishment of the World Trade Organization (WTO) in 1994, numerous European governments, particularly France and Belgium, were in favour of linking labour standards with trade rules through the introduction of a social clause into WTO rules. This was supported by the European Parliament and the Commission. However, Germany and the UK, along with other Member States, opposed any type of social clause, arguing that the WTO is a 'trade organisation, not a social organisation'.[8] As a result, Member States could not agree on adopting a common position in response to a communication issued by the European Commission in 1996 on the trading system and internationally recognized labour standards in the run-up to the WTO's first Ministerial Conference held in Singapore in December 1996. A social clause was not adopted at this conference, the compromise instead being support for and recognition of the ILO's role in promoting core labour standards (Leary 1997). Although consensus was not reached on the issue of a social clause in the WTO context, the EU took the decision by a qualified majority vote in the Council to introduce labour standards conditionality through a unilateral social clause into its Generalised System of Preferences (GSP) trade regime (Orbie and Tortell 2009). Under the GSP, the EU offers tariff preferences to countries which have signed and are effectively implementing the core UN human rights and ILO labour rights conventions. In addition, the EU has created a special incentive arrangement (GSP+), which obliges beneficiary countries to ratify multiple core human and labour rights and environment and good governance conventions in order to benefit from additional tariff reductions. To date, 16 countries benefit from the GSP+.

---

6   For other examples, see Däubler (1989).

7   For a discussion of why labour standards conditionality as part of trade policy in the EU's case can be considered to be hard law, see Trebilcock 2004: 170–85.

8   Quote from UK Minister of Trade Ian Lang, House of Commons Hansard Debates, 6 December 1996.

While the Lisbon Strategy did not make suggestions for an EU external social policy, its new forms of governance nonetheless infiltrated the field. Since the early 2000s, the EU has moved away from using hard law mechanisms and has increasingly turned to soft law instruments in order to promote a social dimension of globalization. At the same time, there has been a shift in focus from the core labour standards mentioned above to broader social and development-related objectives (Orbie and Barbarinde 2008). In 2001, the European Commission indicated that it would not only focus on core labour standards but also on general issues of social governance. Thus, the EU has been active in promoting a European framework for corporate social responsibility internally by introducing voluntary ways of monitoring multinational enterprises' compliance with labour standards and externally through trade incentives, development agreements and cooperation with the ILO. The EU's approach to corporate social responsibility has been described as 'holistic' as it 'includes principles on human rights, labour standards and the environment, unlike other international initiatives which tend to include only one dimension of corporate responsibility, such as environmental issues' (Gatto 2005: 435). However, the frequent lack of a specific connection between labour standards and incentives or sanctions has also been criticized (Faber and Orbie 2007) as it weakens the EU's potential in encouraging higher labour standards.

It must therefore be questioned to what extent the EU has actually developed a global social identity. Its use of hard law – making trade arrangements conditional on the observance of core labour rights – certainly has the potential to improve labour standards in developing countries. A recent study (Gasiorek *et al.* 2010) has shown that the EU's GSP and GSP+ schemes have been relatively successful in raising social standards and the ratification of international conventions. The International Trade Union Confederation (ITUC 2010) also presents evidence of improved labour standards as a result of GSPs. However, other reports (Orbie and Tortell 2009) are less positive and criticize the EU for lack of transparency in applying its trading preferences. Moreover, only 16 countries currently benefit from the GSP+ which has greater potential to promote sustainable development and good governance than the GSP (Gasiorek *et al.* 2010). The difficulty facing the EU in trying to improve labour standards through hard law is not necessarily surprising. The literature examining whether human rights conditionality in trade agreements has led to improved human rights standards is mixed. Overall, there seems to be a lack of a link between the ratification of human rights conventions as part of a trade agreement and higher levels of human rights protection.[9] What seems important to ensure for compliance with higher labour standards (Wells 2006) is to combine effective monitoring of implementation of standards with positive incentives (such as linking increased market access to effective implementation). The ILO can play a major part in such an approach; a potential

---

9 For an overview of the literature and a study examining the hypothesis of compliance, see Hathaway 2002.

which the European Commission has recognized. In 2004, the Commission signed a Memorandum of Understanding with the ILO aimed at enhancing cooperation at all levels in order to make 'the greatest possible contribution to strengthening the social dimension of development cooperation' (European Commission 2004). The Memorandum has led to EU co-funding of ILO initiatives and ILO involvement in the implementation of EU cooperation programmes and projects. Apart from being a useful partner for the EU, involvement with the ILO also serves another purpose. As Orbie and Tortell (2009: 9) argue, 'the Commission's normative and development-oriented role in the ILO is less contested by EU member states than hard law activities related to labour standards conventions'.

The EU's 2020 Strategy – which, unlike the Lisbon Strategy, places emphasis on an external dimension to the EU's social policy – also provides hope that the EU may further develop its own external social policy. An informal meeting of ministers of employment and social security in January 2010 concluded that 'the EU 2020 Strategy should also have an external dimension. [...] [An] objective of the Employment Strategy should be to improve our response to the external dimension of employment, social protection and social inclusion' (Presidency Background Paper 2010). If such an objective were to become a clear target, the EU could go beyond merely stressing (Orbie and Tortell 2009: 8) the exemplary character of the European Social Model and the OMC for international social governance and use the resources that it has at its disposal to combine hard and soft law mechanisms – effective monitoring of labour standards with positive incentives – in order to achieve a social dimension to globalization. This in turn would enable the EU to develop its own global social identity.

The next sections of this chapter consider whether the Lisbon Treaty and the economic crisis have had any impact on the EU's involvement in social policy both internally and externally.

The Lisbon Treaty

The Lisbon Treaty makes a number of changes to the Treaties and to the structure of the European Union, but only few concern the chapters on employment and social policy. It inserted a new provision (Article 151) into Title X of the TFEU on Social Policy which consolidates and clarifies the role of the social partners in the making of social policy through social dialogue. In doing so, it recognizes the diversity of national systems and emphasizes the autonomy of the social partners.[10]

Similarly, the Lisbon Treaty does not alter the extent of the EU's competence in external social policy, though it introduces a number of provisions which have the potential to clarify the scope of the EU's actions. Article 47 of the Treaty on the European Union (TEU) states that the EU 'shall have legal personality', eliminating doubts on whether the EU is capable of entering into international

---

10   For a discussion of the provision, see Bercusson 2009: 728–9.

agreements.[11] Further, Article 4 TFEU states that the Union and its Member States share competence in the social policy field. Building on the CJEU's Opinion 2/91, this seems to partly codify and clarify the relationship between the EU and its Member States also in the area of external social policy. However, Article 4 TFEU does not confirm the Court's suggestion that the EU has exclusive competence in areas where harmonizing legislation has been adopted, leaving uncertainty about this aspect.

Finally, the Lisbon Treaty establishes a High Representative for Foreign Affairs, aided by the European External Action Service to conduct the EU's common foreign and security policy. While the exact scope of the Representative's role is unclear at present, she has the potential to provide a stronger link between the EU and the ILO by supporting the ILO's work during international consultations, encouraging non-EU countries to ratify and implement ILO Conventions on international labour standards and to raise major cases of labour standards violations.

Undoubtedly the main contribution of the Lisbon Treaty to EU internal and external social policy is the Charter of Fundamental Rights, which now has the same legal values as the Treaties (Article 6 TEU). The Charter applies to the actions of the European institutions but also to the Member States when implementing EU law. Thus, an argument could be made that the Commission must respect those rights laid out in the Charter when implementing EU cooperation programmes and projects in third countries.

Perhaps the most compelling practical application[12] of the Charter to the EU's internal social policy lies in its contribution to the identification of a unifying ideology and normalization of social standards, particularly under the OMC. Without such a clear and unequivocal statement of common values, the judicial task of interpreting the existing rights provided by EU law against the backdrop of the OMC's potentially deregulatory guidelines could be severely compromised. Following the elevation of the Charter to a legally binding document, the early signs regarding the Court's willingness specifically to apply the Charter's provisions to the cases before it are promising.[13] The Court demonstrated its enthusiasm for upholding the fundamental principles articulated in the Charter even where there is a conflict with well-established secondary legislation in the recent *Test-*

---

11 Even prior to the Lisbon Treaty, many considered the EU to possess legal personality which would imply that the Lisbon Treaty merely confirmed the status quo. For an overview of the debate, see Gosalbo Bono 2006: 353–7.

12 This argument is further developed in a conference paper entitled 'European Labour Law in Crisis: The Demise of Social Rights?' presented by N. Busby and R. Zahn at the 'Labour Law in Crisis' conference held at Kingston University on 11 May 2012 and at the Social Rights workshop 'Integration or Disintegration? The Future of EU Law and Policy' at the Institute of European Law, Birmingham University on 28 June 2012.

13 See joined cases C-159/10 and C-160/10, *Fuchs and Köhler v Land Hessen* Judgment of 21 July 2011 (nyr) and C-78/11 *Asociación Nacional de Grandes Empresas de Distribución (ANGED) v Federación de Asociaciones Sindicales (FASGA) and others* Judgment of 21 June 2012 (nyr).

Achats case.[14] Although the case might not have been decided differently without the relevant provision of the Charter, the 'new' status of the Charter provides a particularly strong foundation for justification of the Court's judgement. This case thus at the very least reveals the Court's ability to recognize the Charter as the primary tool to be used for the exercise of judicial review where secondary acts of the institutions are potentially incompatible with the fundamental rights guaranteed by its provisions.

By providing a clear statement of the guiding principles of EU law, the Charter has the potential to stimulate a valuable interplay between its contents and the EU's citizens, courts, national governments and the institutions themselves. When placed within its wider constitutional setting, the Charter is at least capable of producing a centrifugal effect by which pre-existing obligations are clarified and strengthened through their interrelationships with associated provisions. Yet although the Charter consolidates modern economic and social rights with the more traditional and well-established civil and political rights, this does not automatically convey equality in application across the whole range of rights. The Charter does little to disturb the *status quo* which has developed over the EU's lifetime. However, by including social rights alongside civil and political rights, the Charter has the potential to realign the underlying rationale of the EU's internal social policy with that of its external social policy by underpinning it with a human rights focus. In this respect, the Charter's significance in the social domain is more than just symbolic, as by its incorporation in the EU's constitutional law, 'the European market order can be said to incorporate a set of core social rights' (Deakin and Browne 2003: 27). This not only has the potential to strengthen the coverage of the European Social Model, it could also give new life to the EU's attempts to develop a global social identity. Overall, therefore, changes made by the Lisbon Treaty could make a positive contribution to the EU's pursuit of an internal and external social policy.

The Economic Crisis[15]

The current economic crisis, the biggest financial and economic downturn since the Great Depression, has its origins in the bursting of the American housing

---

14   C-236/09 *Association Belge des Consommateurs Test-Achats v Conseil des Ministres* [2011] 2 CMLR 38: In this instance, ruling that the equal treatment of men and women provided under Articles 21 and 23 of the Charter cannot be indefinitely subject to derogations introduced under Directive 2004/113/EC (Council Directive (EC) 2004/113 implementing the principle of equal treatment between men and women in the access to and supply of goods and services [2004]. OJ L373/37 also referred to as the 'Recast' Equal Treatment Directive). See also Peripoli 2012 and Watson 2011.

15   This section provides a very brief overview of the current economic crisis in order to provide a background to the discussion on its effects on the EU's internal and external

bubble and the consequent collapse of the sub-prime mortgage market in the United States in 2007 and 2008. The ever-growing number of defaults in the sub-prime mortgage market and the global proliferation of mortgage-backed securities led to uncertainty amongst banks as to the exposure of their counterparties to such toxic assets. As a result of this climate of fear, banks stopped lending to each other thus leading to a shortage of liquidity. Those financial institutions whose business models were predicated on the assumption that they would always be able to satisfy their liquidity requirements by tapping the wholesale markets, such as UK lender Northern Rock, were hit particularly hard by the sudden disappearance of interbank lending. The crisis peaked in the autumn of 2008 when the US government decided not to save the investment bank Lehman Brothers. Governments in the US and Europe had to step in to provide emergency funding for banks in their countries, to guarantee investments, to provide hefty stimulus packages for their economies and, in some cases, to nationalize failing institutions. The financial crisis in turn developed into a global economic crisis as global GDP contracted in 2009. This global recession considerably reduced public revenues and placed a heavy burden on welfare states. In addition, governments in most developed countries were faced with costly rescue packages from bailing out banks in the wake of the financial crisis and had to initiate deep spending cuts and austerity measures in order to reduce their public deficit. At the same time, market confidence in sovereign debt faltered as investors and rating agencies began to doubt the creditworthiness of certain countries in the euro area – notably, Portugal, Ireland, Italy, Greece and Spain. The downgrading of such countries' credit ratings had the effect of raising interest rates for those countries, making it harder for them to service their debt. In October 2009, Greece admitted that it was no longer able to pay its creditors and in February 2010, the country was placed under budgetary supervision by the European Commission. European leaders, together with the Commission and the International Monetary Fund, have since agreed on a number of rescue packages for Greece in exchange for the reform and stabilization of Greece's public finances. In November 2010, Ireland was forced to draw on the financial support of the European Financial Stability Facility in order to service its debts and in April 2011, Portugal received a 78bn-euro bailout, with Cyprus following in June 2012.

The economic crisis has had different effects on the EU's internal and external social policies. Internally, 'increasing financial deregulation and privatisation has put the European Social Model under threat' (Van Reisen, Stocker and Vogiazides 2009: 44). At a national level, spending cuts to reduce public deficits have entailed a reduction in social, welfare and public services. Continued low growth rates have led to some of the highest levels of unemployment in the EU Member States since the Second World War.

---

social policies. Detailed descriptions of the crisis, its effects and possible solutions can be found in Gray and Akseli 2011 or Cassis 2011. An overview of the development of the crisis and its effects on the euro area is provided in Bruun 2012.

At a European level, the response has mainly focused on recovery plans and rescue packages targeted at the financial sector. The rationale behind such support is that 'state guarantees and recapitalisations will allow banks to make more loans available, thus stimulating an increase in investment, which is expected to create and maintain jobs' (Van Reisen, Stocker and Vogiazides 2009: 44). However, this policy has also been criticized by many as ignoring the widening social inequalities which are developing in the Member States. There have been calls (Van Reisen, Stocker and Vogiazides 2009: 44) for the EU to adopt 'measures to integrate those who are excluded from the labour market, invest in social and health services and improve social protection systems'. So far, the EU (European Commission 2009: 2) has restricted itself to 'developing guidelines on the design of labour market policies during the crisis'. Indeed, a summit of EU leaders which was supposed to find a resolution for the growing unemployment problem as a result of the crisis was postponed in order to avoid false promises being made in the run-up to the European Parliament elections in 2009 (Labaki 2009). While a summit was held in February 2010, it focused mainly on the Greek debt crisis rather than the social issues facing the Member States (Illmer 2010).

Although EU institutions have the competence under the Treaty to adopt minimum standards in the area of labour law and social policy, there has been no talk of adopting hard law mechanisms in order to ease the effects of the crisis. Instead, the EU institutions have stressed the importance of the Lisbon Strategy and of Europe 2020 in responding to the economic crisis. Europe 2020 is meant to have a double purpose: 'it should focus on how to overcome the crisis, and in the medium term, it should define the EU's economic and social model, which is needed in order to face the challenges of globalisation.' However, it is unclear what role Europe 2020 can play in overcoming the crisis. As Vanhercke (2011: 15) points out:

> The underlying 'growth, growth, growth' paradigm of Europe 2020 is being challenged; and there is a very real risk that the social dimensions will become swamped by economic considerations [...]. Furthermore, there is a risk that the EU's coordinating role with regard to social protection and social inclusion may be reduced to social inclusion alone, while social inclusion becomes narrowly focused on increasing access to the labour market. Finally, the new governance structure raises serious questions regarding the future operation of the Social OMC: even if it is unlikely that it will be completely abandoned, it is not clear whether and under what form [it] will continue, thereby further weakening the 'social voice' in Europe.

While the European Commission has published evidence (2010b) that an increased use of social dialogue has had a positive impact on companies struggling with the economic crisis, much of this response stems from the national level and a coordinated Europe-wide approach to the social effects of the crisis is lacking. While the use of soft law mechanisms may lead to 'an increased (potential) visibility and importance for social issues' (Vanhercke 2011: 14), they seem inadequate in coordinating an EU-wide response to the devastating effects that the economic crisis has had on national social models.

The lack of a coordinated and effective social policy to deal with the impact of the economic crisis is reminiscent of the EEC's response to the 1973 oil crisis (Weinstock 1989: 19–23). An attempt was made in the 1970s to improve the social dimension to European economic integration through the first Social Action Programme (SAP) which was signed in January 1974. However, with the onset of the crisis, individual states focused on their economic priorities and although the SAP did have some minor successes, enthusiasm at a European level for a concrete social policy evaporated. The value of this comparison is limited as a common currency now mandates EU-wide solutions to the economic crisis at least within the euro area. Yet it seems unfortunate that at the same time the EU has not learned from past experience by taking avail of its legislative competences to use the crisis in order to strengthen the European Social Model. In the current context, Deakin (2012: 35) argues that:

> The financial crisis has given the debate about the role of social policy in the EU a new and very hard edge. Social policy can no longer be seen as a marginal issue for the EU. [...] In the longer run, economies should be put on to a more stable growth path. In the labour market context, this implies a combination of measures aimed at restoring real wage growth, limiting income inequality and providing the basis for long-term productive investment in skills and resources. [However,] [t]his option, while in principle capable of offering a coherent, socially progressive response to the crisis, is not currently on the policy agenda as far as the EU is concerned.

Instead, Deakin (2012: 35–7) predicts that 'the tensions [between economic and social policy] inherent in the [EU's] current policy make it likely that there will be a re-evaluation of the relationship between social and economic policy at some point'. Deakin suggests that such a re-evaluation could take the form of a 'human-developmental view of labour law' as 'the use of human development goals to benchmark national social and economic performance is not just relevant in the context of so-called emerging or transition systems'. Combining social rights and economic growth can also help the EU and its Member States 'to ensure their mutual, long-run sustainability'. Such a strategy is oddly reminiscent of the EU's attempts hitherto to introduce a social dimension to globalization through its external social policy, yet judging by the current lack of initiative it seems that the EU is not yet willing to strengthen its internal social dimension.

Obviously, the pressing need at an EU level is to find satisfactory solutions to the banking and euro area crises. However, ignoring the future development of the European Social Model is a very short-sighted strategy. In an enlarged European Union of 28 Member States with very diverse social protection levels, economic integration needs to be coupled with a certain level of social integration in order to further European integration. The EU has the relevant tools – hard and soft law mechanisms – to develop a clearly defined 'social voice'. It may be that the introduction of the Charter which gives social rights a status where they should not be ignored could be a turning point. However, whether the Charter with its lack of a legislative dimension will provide the necessary impetus for the future development of social rights is doubtful in the current climate. Overall, one must therefore conclude that the economic crisis has had a negative effect on the EU's internal social policy. It has illustrated the weaknesses of the EU's limited competence in the social field and made visible the inadequacies of the new forms of governance under Europe 2020.

By way of contrast, a more positive picture emerges from an examination of the effects of the economic crisis on the EU's external social policy. A report commissioned by the European Parliament in 2010 (Eichhorst *et al.* 2010: 10) found no evidence of a deterioration of social standards as a result of the economic crisis. Conversely, the Report found that:

> From the outside, the EU is perceived as a normative power in social issues and an attractive partner, owing to the unique combination of economic dynamism with a social model. The EU has a good reputation, which can be seen as a major asset when it comes to international dialogue on social issues.

Evidence of the EU's commitment to its external social policy by acting in international fora can be found in the role it played during the negotiation of the ILO's Global Jobs Pact in 2009 (ILO 2009). This Pact attempts to address the social and employment impacts of the international financial and economic crisis by promoting tried and tested policy measures for member countries which put employment and social protection along with environmental sustainability at the centre of crisis responses. The EU played a key role in cooperating closely with emerging economies, developing countries and the social partners during the adoption of the Pact. Moreover, the widening of the Europe 2020 Strategy to include external social policy indicates that the EU remains keen to push for a social dimension to globalization regardless of its internal preoccupations.

It must be recognized at this stage that it is of course easier for the EU to pursue an external social policy. Involvement within and supporting the ILO which does not have enforcement capabilities to ensure observance of its labour standards does not require the EU to seek Member State approval which often acts as a bar to the adoption of internal social measures. Also, the main focus of the EU's external social policy has been on securing the implementation of core labour standards such as freedom of association, elimination of all forms of forced or compulsory labour and effective abolition of child labour. While these are, without a doubt, important goals to work towards, it is arguably easier for the EU to support the abolition of child labour through the use of soft or hard law mechanisms than to get EU Member States to agree on directives setting legally binding minimum standards on specific working conditions within the European Social Model. Social integration within the EU, although patchy, goes much deeper than any attempts to introduce a social side to globalization. Equally, under its current competence, the EU has much greater potential to develop an effective European social model than to visibly improve labour standards in developing countries. It is therefore not surprising that the EU faces stronger political pressures in the pursuit of its internal social policy and is thus less able to act in the face of such pressures.

The development of an external social policy which promotes core labour standards as part of a wider human rights and environmental framework sits comfortably within both the EU's governance agenda, which focuses on incentives, targets and guidelines, and within the Charter's primary aim, which is to reaffirm and clarify the EU's commitment to democracy as expressed through the language of human rights. Promoting an external social policy either through trade agreements or within the ILO is thus a diplomatic way of showing that the EU is taking social rights seriously while avoiding a clash with its Member States. Individual Member States such as the UK have adopted a similar tactic. Despite huge budget cuts which have had a profound effect on the country's domestic economy, the UK's development and aid budget (which admittedly makes up a small percentage of the overall budget) has remained untouched and is set to increase (HM Treasury 2010). Due to the limited nature of EU competence in external social policy, it is perhaps not surprising that the economic crisis has had little impact.

Concluding Remarks

This chapter set out to explore potential parallels between the EU's internal and external social policies and the extent to which the Lisbon Treaty and the current economic crisis have had an effect on these policies. Both policies begin from different starting points and are founded on different rationales; the EU's internal social policy is based around a theory of economic integration, whereas its external social policy has evolved around a human rights and development argument. However, the mechanisms used to achieve both social policies throw up interesting similarities; an initial preference for hard law mechanisms followed by a shift to new forms of governance and a reliance on soft law. There are signs that a combination of both types of mechanisms – for example, linking enforceable targets with incentives – may be a successful strategy to pursue. However, such a hybridization of hard and soft law has been sporadic in practice. This does not mean to say that there has been convergence between the EU's internal and external social policies nor that this is a desirable outcome. The EU's internal social policy seeks to approximate national labour laws in order to facilitate economic integration whereas the EU's external social policy encourages respect of core labour standards. The effects of the economic crisis make visible the different approaches underpinning the EU's social policies. From the lack of recent initiatives taken in the field of internal social policy during the economic crisis, it seems that the European Social Model is itself in a crisis. There have been almost no hard law developments since 2002 and while the Europe 2020 Strategy sets ambitious targets, there are question marks over its ability to effectively tackle the negative impact of the crisis on employment and social welfare across the EU. The EU seems to be reluctant to take action in the social sphere despite it being necessary to counter the effects of the economic crisis, thereby giving the impression that the direction of its future social model is yet to develop. This feeling of crisis is not present in the EU's external social policy. Although there are doubts as to whether the EU has developed a global social identity, recent initiatives such as the renewal of the GSP and GSP+, the EU's involvement in the ILO's Global Jobs Pact and the inclusion of external social policy in the Europe 2020 Strategy suggest that the EU is willing to take on a more active role in promoting an external social policy. A more positive picture emerges following the introduction of the Charter of Fundamental Rights as a legally binding instrument. The Charter equips the EU's internal social policy with a stronger human rights focus which would make it difficult to see social policy only as a facilitator of economic integration. Rather, it gives social rights a status in EU law where they cannot be ignored. Similarly, in the area of external social policy, the codification of human rights within the EU's constitutional legal order could give the European institutions greater legitimacy and encourage accountability when promoting social rights abroad. Thus, overall, the Charter may have a positive effect on the EU's social policies; its use by the CJEU has certainly been encouraging.

Bibliography

Armstrong, K. 2005. *The Open Method of Co-ordination and Fundamental Rights: A Critical Appraisal* Draft Paper for Discussion at the 'Fundamental Rights and Reflexive Governance' Seminar: Columbia Law School, New York, 4th November 2005.

Armstrong, K. 2010. *Governing Social Inclusion – Europeanization Through Policy Coordination.* Oxford: OUP.

Armstrong, K. and Kilpatrick, C. 2007. Law, Governance, or New Governance? The Changing Open Method of Coordination *CJEL* 13, 649–77.

Ashiagbor, D. 2004. Soft Harmonisation: The 'Open Method of Coordination' in the European Employment Strategy *European Public Law* 10, 305–22.

Bercusson, B. 2009. *European Labour Law.* 2nd Edition. Cambridge: CUP.

Bruun, N. 2012. Economic Governance of the EU Crisis and Its Social Policy Implications, in *The Lisbon Treaty and Social Europe*, edited by N. Bruun, K. Lörcher and I. Schömann. Oxford: Hart, 261–76.

Cassis, Y. 2011. *Crises and Opportunities.* Oxford: OUP.

Däubler, W. 1989. Sozialpolitik in der EG – ein Überblick über den Diskussionsstand, in *Sozialstaat EG? Die andere Dimension des Binnenmarktes*, edited by W. Däubler. Gütersloh.: Bertelsmann Stiftung, 35–160.

Dawson, M. 2011. *New Governance and the Transformation of European Law: Coordinating EU Social Law and Policy*. Cambridge: CUP.

Dawson, M. and de Witte, B. 2012. The EU Legal Framework of Social Inclusion and Social Protection: between the Lisbon Strategy and the Lisbon Treaty, in *Social Inclusion and Social Protection: Interactions between Law and Policy*, edited by P. Ploscar, B. Cantillon and H. Versheuren. Mortsel: Intersentia, 41–70.

De la Porte, C. 2002. Is the Open Method of Coordination Appropriate for Organising Activities at European Level in Sensitive Policy Areas? *European Law Journal* 8(1), 38–58.

De la Porte, C. and Pochet, P. 2012. Why and how (still) study the Open Method of Co-ordination (OMC)? *Journal of European Social Policy*. 22(3), 336–49.

DeSchutter, O. 2005. The Implementation of Fundamental Rights Through the Open Method of Co-ordination, in *Social Rights and Market Forces: Is the Open Coordination of Employment and Social Policies the Future of Social Europe?* edited by O. De Schutter and S. Deakin. Brussels: Bruylant.

Deakin, S. 2012. The Lisbon Treaty, the *Viking* and *Laval* Judgments and the Financial Crisis: In Search of New Foundations for Europe's 'Social Market Economy', in *The Lisbon Treaty and Social Europe*, edited by N. Bruun, K. Lörcher and I. Schömann. Oxford: Hart, 19–44.

Deakin, S. and Browne, J. 2003. Social Rights and Market Order: Adapting the Capability Approach, in *Economic and Social Rights under the EU Charter of Fundamental Rights*, edited by T. Hervey and J. Kenner. Oxford: Hart, 27–44.

Eichhorst, W., Kendzia, M., Knudsen, J.B. and Wahl-Brink, D. 2010. *External Dimension of EU Social Policy*, IZA Research Report No. 26 available at http://www.iza.org/en/webcontent/publications/reports/report_pdfs/iza_report_26.pdf [accessed: 23 August 2012].

European Commission. 1996. The trading system and internationally recognised labour standards COM(1996)402.

European Commission. 2001. Promoting core labour standards and improving social governance in the context of globalisation COM(2001)416.

European Commission. 2002. European Benchmarks in Education and Training: follow-up to the Lisbon European Council COM(2002)629.

European Commission. 2004. *Memorandum of understanding concerning the establishment of a strategic partnership between the ILO and the Commission of the European Communities in the field of development*, Brussels and Geneva 15–16 July available at http://ec.europa.eu/europeaid/what/social-protection/documents/memorandum_of_understanding_ec_ilo_en.pdf [accessed: 1 February 2013].

European Commission. 2009. *Economic Crisis in Europe: Causes, Consequences and Responses*, European Economy 7/2009 available at http://ec.europa.eu/economy_finance/publications/publication15887_en.pdf [accessed: 23 August 2012].

European Commission. 2010a. Europe 2020: A strategy for smart, sustainable and inclusive growth, COM(2010)2020.

European Commission. 2010b. *Industrial Relations in Europe 2010 Report* available http://europa.eu/rapid/pressReleasesAction.do?reference=MEMO/11/134 [accessed: 23 August 2012].

European Commission. 2012. *Towards a Job-Rich Recovery*, COM(2012)173.

European Commission and International Labour Organization, 2004. Memorandum of understanding concerning the establishment of a strategic partnership between the ILO and the Commission of the European Communities in the field of development, available at http://ec.europa.eu/europeaid/what/social-protection/documents/memorandum_of_understanding_ec_ilo_en.pdf [accessed: 23 August 2012].

European Council. 2000. *Presidency Conclusions – Lisbon European Council* Brussels: European Council.

Faber, G. and Orbie, J. 2007, *European Union Trade Politics and Development*, Oxon: Routledge.

Gasiorek, M. *et al.* 2010. *Mid-term Evaluation of the EU's Generalised System of Preferences*, Final Report, CARIS, Brussels: European Commission, DG Trade.

Gatto, A. 2005. Corporate Social Responsibility in the External Relations of the EU *Yearbook of European Law* 24 (1), 423–62.

Goetschy, J. 2009. The Lisbon Strategy and Social Europe: two closely linked destinies, in *Europe, Globalization and the Lisbon Agenda*, edited by M.J. Rodrigues. Cheltenham: Edward Elgar, 74–90.

Gosalbo Bono, R. 2006. Some Reflections on the CFSP Legal Order. *Common Market Law Review*. 43, 337–94.

Gray, J. and Akseli, O. 2011. *Financial Regulation in Crisis?* Cheltenham: Edward Elgar.

Hathaway, O.A. 2002. Do Human Rights Treaties make a Difference? *Yale Law Journal*,111, 1935–2042.

Hatzopoulos, V. 2007. Why the Open Method of Coordination is Bad For You: A letter to the EU. *European Law Journal* 13(3), 309–42.

Heidenreich, M. and Zeitlin, J. (eds) 2009. *Changing European Employment and Welfare Regimes: The Influence of the Open Method of Coordination on National Reforms*. London: Routledge.

HM Treasury. 2010. *Spending Review 2010*, London: HM Treasury.

Illmer, A. 2010. EU leaders hold summit to tackle unemployment, crisis in Greece. *Deutsche Welle*, 11th Februrary.

ILO. 1956. *Social Aspects of European Collaboration (Ohlin Report)*, Geneva: ILO Studies and Reports.

ILO. 2004. *A Fair Globalization: Creating Opportunities for All*, Geneva: ILO.

ILO. 2009. *Recovering from the Crisis: A Global Jobs Pact*, Geneva: ILO.

ITUC. 2010. *Internationally Recognised Core Labour Standards in Croatia*, Report for the WTO General Council Review of the Trade Policies in Croatia. Brussels: ITUC.

Labaki, M. 2009. Exit le sommet sur l'emploi. *Le Soir*, 21st March.

Leary, V. 1997. The WTO and the Social Clause: Post-Singapore. *EJIL*. 1, 118–22.

Marginson, P. 2006. Europeanisation and Regime Competition: Industrial Relations and EU Enlargement. *Industrielle Beziehungen* 13(2), 97–117.

Orbie, J. and Barbarinde, O. 2008. The social dimension of globalisation and European Union development policy: promoting core labour standards and corporate social responsibility. *Journal of European Integration* 30(3), 459–77.

Orbie, J. and Tortell, L. 2009. From the social clause to the social dimension of globalisation, in *The European Union and the Social Dimension of Globalisation*, edited by J. Orbie and L. Tortell. Oxon: Routledge, 1–26.

Peripoli, A. 2012. Is the ECJ finally putting the Charter to work?, *LQR*, 128(2), 212–16.

Presidency Background Paper. 2010. Follow-up to the informal meeting of Ministers of Employment and Social Security 28th and 29th January, Brussels: Council of the EU.

Report by a Group of Experts. 1956. *Social Aspects of European Economic Co-operation*. Studies and Reports, New Series, No. 46, Geneva: ILO.

Sabel, C. and Zeitlin, J. (eds) 2010. *Experimentalist Governance in the European Union*. Oxford: OUP.

Schiek, D. 2012. *Economic and Social Integration: The Challenge for EU Constitutional Law*. Cheltenham: Edward Elgar.

Scott, J. and Trubek, D. 2002. Mind the Gap: Law and New Approaches to Governance in the European Union. *European Law Journal* 8(1), 1–18.

Streeck, W. 1995. From Market-Making to State-Building? Some Reflections on the Political Economy of European Social Policy, in *European Social Policy Between Fragmentation and Integration*, edited by S. Leibfried and P. Pierson. Washington, D.C.: The Brookings Institute, 389–437.

Trebilcock, M. 2004. Trade Policy and Labour Standards: Objectives, Instruments, and Institutions, in *Hard Choices, Soft Law*, edited by J. Kirton and M. Trebilcock. Aldershot: Ashgate, 170–85.

Van Reisen, M., Stocker, S. and Vogiazides, L. 2009. *Europe's response to the global financial crisis*, Social Watch Report available at http://www.socialwatch.org/sites/default/files/eepa-eurostep2009_eng.pdf [accessed 23 August 2012].

Vandenbroucke, F. 2012. *Europe: The Social Challenge*, Brussels: OSE.

Vanhercke, B. 2011. *Is 'The Social Dimension of Europe 2020' an Oxymoron?* Paper to the CELLS Conference: The European Union's economic and social model – still viable in a global crisis?, Leeds, 8th–9th December 2011.

Watson, P. 2011. Equality, fundamental rights and the limits of legislative discretion: comment on *Test-Achats. ELRev*, 36(6), 896–904.

Weinstock, U. 1989. Europäische Sozialunion – historische Erfahrungen und Perspektiven, in *Sozialstaat EG? Die andere Dimension des Binnenmarktes*, edited by W. Däubler. Gütersloh: Bertelsmann Stiftung, 15–34.

Wells, D. 2006. Best Practices in the Regulation of International Labour Standards: Lessons of the U.S.-Cambodia Textile. *Comparative Labour Law and Policy Journal* 27, 357–76.

World Commission on the Social Dimension of Globalisation. 2004. *A fair globalisation: creating opportunities for all*, Geneva: ILO.

Zeitlin, J. and Pochet, P. (eds) 2005. *The Open Method of Coordination in Action: The European Employment and Social Inclusion Strategies*. Brussels: PIE-Peter Lang.

Chapter 9

The EU as a 'Virtuous International Actor': Human Rights Indicators and Global Governmentality

Bal Sokhi-Bulley*

Introduction

Despite the view that 'human rights are an elusive and in many ways unobservable social phenomenon, which are not always tractable for measurement' (Landman and Carvalho 2010: 44), the use of *indicators* to measure human rights is now an increasingly popular way of determining whether progress in rights has been made and of holding human rights actors to account. Rights are, moreover, associated with a good, correct or exemplary form of governing – guidelines compiled by the United Nations Development Programme (UNDP 2004: 3) define a 'governance indicator' as 'a measure that points out something about the state of governance in a country [… and is] usually narrowed down to measure more specific areas of governance such as […] human rights'. The UNDP thus makes the link between good governance and human rights – 'good' governing within states should imply 'good' human rights practices. The language of 'good governance' has now permeated the European Union – in particular, the Commission's White Paper on Governance (European Commission 2001) identifies a need to set up new agencies (a departure from the Classic Community Method)[1] in order to ensure that 'good governance' is maintained throughout the EU. It was this sentiment that led to the establishment of a new agency for fundamental rights protection in the EU, the Fundamental Rights Agency of the European Union (FRA) in March 2007.[2]

---

* The author would like to thank Thérèse Murphy for providing the inspiration for this chapter and Dan Bulley for reading the numerous previous versions. I would also like to thank Dagmar Schiek and the School of Law at Leeds for the excellent and productive CELLS conference in December 2011, where this work was originally presented.

1 The CCM is defined in the Commission's White Paper on Governance (European Commission 2001) as 'premised on the Commission's exclusive right of legislative initiative and the legislative powers of the Council of Ministers and the European Parliament' – i.e. mechanisms designed to produce law at the EU level. See also Scott and Trubek 2002.

2 Council Regulation (EC) 168/2007 establishing a European Union Agency for Fundamental Rights [2007] OJ L 53/1.

Coupled with the 'good governance' agenda put forward in the EU's external relations, in the form of agreements on trade and cooperation with Third Countries (e.g. Cotonou) and required by the EU's accession criteria (Copenhagen Criteria), this new agency symbolizes a clear internal link between good governance and human rights.[3]

Over the last four and a half years since its establishment, the FRA has been increasingly active in its role of providing 'assistance and expertise' to Union institutions and Member States with respect to fundamental rights issues (Regulation 168/2007, Article 6). It has conducted a number of surveys, notably in the area of discrimination against minorities and LGBT persons,[4] it has produced annual and thematic reports[5] and has secured relationships with NGOs and other bodies (e.g. universities, churches) that it works in partnership with to secure rights in Europe (Regulation 168/2007, Article 7–10). Most recently the FRA, under request from the Commission, has conducted a symposium on developing indicators to measure fundamental rights in the EU (FRA 2011b).[6] The move towards developing indicators for measuring rights in the EU, and the implications that this has for the EU's identity as a 'virtuous' global human rights actor, is the focus of this chapter.[7]

The chapter argues that rights indicators act as techniques of regulation and control that help shape the global rights identity of the EU. I aim to, first, explain how the indicators being developed within the EU framework act as regulatory techniques – i.e. as technologies of 'governmentality'. I briefly describe that governmentality is both a process and a way of thinking about the problems of governing that is taken from Michel Foucault's later work. The indicator examples I look at are the more developed indicators on the rights of the child and the emerging indicators on violence against women. I examine the features that allow these indicators to manage conduct (of the EU's Member States, for instance). Second, the chapter aims to show how these features of managing conduct – i.e. the features of governmentality – ultimately manage the identity of the EU so that it is recognized as a global human rights actor. This is an interesting development insofar as the growth of rights indicators reflects a change in the EU's *internal*

---

3   Consolidated version of the ACP-EU Partnership Agreement ('Cotonou Agreement'), 22 June 2010. Available at: http://ec.europa.eu/europeaid/where/acp/overview/cotonou-agreement/index_en.htm [accessed 28 August 2012]. For the Copenhagen Criteria see http://europa.eu/legislation_summaries/glossary/accession_criteria_copenhague_en.htm [accessed 28 August 2012]. See also Williams 2004.

4   European Union Minorities and Discrimination Survey (EU-MIDIS) – survey results, available at: http://fra.europa.eu/fraWebsite/eu-midis/index_en.htm [last accessed 2 December 2010]. See also FRA 2008, 2009b, 2009c and 2009d.

5   For example, on children's rights, the rights of Roma, the rights of Muslims – FRA 2010b, 2009c and 2009d.

6   See the FRA Symposium Website, at: http://fra.europa.eu/fraWebsite/symposium2011/index.html [last accessed 20 November 2011].

7   The phrase 'virtuous global human rights actor' is inspired by de Búrca 2010.

human rights policy – the EU's global identity as a human rights actor shows the Union changing *internally* and not simply promoting rights in its external policies. The chapter, finally, problematizes indicators as tools of governing behaviour and questions the resultant 'virtuous' global rights actor image. Whilst indicators have been associated with progress in rights, with holding actors to account and with 'searching reality at a deeper level',[8] there are questions to be asked about the method of data collection, about who collects the data and indeed what the data represents (Merry 2011, Rossga and Satterwaite 2009). There are also questions over participation of so-called 'victims' of rights violations in the discourse of indicator development. Moreover, and crucially for the subject of this edited collection, the resultant virtuous, global human rights actor image of the EU on a changing global landscape is problematic, as it is constructed as a mathematical, apolitical equation that ignores the power relations involved in its construction.

Indicators: A Definition

A Global Standard of Measurement

The indicators initiative was formally begun by the UN Office of the High Commissioner for Human Rights (OHCHR) in 2005 (see further Rossga and Satterwaite 2009). Originally used in development, indicators became popular within the human rights field as a means of holding human rights actors to account.[9] This overarching accountability function can be further divided into three roles, indicators are to: first, monitor compliance with and fulfilment of human rights commitments; second, they are to measure the progress of human development in human rights terms; and third, they are to measure the success/impact of particular rights-based policies or development programming (Rossga and Satterwaite 2009: 257). The European Commission has previously been involved with the UNDP in developing 'governance indicators' to measure the various aspects of democracy, human rights and governance (UNDP 2004). The Commission has, furthermore, been involved in the development of indicators in a range of areas that are relevant to fundamental rights, including poverty and social exclusion, education, pensions and health care (Kjærum 2011).

The idea behind the involvement of the FRA is that it will build on the Commission's work to add at least three dimensions to existing indicators, making them more rights-friendly (Kjærum 2011: 3–4): first, they would add a measurement of enforceability – fundamental rights must be dependent

8   Mr Ciobanu-Dordea, Director in charge of Equality, DG Justice, European Commission, in FRA 2011b: 6.

9   Note the HDI (Human Development Index), HPI (Human Poverty Index), GDI (Gender-related Development Index) and GEM (Gender Empowerment Measure) – indices presented in the Human Development Reports in 1990.

on enforcement mechanisms, which would track issues like the existence of complaints mechanisms and how often they are used. Second, they would add a measurement of substance – they must be based around the substance of the rights themselves. So, for example, indicators on health care would include questions that relate to the availability of family planning services and sexual health services catering for the needs of LGBT persons, for instance. Third, they would add a measurement of equality – that is, require data to be disaggregated on the basis of grounds including gender, age, disability, religion or sexual orientation. It was the European Commission that asked the FRA to develop indicators to measure how child rights are implemented, the first of five key areas in which indicators to measure rights will be developed (the other areas are: data protection, access to justice, Roma and the right to education, and persons with disabilities). In addition, there are four further areas for potential indicator development: violence against women, discrimination and hate crimes against Jews, discrimination and victimization of LGBT persons, and discrimination against Roma. The role of the Agency in developing indicators is to *collect and analyze reliable and robust data* on fundamental rights in the EU – using this data, it is then to offer 'assistance and expertise' to the EU institutions and its Member States (Regulation 168/2007, Article 6). This role, whilst phrased as a departure from 'monitoring' Member States' observance of human rights, has strong characteristics of 'surveillance' that suggest a regulation and control function (Sokhi-Bulley 2011).

The Rights of the Child and Violence Against Women Indicators

The FRA was asked by the European Commission to develop indicators to measure how child rights are implemented, protected, respected and promoted across the EU in 2007, following its Communication 'Towards a Strategy on the Rights of the Child' (European Commission 2006). It follows the OHCHR model of three broad types of indicator: structural (reflecting existing legal institutions and instruments), procedural (reflecting national procedural efforts to implement the structural provisions) and outcome (reflecting individual and collective achievements in the realization of the rights of children in a given context). These are to comply with four general principles: participation (as per Article 12 of the UN Convention on the Rights of the Child (CRC) – listening to children's views), non-discrimination (as per Article 2 of the CRC – accommodate diversity to capture the variety of childhood experience), best interests (as per Article 13 CRC – to ensure that the interests of the child are the paramount concern of all stages of regulation, policy and decision-making) and, finally, life, survival and development rights (Article 6 CRC – guaranteeing the child the best possible conditions for personal development) (FRA 2009a). The indicators will be developed in four core areas, namely: family environment and alternative care, protection from exploitation and violence, adequate standard of living and education, citizenship and cultural activities. Each area is divided again into 'indicator groups'. So, for instance, the indicator area 'protection from exploitation and violence' is split into indicator group a) child trafficking, b) sexual and economic exploitation and c) violence against children. Each indicator group contains information on 'why the indicator is important to measure', its basis in the CRC and other international legal instruments, its relevance to the EU (related law) and finally the indicator list. There are sub-groups within the groups (e.g. 'identification of victims' is a sub-group within the group 'child trafficking') (FRA 2010b).

Following instruction from the European Parliament and the Council of the EU,[10] the FRA is to carry out an EU-wide survey in 2011–12 on violence against women, with the objective of obtaining 'robust, comparable data that policy makers need to shape informed, targeted policies to combat such violence'.[11] The survey results are to be made public in 2013 and contribute to the development of harmonizing legislation to combat violence against women and to develop indicators to measure national procedures in process to combat such violence. The survey aims to capture experiences of 'everyday' violence – including physical, sexual and psychological violence, harassment and stalking of women from the age of 15 and before the age of 15 also to allow for a complete picture of women's experiences over their lifetime. The survey is intended to examine violence in different settings, for example the home and the workplace and investigate *how* the violence is carried out – including through the use of internet-based network sites and text messaging.

In the following section, I highlight features of the indicators on the rights of the child and on violence against women that make it possible to identify processes of governmentality at work in the FRA/EU rights model.

Indicators as Techniques of Global Governmentality

Governmentality as a (Thought) Process

> Would any of you ever consider driving at night in the countryside without turning your headlights on? [...] If we want to move fundamental rights from globally agreed, abstract, rhetorical standards, to the level of local, practical implementation, then policy makers need headlights; they require a solid base of evidence [...] [L]et us turn on the headlights, so that we can drive progress forward without losing our way. (Kjaerum, 2011)

---

10   European parliament resolution on the elimination of violence against women (26 November 2009) and Council of the European Union, Conclusions on the eradication of violence against women (8 March 2010).

11   European Union Agency for Fundamental Rights (FRA), 'Factsheet on Gender-based violence against women – an EU-wide survey', 28/10/2011. Available at: http://fra.europa.eu/fraWebsite/attachments/FRA-2011_Factsheet_Violence-against-women_EN.pdf [last accessed 7 November 2011].

Morten Kjærum, Director of the FRA, makes this analogy between indicators and headlights. Whilst it may indeed be the case that indicators, like headlights, direct the way forward and make progress along the route possible, the analogy ignores questions like: Who is driving? What type of vehicle are they driving? Does anyone object to driving in that area? Who else is on the road? In other words, as well as recognizing that indicators allow for the monitoring and possibility of progress in rights, it is important to question the processes that they involve: how they are produced (a question that also asks who is involved in their formulation) and how the knowledge that they make possible engenders relations of power.

Indicators are, this chapter argues, a form of managing the behaviour of actors involved in rights. They thus enable a *governmentality of rights* – which refers to a critical understanding of government as the 'conduct of conduct' (Gordon 1991: 2) or the control of behaviour of a person, persons or actors. For the purposes of rights discourse, these actors include the Member States, human rights NGOs, national human rights institutions and research bodies (e.g. universities). Governmentality does not, therefore, refer to a conventional understanding of government:

> 'Government' did not refer only to political structures or to the management of states; rather, it designated the way in which the conduct of individuals or of groups might be directed – the government of children, of souls, of communities, of the sick ... To govern, in this sense, is to control the possible field of action of others. (Foucault 2002a: 341)

Governmentality refers, rather, to a concern with 'the ensemble formed by the *institutions, procedures, analyses, reflections, calculations and tactics* that allow the exercise of [a] very specific albeit complex form of power, which has as its target population' (Foucault 2002b: 219–20). It is a concern, in other words, with the nature and practice of government: 'who can govern; what governing is; who or what can govern' (Gordon 1991: 2).

Indicators and the Features of Managing Conduct

Within the EU/FRA's indicator model, it is possible to identify three features of the management of rights actors: first, governmentality is made possible by the presence of a complex network of experts and, second, by the existence of data in the form of statistics. Third, the latter two features mean that governmentality happens 'at a distance' (Rose 2000: 324).

The FRA, first, consists of a multiplicity of *actors* at the national and EU level. There are the bodies of the Agency itself (the director, management board, executive board and scientific committee). There are the points of contact at the national level in the form of national liaison officers, as well as data collection bodies – RAXEN (groups of experts collecting data on issues concerning racism, xenophobia and related intolerances)[12] and FRALEX (the FRA's 'group of legal experts', who report on legal aspects of fundamental rights issues in all Member States). There are also 'other bodies' with which the FRA is to have a relationship of 'cooperation' (Regulation 168/2007, Articles 7–10) – these include the Council of Europe, NGOs (dealing with human rights), national human rights institutions, trade unions and universities. Moreover, the work on indicators is being conducted through cooperation with a number of other non-state actors, including: the Organization for Security and Cooperation in Europe (OSCE), the United Nations Office on Drug and Crime (UNODC), UNICEF, the International Labour Organization (ILO), the International Organization for Migration (IOM), and the OHCHR. These actors are experts in rights and rights measurement by virtue of the fact that they share an expertise – that is, they share 'expert knowledge' (Kennedy 2005). There is no hierarchical relation between the experts – rather, they exist in the 'shape of a net' (Latour 2011: 799) through which knowledge/information is passed via various channels (e.g. reports, surveys, blogging). The experts are thus part of a move to 'strengthen the fundamental rights architecture in the EU' (FRA 2010a), which is structured as a panopticon and resembles the operation of power as panopticism (Foucault 1991: 195–228).

The FRA engages through its expert networks in a type of monitoring that can be termed surveillance (Sokhi-Bulley 2011). The mandate of the FRA explicitly rules out *monitoring* the fundamental rights situation within the Member States – the FRA's function is, rather, to collect information and data and to provide assistance and expertise on the basis of that data. The FRA's Summary Report on 'Developing indicators for the protection, respect and protection of rights of the child in the EU' states, 'these indicators are not intended to scrutinise the Member States' implementation of their obligations under EU law, nor are they intended as an additional means of monitoring Member States' compliance with the UN CRC' (FRA 2009b: 8). However, despite this wording, the FRA's architectural structure means that Member States are permanently and automatically observed by the FRA's experts, according to an indicators standard – which resembles panopticism. The implementation of the indicators on the rights of the child will be assessed by means of a 'rights of the child scoreboard' that will highlight 'best practice' in Member States (FRA 2010b: 13). The Member States will thus be observed to ensure that good/best practice is being carried out as dictated by the indicators. Panopticism requires, however, the presence of a totalizing and permanent gaze,

---

12   Regulation 168/2007, Articles 11–15. RAXEN operates in each of the Member States in the form of 'National Focal Points' (NFPs), typically made up of bodies such as anti-racist NGOs, university research centres, institutes for human rights or government-affiliated organizations. The FRA announced on 12 September 2011 that it will host the first kick-off meeting of the NFPs of a new FRA Research Network (FRANET), which will work for both the FRA and the European Institute for Gender Equality (see http://fra.europa.eu/fraWebsite/news_and_events/2011-events/evt11_12sep_en.htm [last accessed 22 September 2011]).

a 'supervisor' of sorts that can be likened to the 'warden' in the prison model. There is no equivalent supervisor in the FRA indicator model; neither are all areas of Member State action visible at all times. Hence the model can perhaps more accurately be described as what Bruno Latour calls an 'oligopticon' – a 'series of partial orders, localized totalities, with their ability to gaze in some directions and not others' (Amin and Thrift 2002: 92). That is, the FRA can survey, through its expert networks, pieces and fragments of the Member States fundamental rights structure and determine where it is placed on the indicator scoreboard.

The rights of the child indicators were developed after extensive expert consultation with key EU, national and international stakeholders, policy makers and children's rights specialists and an 'intensive consultation process' which contained elements of direct face-to-face interaction and online communication (FRA 2010b: 11–12). The consultation thus involved an online discussion forum, an online survey, a consultation meeting (held in Vienna on 25 April 2008), personal interviews with officials from the Commission, the Council of Europe, UNICEF's Innocenti Research Centre and representatives from European children's rights networks and NGOs and invitations for feedback (FRA 2010b: 11–12). The extensive expert gathering and consultation process illustrates the breadth of the oligopticon and the FRA's auditing role as enabled by indicators. Whilst the FRA is not to monitor Member State compliance with internationally agreed standards on rights protection, it is to '*actively promote the use of these indicators within the Member States* with a view to gradually developing a more coordinated approach to data collection improving data comparability' (FRA 2010a: 7). The FRA is therefore to actively encourage the monitoring of monitoring (Rossga and Satterwaite 2009: 278) – it incites the Member States to monitor themselves.

The second feature of governmentality that I mentioned previously is *statistics* – the collection of information and data in the form of statistics is an important tactic of government. Statistics resemble for Foucault the 'secrets of power' (2007: 275) since they enabled the specific phenomena of the population to be qualified and managed. Although the UNDP (2000: 90) claims that rights could never be measured fully merely by statistics, statistics do come to represent the whole 'truth' about rights within a Member State. That is, figures on the presence of equality bodies, on the number of complaints lodged on the basis of discrimination, for instance, determine whether we see that state as exercising 'good practice' when it comes to the promotion and protection of human rights – and hence good governance. So, as the UK Country Report (Thematic Study) on Child Trafficking (Harris, Sandland, and Akullo 2009: 32) shows, Member States (in this case through data compiled by a university human rights centre) will be required to provide evidence of, for instance, the existence of monitoring mechanisms such as national rapporteurs, training strategies, awareness-raising campaigns and direct participation of local communities and minority groups. The thematic country reports are also required to provide evidence of 'good practice' – the UK Trafficking report lists NGOs and government initiatives that have met the indicator criteria. For instance, the report mentions 'NRUC – National Register of Unaccompanied Children which ensures continuity of care for unaccompanied asylum seeking children' and 'Every Child Matters' – a Government approach that places a responsibilities on all practitioners ensuring that every child has the support it needs to 'Be healthy, Stay safe, Enjoy and achieve, Make a positive contribution and Achieve economic well-being' (Harris, Sandland and Akullo 2009: 103–4). The statistics effectively construct those states that do not show the right figures as 'bad states' and examples of how not to do 'good governance'. They are able to do this because numbers are scientific fact – they do not require intimacy, trust or political correctness (Rossga and Satterwaite 2009).

Moreover, the indicator group 'violence against children' contains indicators on measuring prevention of violence in Member States. These include: evidence of designated public funding for positive parenting education campaigns and evidence of legal provisions requiring schools to have adopted a child protection policy. It is for the Member States to ensure that they comply with the 'benchmarks' set by these indicators – they must manage their behaviour so that it complies with these benchmarks by ensuring that the requisite laws are in place. The penalty for not doing so is recognition of 'bad practice', 'bad governance techniques' and hence a label of 'bad member state'. The FRA is already using such terminology to identify Member States' 'good practice', 'promising practice' and 'achievements' as behaviour that ought to be 'emulated' in its annual and thematic reports (FRA 2011a). Indicators thus operate as 'technologies of the self', encouraging self-government of Member States. Crucial features of this self-government are that it is based on freedom (i.e. freely complied with); it does not involve any element of coercion but rather emphasizes an acceptance of responsibility for management of one's own behaviour.

With respect to the collection of statistics using the violence against women indicators, it will be interesting to observe how the FRA and its experts define 'everyday' experiences of violence and how far they extend definitions and interpretations of forms of violence which are not specifically mentioned in its mandate (e.g. text messaging). The mandate is the Charter on Fundamental Rights of the EU and it should be noted that violence against women *can*, though not explicitly referred to, be linked to several of the Charter provisions, such as human dignity (Article 1), the right to life (Article 2), integrity of the person (Article 3), the prohibition against torture (Article 4), the right to liberty and security of person (Article 6) and non-discrimination (Article 21). Similar to the approach to child rights indicators, the FRA will opt for a UN indicator model. The UN Special Rapporteur on Violence Against Women has had a significant contribution to the development of rights discourse in the definition of 'gender-based violence'. In her 2008 annual report to the human rights council, Yakin Ertürk proposed a 'grave violence against women' indicator (Ertürk 2008) – 'grave violence' is not included in the definition of gender-based violence outlined in the Declaration on the Elimination of Violence Against Women of December (UN 1993). This illustrates how rights experts are directly involved in developing the content of rights (beyond the Treaties), setting new benchmarks and thereby the discourse of international human rights through the development of human rights indicators. These will constitute new interpretations of 'violence', which means that the FRA is developing our understanding of rights and rights protection, what we need protecting from and who the victims of 'violence' are. Hence the FRA is developing rights language through indicators. The special rapporteur, Rashida Manjoo, in 2010 repeated this as 'gross violence' (2010: especially at 13 and 14) used to recognize different categories of victims and thereby determine how reparation programmes for these victims will be selected. Grave, or gross, violence indicators are also to be used to ensure a system of 'layered compliance' by states. The indicators thus, first, define the human rights situation within states (the presence of (grave) violence); second, they help identify the good/bad states; and third, they label the victim of rights violation. These might be the ethnic minority woman, the inhabitant of rural areas, the migrant woman, the refugee woman or the prostitute.[13] Indicators developed by the EU's/FRA's rights experts will similarly identify 'good' or 'bad' governance in Member States and thereby encourage the States to audit themselves to ensure they maintain the more preferable label.

The third and final feature of governmentality is that the FRA thus governs using experts and statistics, 'at a distance' through rights indicators. The FRA's observance of the Member States' monitoring of rights and its collecting of statistics resembles a type of *auditing*. It does not exercise 'monitoring in a legal sense' (a function reserved only for the Commission) but it monitors the way in which the Member States monitor rights. It conducts thus a monitoring of monitoring (Rossga and Satterwaite 2009: 278). What is important here in terms of governmentality is that whilst the FRA remains within the limits of competence (and does not strictly 'monitor'), the oligoptic structure of its experts and their compliance with indicators standards mean that the Member States monitor themselves. They therefore govern themselves – using the indicators as codes of conduct or a 'toolkit' (FRA 2010b: 7) by which to regulate their behaviour. Moreover, the experts, though knowable, do not come into contact with the 'governed/governor' – i.e. the Member State and its population. Information is rather collected and passed on through information technology – such as the FRA's website. Where surveys are conducted and individual citizens come into contact with FRA experts directly, this represents only a small percentage of the population and the 'governing' relation is still distinct from the person sitting conducting the interview. The statistics compiled by the FRA, moreover, distance the reality of the situation from the people it affects or concerns. This is the effect of numbers – to reduce intimacy and local situations into a general, scientific, quantifiable fact.

---

13   These are some of the labels consistently attached to vulnerable groups in the special rapporteurs' annual reports. See for example Ertürk, 2008: 5, 14 and footnote 14.

Managing the Identity of the Union – The EU as a Virtuous, International Human Rights Actor

We have now examined how indicators engender power relations of governmentality 'at a distance', using expertise and statistical data. The observation that indicators, when observed from a governmentality perspective, allow for governing processes has previously been made by academics working in the field of human rights and in anthropological studies (Davis, Kingsbury and Merry *et al.* 2012, Ilcan and Philips 2008, Merry 2011, Rossga and Satterwaite 2009). What specifically interests this chapter are the implications of the FRA developing and using rights indicators in terms of governing the identity of the EU. A global governmentality by rights, through indicators, promotes the identity of the EU as a virtuous, international human rights actor. It is 'virtuous' in the sense that it is a) declaring less government (in line with a Western neoliberal consensus,[14] direct governmental regulation is seen as 'bad' and outdated) and b) supposedly promoting and protecting norms that have by consensus reached the status of values to be upheld above all national differences – i.e. human rights. It is fair to say that the EU has long been developing a global human rights actor image. The incitement to rights discourse began in the 1960s with the burgeoning of the jurisprudence of the Court of Justice of the European Union (CJEU) to replace the absence of reference to human rights in the original treaties.[15] The Court gave a number of monumental judgements in which it began to establish that the EU is a rights-based Union. A codification of the CJEU's case law happened in 1992 with the Treaty on European Union (TEU), which confirmed in Article 6(1) the norm that the Union '*respects the principles of liberty, democracy, respect for human rights and fundamental freedoms, and the rule of law*'.[16] A significant change to the norm came with the

---

14   I use Western neoliberal consensus to encompass the following ideas: that rights are a defence against the (excessive use of) power by the state. Moreover, they are 'that which we cannot not want' (Brown 2002: 421) and as such are consensually not optional. Finally, rights themselves are arguably products of Western liberal ideals and 'the fulfilment of the Enlightenment promise of emancipation and self-realisation' (Douzinas 2000: 2). The consensus is not affected by the fact that the Western EU States have distinct welfare approaches (see ahead at p. 199).

15   Cases of particular relevance are 29/69 *Stauder v City of Ulm* [1969] ECR 419, 11/70 *Internationale Handelsgesellschaft mbH v Einfuhr-und Vorratsstelle für Getreide und Futtermittel* [1970] ECR 1125, 4/73 *Nold v Commission* [1974] ECR 491, 36/75 *Rutili v Minister for the Interior* [1975] ECR 1219, C-36/02 *Omega Spielhallen-und Automatenaufstellungs-GmbH v Oberbürgermeisterin des Bundesstadt Bonn* [2004] ECR I-9609.

16   Treaty on European Union (Maastricht Treaty, as amended). Note that this provision has been amended by the Lisbon Treaty (Treaty of Lisbon amending the Treaty on European Union and the Treaty establishing the European Community). The new Article 6 refers to the Union recognizing the rights, freedoms and principles set out in the Charter of Fundamental Rights of the European Union (Article 6(1)), establishes that the Union shall

Treaty of Amsterdam in 1997, which amended the wording of Article 6(1) so that it read: 'the Union is *founded on* the principles of liberty, democracy, respect for *human rights and fundamental freedoms*, and the rule of law'. There is more to this than word play. Interestingly, while the original treaties made no reference to human rights as foundational principles, they became not only the new vision of the EU but, according to the Treaties, always had been.[17] The EU's global rights actor image was more recently strikingly announced by the CJEU in the prominent *Kadi* case – where the CJEY used its previously established human rights doctrine to promote a global EU identity that does not respect the priority of international (UN) law over and above the protection of Union rights. The Court chose to take a stance against both the Council of Europe and, crucially, the UN Security Council in overruling a Resolution denying the respondents their fundamental rights to free movement under EU law.[18] Whereas its status as a 'good international citizen' in this regard has been questioned (de Búrca 2010), there is no mistaking the significance of this judgement for the EU pronouncing itself as a human rights actor in its own right.

Moreover, the CJEU's judgement in *Kadi* shares an important characteristic with the recent development in human rights indicators by the FRA: Both show an advancement of the EU's *internal human rights policy*. The EU's external human rights engagement is known – it required countries wishing to join the EU Members' club to abide by the standards of democracy, rule of law and protection of fundamental rights (Copenhagen Criteria). Similarly, its international trade agreements contain a human rights clause (Cotonou Agreement). However, in terms of holding its own Member States to account or 'monitoring' their human rights situation, there has been little movement. The development of rights indicators thus signifies an internal process to support the outward image. This internal process has come about through observing how Member States measure rights (using indicators) and thereby being able to rank them on a scoreboard of rights that ultimately reflects a virtuous actor engaged in good governance (the Union).

The value of recognizing indicators as tools of governmentality is that it highlights that indicators allow for government under a banner of good governance. The FRA, as an agency, resembles a governance structure. It is not specifically provided for in the treaties and came about from the Commission's desire to ensure 'better application of rules' through regulatory agencies (European Commission 2001). It, and its fundamental rights mandate, is thus explicitly part

---

accede to the European Convention for the Protection of Human Rights and Fundamental Freedoms (6(2)) and acknowledges fundamental rights shall constitute general principles of the Union's law (6(3)).

17   There has been extensive comment on the historical construction of human rights. See for example Alston and Weiler (1998), de Búrca (1995) and Williams (2004).

18   Cases C-402 and 415/05P *Kadi (Yassin Abdullah) & Al Barakaat International Foundation v Council and Commission (Kadi I)* [2008] ECRI-6351.

of the 'governance' agenda of the EU – i.e. the development of rights language through the creation of a new institution to ensure better protection and promotion of rights through the collection and dissemination of reliable and comparable data is part of 'good governance'. What is of concern is that the Commission promotes its good governance agenda as part of a reform movement towards 'less government' – stating that 'we need to *govern ourselves better, together*'.[19] The EU-sponsored 'New Modes of Governance Project' sums up this understanding of 'governance' succinctly as 'governance *without government*'.[20] This feeds into a wider, Western acceptance that limited government is good and virtuous and that the old style of central regulation is 'bad' and wrong. The EU is therefore able to promote and maintain a 'virtuous' global image under a banner of less government and protection of human rights in comparison, geopolitically, to 'failing' actors/ states (labelled as such because they are seen to be totalitarian) such as North Korea or Iran. However, as the examination of indicators on rights as shown, these particular tools are techniques of governmentality – not only governance – allowing for Member States to regulate themselves according to a previously agreed upon human rights standard. It is thus not less governance but more, and better, government – better in the sense that it is more ingrained within a complex actor-network, it is distanced, it is more efficient and the 'governed' are at once the governed and the governor (they manage themselves). What is therefore happening in the EU is government(ality)[21] by rights.

Conclusion

It remains to problematize indicators as tools of governing behaviour (of Member States, for instance) and to question the EU's resultant apolitical 'virtuous' global rights actor image. I make three points here. First, recognizing indicators as techniques of governmentality raises the question of participation (of the 'governed'). Rossga and Satterwaite (2009) address this issue by calling for indicators that measure participation of the populace in decisions affecting human rights. How will it be possible to actually ensure effective participation of children in the protection of their rights? Or of women who suffer a form of gender-based violence? This is a question of ensuring that the actual rights are observed rather than the indicator being designed *or* an image of the EU as a global rights actor on a par with other international organizations on the global rights stage being represented as a result of indicator development. Measuring whether specialist training is provided for personnel involved in determining the immigration status

---

19 European Commission 2002: 2.

20 An integrated project coordinated by the European University Institute and funded by the EU under its Sixth Framework Programme, 2004–2008 http://www.eu-newgov.org/index.asp [accessed 26 January 2007].

21 I use 'government(ality)' to suggest that government is always also governmentality.

of children, for instance (under the indicator group 'adaptability of immigration processes to the vulnerabilities of separated children') does not ensure that specialist training from legal professionals, interpreters and so on is provided. Similarly, identifying whether national law extends the definition of 'family' in a way that more accurately reflects the reality if children's family life (as per indicator group 'existent of provision favouring family reunification for children where it is in their best interests') does not actually create a family environment for children in need. There is a limit to what statistics can achieve.

This leads to a second problematic issue, which is that the statistical data which indicators collect is essentially a numerical representation of a political situation. The representation as a number removes all cultural and political context. Whilst 'European', the EU's Member States have distinct approaches to family, education and child welfare – these features are lost in indicators. This risks reducing the subjects of rights to numerical entities rather than individuals with different cultural and contextual needs and preferences. Moreover, the numbers only represent data that was deemed to be 'robust', 'reliable' and 'comparable'. What of data that cannot be collected because it will not be given or is not obtainable? As Rossga and Satterwaite note, one UN member involved in the creation of indicators concerning children's rights exclaimed: '[P]eople try to get the information that they can. What is available? What information can you get? Because if you can't get this information, you can't get it' (2009: 282). There are thus sites of violation and struggle that indicators will miss because the information simply is not available. Violence against women is an understandably sensitive and painful topic which will require overcoming the barrier of women not wanting to speak of their experience and promoting active awareness of rights so that women are encouraged to seek help from the law (Merry 2003).

Following on from the idea that governing through indicators is a form of government, not simply governance, the third effect is that government is concealed. Why should this interest us? Because the government is happening through rights. Rights indicators as developed by the FRA/EU regulate the behaviour of states (and as a result its citizens and other actors with which the FRA engages, such as NGOs) and this goes against the liberal foundation of rights as tools *against government*. Moreover, the government is happening through experts which have not been democratically appointed, raising issues of a democratic deficit in governing. We can know who the experts are in theory but the reality of the complex network of actors, the oligopticon, makes this almost impossible – it certainly makes the key feature of accountability in government impossible.

Where does this leave us? The chapter has argued that through the development of fundamental rights indicators by the FRA, the EU is promoting global governmentality by rights through a good governance agenda and that this reveals how a global image of itself as a virtuous international human rights actor is able to be represented. I am not arguing against rights indicators. Rather, I have tried to argue, first, that indicators on fundamental rights, whilst they have the potential to act as 'headlights', also have the inevitable characteristic of technologies of government – and they ought therefore to be 'resisted' (i.e. ceaselessly interrogated) through critique. This entails constant dialogue and deliberation that seeks to persistently review the participation of 'the governed' (e.g. children, vulnerable women) in measurement of rights protection, that appreciates the limits of numbers as evidence that the actual rights themselves are being protected and that recognizes the governing potential of rights rather than accepting, uncritically, that we are governed less. I have also argued, second, that whilst the EU's 'virtuous international actor' image results from a change in the EU's internal human rights policy to comply with indicator standards – and this is positive because it reveals actual change within the EU's internal rights framework[22] – the image is nevertheless a recently realized numerical representation. That is, in the interests of measurement and of symbolizing protection of European rights in Europe, culture, history, politics and power have been lost. Whilst the EU shares the global rights stage with the UNDP, the UN OHCHR and other international actors such as the ILO, it is constructing a problematic identity that has forgotten its colonial past. That is, the less-than-'virtuous', colonial heritage of the Union is forgotten as the new rights image is created. The Union has re-written its history and claimed that it has always been 'founded on' the principles of respect for fundamental rights (democracy and the rule of law).[23] It sees respect for fundamental rights as a condition of membership (as per Cotonou). The positive aspect of what I have described as the construction of the EU as a global rights actor is that it has resulted from a change in its *internal* human rights policy – the Member States are monitoring themselves so as to fulfil the demands of 'good governance' as required by indicators. The indicators mean that the EU (the Member States) are themselves observed as well as observing – and thereby controlling and regulating – that which is 'outside' the Union. It is important to remember that rights demand this self-reflexive aspect if they are to be more than criteria for membership of a Union that has re-written its own rights history and if we are to engage with the promises and limits of the EU to represent *rights*, rather than representing a virtuous global identity based on rights.

---

22   Note the new Trafficking Directive (Directive of the European Parliament and of the Council (EU) 2011/36 on preventing and combating trafficking in human beings and protecting its victims, and replacing Council Framework Decision 2002/629/JHA [2011] OJ L 101/1). The Directive would integrate existing standards of Council Directive (EC) 2004/81 on the residence permit issued to third-country nationals who are victims of trafficking in human beings or who have been the subject of an action to facilitate illegal immigration, who cooperate with the competent authorities [2004] OJ L261/19 and Council Framework Decision (JHA) 2002/629 on combating trafficking in human beings [2002] OJ L203/1 into one central piece of EU legislation.

23   Note the wording of the old Article 6 TEU, see above.

Bibliography

Alston, P. and Weiler, J.H.H. 1998. An 'Ever-Closer Union' in Need of a Human Rights Policy: The European Union and Human Rights. *European Journal of International Law*, 9, 658.

Amin, A. and Thrift, N. 2002 *Cities: Reimagining the Urban.* Cambridge: Polity Press.

Brown, W. 2002. Suffering the Paradoxes of Rights. in *Left Legalism/Left Critique*, edited by W. Brown and J. Halley. London: Duke University Press, 420–34.

Davis, K., Kingsbury, B. and Merry, S.E. 2012. Indicators as a Technology of Global Governance. *Law and Society Review*, 46(1), 71–104.

de Búrca, G. 1995. The Language of Rights in European Integration in *New Legal Dynamics of European Union*, edited by J. Shaw and G. More. Oxford: Clarendon, 29–54.

de Búrca, G. 2010. The European Court of Justice and the International Legal Order after Kadi. *Harvard International Law Journal*, 51(1) 1–49.

Douzinas, C. 2000. *The End of Human Rights: Critical Legal Thought at the Turn of the Century.* Oxford: Hart.

Ertürk, Y. 2008. (Special Rapporteur on violence against women, its causes and consequences). *Indicators on violence against women and State response.* (Geneva: UN).

European Commission. 2001. 'European Governance: A White Paper', COM(2001)428 final, 25 July 2001.

European Commission. 2002. Communication from the Commission, 'European Governance: Better Lawmaking', COM (2002) 275 final, 5 June 2002.

European Commission. 2006. Communication 'Towards a Strategy on the Rights of the Child' (COM(2006)367 final).

Foucault, M. 1991. *Discipline and Punish: The Birth of the Prison.* London: Penguin.

Foucault, M. 2002a. The Subject and Power, in *Power: Volume 3: Essential Works of Foucault 1954–1984*, edited by J. Faubion. London: Penguin, 326–48.

Foucault, M. 2002b. Governmentality in *Power: Volume 3: Essential Works of Foucault 1954–1984*, edited by J. Faubion. London: Penguin, 201–22.

Foucault, M. 2007. *Security, Territory, Population.* Basingstoke: Palgrave Macmillan.

FRA (European Union Agency for Fundamental Rights). 2008. Homophobia and Discrimination on the Grounds of Sexual Orientation in the EU Member States: Part I: Legal Analysis. Available at: http://fra.europa.eu/fraWebsite/lgbt-rights_en.htm [accessed 17 October 2011].

FRA (European Union Agency for Fundamental Rights). 2009a. Developing indicators for the protection, respect and promotion of rights of the child in the European Union', Summary Report. Available at: http://fra.europa.eu/fraWebsite/attachments/RightsofChild_summary-report_en.pdf [accessed 7 November 2011].

FRA (European Union Agency for Fundamental Rights). 2009b. EU-MIDIS at a Glance: Introduction to the FRA's EU-wide Discrimination Survey. Available at: http://fra.europa.eu/en/publication/2011/eu-midis-glance-introduction-fras-eu-wide-discrimination-survey [accessed 15 February 2013].

FRA (European Union Agency for Fundamental Rights). 2009c. EU-MIDIS European Union Minorities and Discrimination Survey: Data in Focus Report 2: Muslims. Available at: http://fra.europa.eu/fraWebsite/research/publications/publications_per_year/2009/2009_en.htm [accessed 17 October 2011].

FRA (European Union Agency for Fundamental Rights). 2009d. EU-MIDIS European Union Minorities and Discrimination Survey: Data in Focus Report: The Roma. Available at: http://fra.europa.eu/fraWebsite/research/publications/publications_per_year/2009/2009_en.htm [accessed 17 October 2011].

FRA (European Union Agency for Fundamental Rights). 2009e. Homophobia and Discrimination on the Grounds of Sexual Orientation in the EU Member States: Part II: The Social Situation. Available at: http://fra.europa.eu/fraWebsite/lgbt-rights_en.htm [accessed 17 October 2011].

FRA (European Union Agency for Fundamental Rights). 2010a. National Human Rights Institutions in the EU Member States: Strengthening the Fundamental Rights Architecture in the EU I. Available at: http://fra.europa.eu/fraWebsite/attachments/NHRI_en.pdf [accessed 20 November 2011].

FRA (European Union Agency for Fundamental Rights). 2010b. Developing indicators for the protection, respect and promotion of the rights of the child in the European Union (Conference edition). Available at: http://fra.europa.eu/fraWebsite/research/publications/publications_per_year/2010/pub-rightsofchild-summary_en.htm [accessed 28 August 2012].

FRA (European Union Agency for Fundamental Rights). 2011a. Fundamental Rights: Challenges and Achievements in 2010, Luxembourg: Publications Office of the European Union. Available at: http://fra.europa.eu/fraWebsite/attachments/annual-report-2011_EN.pdf [accessed 14 September 2011].

FRA (European Union Agency for Fundamental Rights). 2011b. Using Indicators to measure fundamental rights in the EU: challenges and solutions, 2th Annual FRA Symposium, Vienna 12–13 May, FRA Symposium Report. Available at: http://fra.europa.eu/fraWebsite/attachments/FRAsymp2011-outcome-report.pdf [accessed 20 November 2011].

Gordon, C. 1991. Governmental Rationality: An Introduction, in *The Foucault Effect: Studies in Governmentality*, edited by G. Burchell, C. Gordon and P. Miller. Chicago: Chicago University of Chicago Press, 1–52.

Harris, D., Sandland, R. and Akullo, M. 2009. *FRA Thematic Study on Child Trafficking [United Kingdom]*. Available at: http://fra.europa.eu/fraWebsite/research/background_cr/cr_child_traff_0709_en.htm [accessed 29 August 2012].

Ilcan, S. and Philips, L. 2008. Governing Through Global Networks: Knowledge, Mobilities and Participatory Development. *Current Sociology*, 56(5), 711–34.

Kennedy, D. 2005. Challenging the expert rule: The politics of global governance. *Sydney Law Review*, 27(1), 5–28.

Kjærum, M. 2011. Director of the European Union Agency for Fundamental Rights, *Speech at FRA Symposium*, Vienna, 12–13 May. Available at: http://fra.europa.eu/fraWebsite/attachments/MK-speech-fra-symposium2011.pdf [accessed 7 November 2011].

Landman, T. and Carvalho (eds). 2010. *Measuring Human Rights*. Abingdon: Routledge.

Latour, B. 2011. Networks, Societies, Spheres: Reflections of an Actor-Network Theorist. *International Journal of Communication* 5, 796–810.

Manjoo, R. 2010. (Special Rapporteur on violence against women, its causes and consequences) *Reparations to women who have been subjected to violence*. Geneva: UN.

Merry, S.E. 2003. Rights Talk and the Experience of Law: Implementing women's Rights to Protection from violence. *Human Rights Quarterly*, 25(2), 343–81.

Merry, S.E. 2011. Measuring the World: Indicators, Human Rights and Global Governance. *Current Anthropology*, 52(3), 83–95.

Rose, N. 2000. Government and Control. *British Journal of Criminology*, 40(2), 321–39.

Rossga, A. and Satterwaite, M. 2009. The Trust in Indicators: Measuring Human Rights. *Berkeley Journal of International* Law, 27 (2), 253–315.

Scott, J. and Trubek, D. 2002. Mind the Gap: Law and New Approaches to Governance in the European Union. *European Law Journal* 8(1), 1–18.

Sokhi-Bulley, B. 2011. The Fundamental Rights Agency of the EU: A New Panopticism. *Human Rights Law Review*, 11(4), 683–706.

United Nations. 1993. United Nations Declaration on the Elimination of Violence Against Women, adopted by the General Assembly on 20 December 1993, Un Doc. A/RES/48/104.

United Nations Development Programme (UNDP). 2004. *Governance Indicators: A User's Guide*. New York: UNDP Oslo Governance Centre.

United Nations Development Programme (UNDP). 2000. *Human Development Report 2000: Human Rights Development*. Available at: http://hdr.undp.org/en/media/HDR_2000_EN.pdf [accessed 15 January 2009].

Williams, A. 2004. *EU Human Rights Policy: A Study in Irony*. Oxford: Oxford University Press.

Index

www.ingramcontent.com/pod-product-compliance
Ingram Content Group UK Ltd.
Pitfield, Milton Keynes, MK11 3LW, UK
UKHW020353010325
455677UK00021B/436